S0-BQX-917

THE WORLD OF THE SUFI

An anthology of writings about Sufis and their work

Introduction by
IDRIES SHAH

THE OCTAGON PRESS
LONDON

Individual Copyrights are owned as follows, and the items are reproduced herein by permission:

Introduction, Copyright © 1979 by Idries Shah
The Classical Masters and Learning and Teaching © 1979 by The Institute for the Study of Human Knowledge
Sanai and Sufism in the 20th Century West © 1978 by David Pendlebury
The Mulla Nasrudin Tales in A Naqshbandi Circle © 1967 by Raoul Simac
Indian Thought and Sufis © 1961 by Dr. Tara Chand
Specialized Techniques in Central Asia © 1962 by Ja'far Hallaji
Sufism and Psychiatry and Report on Mysticism © 1977 by Dr. A.J. Deikman
Sufi Studies Today © 1968 by William Foster
Sufi Studies: East & West © 1976 by Dr. Leonard Lewin
Abshar Monastery © 1964 by Julian Shaw
The Pointing Finger System © 1968 by Sheikh Ahmed Abdullah
The Known and the Unknown in Studies © 1968 by John Grant
Emulation and Cycles of Study © 1968 by Ali Sultan
Learning by Contact © 1968 by Rustam Khan-Urff
Meditation Method © 1968 by Mir S. Khan
A Sufi Organization in Britain © 1961 by Arkon Daraul
A Dervish Assembly in the West © 1961 by Selim Brook-White
Use of the Five Gems © 1968 by Edouard Chatelherault

All other papers are Copyright © by The Octagon Press Ltd.

Published by The Octagon Press
with the aid of a grant from The Sufi Trust

ISBN 900860 66 9

Published 1979
Reprinted 1984

Printed and bound in Great Britain by
Redwood Burn Limited, Trowbridge, Wiltshire

CONTENTS

iii

1. INTRODUCTION

According to the Sufis, human beings are ordinarily cut off from Objective Reality, which is the origin of everything. Human faculties, although perceptive, are limited: like a radio set which can receive only certain electromagnetic waves and not other parts of this band; all perceptions exclude external impulses as well as receiving others.

The perceived world, again according to this assertion, is therefore a distortion. The inability to transcend the barrier of limited senses explains human subjectivity: and secondary effects are usually perceived as primary ones.

So Rumi says, in his *Fihi ma Fihi*: 'If a sleeve moves, it is because the hand moved. But if the hand moves, the sleeve does not always have to move. So if you look at the caused and do not know the causer, you imagine that the "sleeve" is something which has a life of its own'.*

The Sufis further assert that they can penetrate beyond the apparent to the real in this sense, and Sufism is the method or, rather, provides the methods, for this enterprise.

They further state that theirs is a spiritual path, because their experience, in their judgment, verifies that the Objective Truth, the First Cause, that which lies beyond appearances, is divine.

The methods which are adopted to pierce the veil between truth and humankind are, accordingly, those chosen by experienced Sufis (nobody who has not completed this journey can properly be called a Sufi; someone who is only trying is known as a seeker, a

---

*Professor B. Faruzanfar's 1952 Tehran edition of *Fihi ma Fihi*, Section 63 of the Persian text.

1

dervish, and by other names), the ones which their own overview tells them are appropriate for the current time, place and people.

This explains why so many Sufis have worked in so many fields, and why so many Sufi schools have had so many different conceptions of the path. Sufism is, in operation, pragmatic. Most of the supposedly Sufi organizations, exercises and 'orders' are in fact only of archaeological interest. Those who know do not need them: those who do not must find those who know, not the obsolete garments of previous formulations.

It cannot be denied, even from an outside point of view, that someone who has been along a certain path may be able to conduct others by that route, or find a better one: both enterprises being more promising than a route from an old map which has been rendered irrelevant by a landslide. Whether acceptable by outward minds or not, the contention cannot be faulted if the premises are conceded.

If this is so, then, it may be asked, what is the use of the map which is now said to be superseded? Why collect accounts of former enterprises and their activities?

The answer is that these materials have a use other than the leading of a disciple from A to Z. Just as it would be absurd to imagine that an orange was only taste, only colour, only flavour or only a vehicle for seeds in its value to us, so with Sufi expressions. On one of the lowest, but yet fundamental, levels, the value lies in removing misconceptions about humanity in human thinking and about narrowness in Sufi studies.

It is easy to illustrate one of the important uses of this kind of material from an experiment carried out in the case of the present book.

The manuscript of the work which you are now reading was given to specialists in several fields, and to a number of general readers and metaphysicians, all of them with some interest in Sufism and the Sufis.

The results were illuminating. A psychiatrist was delighted at the psychological content but confessed

2

himself uncomfortable with the religious and literary material. A theologian was distressed by the 'mystical content' but loved the 'spiritual beauty' which he found herein. An historian and orientalist was thrilled by the new information not available elsewhere: but at the same time annoyed that Sufi studies should have been embraced by modern workers in the soft sciences, such as psychologists. A literary critic felt that 'the work of the great thinkers and writers in this tradition should be retained; the rest, excised'.

In other words, each wanted to regard the Sufi expression as a part of his or her own field. Each, too, when questioned, admitted to preferring that the relevance to any other field be censored or suppressed.

This reaction (for it is only one reaction in pattern, though apparently several because expressed variously in literary, scientific, academic and other category-terms) well delineates the mentality of a number of typical contemporary people. It gives us a means of assessing them and, it is to be hoped, gives them a means of noting their own limitations.

And there are other contents in this material which can take effect long before any learning in Sufism can be promoted, but which can nevertheless pave the way for it.

Happily there were other, and sufficiently wholesome, responses to the materials, which alone could justify publication.

We could have pleased every one of our specialists by splitting the manuscripts into narrow categories, adding more material in the same field, and publishing each fragment as a separate book.

The list of titles would then have read, at least in part:
Sufism: The Classical Tradition
Humour and the Sufis
Sufism in Eastern Religion
Modern Psychology and Sufi Thought and Action
Sufi Spiritual Practices
Visits to Sufis
The Sufis in Literature: East and West

3

And so on. The only problem left would have been that the Sufic content, value and impact would have disappeared. There was once a boy, you may recall, who dismembered a butterfly. Looking at the piles of wings, antennae, legs, head and body, he exclaimed: 'There are the parts all right: but where has the *butterfly* gone?' This behaviour is so well understood in the East that there is a term derived from this story 'Pai-magas' (fly's-leg), to refer to perhaps interesting but ultimately incomplete specialization.

Because certain subjects have been made specializations, and because there is a habit of putting labels on things (both admirable tendencies if kept within proper bounds) the habit of collecting butterfly-legs has come to be accepted very widely as equal to, or a suitable substitute for, the study of butterflies. Many people will deny this, talking about 'fragmentation, classification and holisticism', but you only have to talk to many of them for a time and watch their behaviour and methods of thought to know that, in general, these tend to be parrot-cries.

In case anyone jumps to conclusions, let me say here that this book is not a reconstructed butterfly. It contains material within a very wide range, both of subject and of competence and relevance. As an anthology of readings it seems to me to contain a great deal that is useful: but much will depend upon what assumptions are brought to its reading.

If my own experience is anything to go by, the book will produce as many reactions as there are types of people reading it. Unless carefully warned, reactions to books include some very superficial behaviour. Some of the readers might embark on journeys to the East, others might lose no time in trying out exercises, yet others are likely to use it to manifest a desire for acceptance or rejection: to like or dislike it.

I say this because I have noted that there is a tendency to employ books to help one work out a desire already

4

existing in the mind, regardless of the balance of the material. As responses to one and the same book I have found people (or, rather, they have found me) who have gone on long journeys, rushed to look for texts mentioned in the book, tried to spread the good word, plunged into the world or fled it. I sometimes have a fantasy that I would like to put them all into a room and have them fight out which of their highly selective interpretations is the 'right' one.

This kind of behaviour ignores, of course, the fundamental priority: the question as to whether the admittedly heroic seeker is equipped for the particular effort which has taken his fancy: for fancy it is in such cases.

I once gave a lecture, in the United States, during the course of which I made much play of the fact that to adopt so-called spiritual exercises and to try to use them without knowledge was positively to be avoided. At the end of the lecture I was surrounded by people who wanted to be given lists of exercises.

In another lecture, before an assembly of scholars, and at their invitation, I spoke at length about the fact that Sufism is not and cannot be a scholarly specialization, nor does it contain any such specializations.

The first question I got at the end of this lecture was:

'Yes, but what are the actual scholarly specializations within Sufism?' When I asked whether the rest of the audience wanted an answer to this, nearly all the assembled savants held up their hands.

So, as can easily be demonstrated, both the metaphysical and the academic are relatively rigid sets of mind labouring under a similar restriction: lack of flexibility and a feeble ability to absorb new material. The Sufi, in common with others, of course, has a different point of view. He may help others to attain it (or perhaps rather to reclaim it) though indoctrination and habit, plus vanity and emotionality, can prevent the useful absorption of what is in fact only common sense.

The employment of materials such as those in this

5

book for information-gathering or emotional stimulus would yield no more (even if no less) than any other book adopted for such secondary purposes.

In the Sufi phrase:

'The colour of the water seems to be the colour of the glass into which it has been poured'.

Idries Shah

2. THE CLASSICAL TRADITION OF THE SUFI

2/i.

The Classical Masters

Peter Brent

It is impossible to be clear about beginnings — a tradition winds back through the centuries; one says, 'Here it commenced' or 'That was the man who spoke the first word', but however firm one's tone of voice, however dogmatic one's assertion, one cannot lay bare the earliest, the primal root. This is the more true the more imprecise the tradition; it is absolutely true of a tradition in which from Master to disciple there has been handed down through the generations something as nebulous as an awareness, a manner of being, a process of learning, an alteration of perception, the development of an inner conviction, an imprecisely defined method for achieving an incommunicable experience. Even the word we have chosen to describe the tradition (not one picked for that purpose by those whose tradition it naturally was) is surrounded by a haze of discussion, even of acrimonious argument.

What is the derivation of 'Sufi'? It comes, say some, from *ashabi-sufa,* 'sitters in the shrine', mendicants who made their home in the porch of the temple and whom the Prophet, Mohammed, used at times to feed. But even those who accept this derivation dispute its meaning: the *ashabi-sufa,* they say, were those who sat on benches outside the mosques and debated matters theological

7

with the orthodox. Others choose a different root for the word, settling on *safa*, 'purity' or 'sincerity', to mark the special characteristic of those who set out upon the Sufi way. Some believe that the Greek *sophia*, 'wisdom' or 'knowledge', lies near the root of the matter. Many think *suf*, 'wool', to be the relevant word, for those who took to the self-disciplined life of the ascetic wore long robes of wool, cowled, distinctive and practical for a wanderer forced often to sleep on the hard earth. But for others again, the word needs no derivation, being simply itself: the sound *soof*, they say, has its own power, a value based on the universe's hidden currents of meaning.

The debate over the name, however, is no more than a surface indication of the more important dispute about the origins of the Sufi teaching itself. This in turn concerns the qualifications considered necessary in those wishing to learn the Sufi way to self-development. Many commentators, indeed most, insist that the *tariqah*, the Spiritual Path, is open only to those who come to it by way of the *shari'ah*, the holy law of Islam, based on the Koran and dependent upon theological exegesis. Thus to be a Sufi you have first to be a Moslem. The reason for this, they say, is that the origins of Sufism and those of Islam are inextricably intertwined, and the Prophet himself, as his profound mystic experiences prove, was not merely a Sufi, but the first and greatest of Sufis.

If this were truly the case, then the ideas and practices of Sufism would be, even in part, inaccessible to all those who have not first adopted Islam. Yet writers and teachers have for years busily spread the news of precisely these ideas and practices throughout the West. Has their interest been a purely scholarly one or, when it has not, have they been either misguided or fraudulent in their endeavours? J. Spencer Trimingham in his *The Sufi Orders in Islam* writes that Sufis 'differed considerably in their inner beliefs, but their link with orthodoxy was guaranteed by their acceptance of the law and ritual practices of Islam. All the same they formed inner coteries in Islam and introduced a hierarchal structure

8

and modes of spiritual outlook and worship foreign to its essential genius'. It is a view that suggests that an approach to the Sufi structure and modes of action might not after all have to pass by way of orthodox Islamic law. (One may not, on the other hand, have to go as far as some and see the origins of Sufism, not in Islam at all, but in such mystic traditions as those of the Zoroastrian *magi* of Persia.)

What do the great names of Sufi tradition say? Jalaluddin Rumi is still called, seven centuries after his death, *Mowlana,* Our Master, by the Sufis, and not only the Sufis, of today. He is, above all others perhaps, the essential voice of Sufism, positive, unconventional, at times sardonic, at times admonitory or anecdotal, his verse impregnated with an awareness of profound love — but a love that makes it sinewy, not sugary — and of the exaltation of transcendental experience. He casts aside the trammels of theology when he deals with the central, inescapable issue, the relation between humanity and the divine:

> I adore not the Cross nor the Crescent, I am not Christian nor Jew. . .
> Not from Eden and Paradise I fell, not from Adam my lineage I drew.
> In a place beyond uttermost place, in a tract without shadow or trace,
> Soul and body transcending I live in the soul of my loved one anew.

The loved one here is both the Sufi guide and the divine itself. And a contemporary of his, the Sufi Master Nafasi, wrote of God's proximity to mankind, 'The beautiful truth is that He is ever near to those who seek Him, regardless of their creed or belief'.

Scholars argue that Rumi, and the other great thinkers and teachers through whom Sufism developed, can only be considered in the Islamic context within which they grew and worked. It was that religion which they practised, its tenets and rituals that they drew from and illuminated. And in a broad sense this must be true, since we are all the products of the cultures from which we spring. But to say that Sufism, an approach to the Absolute by way of self-discipline, heightened perception, retrained intelligence and profound emotion, must be restricted to those who come to it through the gateway of Islam's *shari'ah* seems on the face of it almost perversely narrow. When, in mid-14th century, the ruler of Fars decreed in an excess of puritan zeal that all the inns of the town must close, Hafiz, among the greatest of Sufi poets, and one who understood better than most the metaphor 'God-intoxicated', wrote:

> They have closed the doors of the wine taverns;
> O God suffer not
> That they should open the doors of the house of deceit and hypocrisy.
> If they have closed them for the sake of the selfish zealot
> Be of good cheer, for they will reopen them for God's sake.

And what is one to make of this short tale from Rumi's *Discourses*? 'I spoke one day to a group of people, among whom were some non-Moslems. In the midst of my speech they wept and experienced ecstasy. Only one out of a thousand Moslems understood why they wept. The master then declared: "Although they do not understand the inner spirit of these words they comprehend the underlying feeling, the real root of the matter".' If we who are not Moslems listen carefully, may we too not comprehend 'the root of the matter'?

It seems likely that certain elements in the Sufi tradition are indeed older than Islam itself. It is hard to believe that a mystic tradition should have had a sudden untrammelled beginning in the seventh century, without being heavily influenced by existing ideas, especially when one remembers that Islam itself is a self-aware continuation of the monotheism already long developed in Judaism and Christianity. There is also the discomfort with which, as Trimingham and others have suggested, Sufism seems at times to sit within Islam, a consequence perhaps of the incompatibility between the religion of

10

revelation and the religion of continuing mystical experience. A once-for-all appearance on the human plane of the divine, as postulated by Christians, for example, tends to be codified in precepts, transfixed by tradition and animated only by ritual; on the whole, later generations are not permitted to obscure it by their own directly personal experience of the Absolute. Yet in Islam, both traditions co-exist, suggesting that some part of the mystical convention may have its beginnings not in the primary prophetic Message, but elsewhere. For that convention supplies legitimacy to its adherents, equivalent to that supplied by revelation to the theologians, through a continuing chain of inductor and inducted, linked always by the relation between an unforced authority and a willing submission, and stretching back across the centuries. It is this chain of Master and disciple, known in Sufism as the *silsilah*, that itself provides the necessary authority for the latest neophyte desiring to add his link to it.

The Master personifies that authority, as he does the inner experience which is both the basis and the purpose for that authority's existence. Again, such systems of tuition, where they exist elsewhere in the world, in Hinduism's *Guru-shishya parampara*, for instance, have their roots in a pre-literate world where all instruction had to be oral, and those who taught were therefore the living embodiment of the culture they transmitted. There are many other reasons, of course, why tuition in mysticism should be by means of a similar direct transmission, and yet one wonders whether its very structures do not reveal how very deep and ancient the roots of Sufism are.

The argument, however, has centred on what the *exclusive* origins of Sufism might be. One profound lesson that the philosophies of Asia can teach is that many desperate disagreements based on the disruptive 'either-or' of which scholastic thinkers are so fond can be resolved by a reconciling 'both'. This is probably such a case. If historical Islam itself has its roots in monotheism already well known in Arabia, so may Sufism have arisen

11

out of already established mystical schools. Yet the story of Mohammed and his mission, of his relation with the divine and the transmission of the Koran, is, of course, one in which profound mystical certainties are both implicit and explicitly described. Nor is there any question that the images and metaphors, the philosophical concepts and cultural counters of the Sufi sages have always been those of Islam. It seems probable that, like so much else, the beginnings of Sufism are multiple, complex: as Idries Shah writes in his *The Sufis*, 'That is why, in Sufi tradition, the "Chain of Transmission" of Sufi schools may reach back to the Prophet by one line, and to Elias by another'. Nor need there be any conflict between the mystics and the orthodox: 'Because the Sufis recognized Islam as a manifestation of the essential upsurge of transcendental teaching, there could be no interior conflict between Islam and Sufism. Sufism was taken to correspond to the inner reality of Islam, as with the equivalent aspect of every other religion and genuine tradition'.

Like all mystical doctrines, Sufism (a term, incidentally, unknown until recent decades — it was coined by a German in the 1820s — and thus never used by the famous Sufi poets and philosophers of the past) postulates an Absolute and goes on to assert that we can attain an awareness of it. This Absolute has been defined in terms both secular and religious. It has been called the Reality of Existence, the Reality of Being. Being is of its nature singular, since nothing that exists does so to a greater degree than anything else: it either is or it is not. This singularity is the Divine. Set within the ideologies of Islam, it becomes specific. Personified, it becomes the object of a transcendent love. Yet one may ask, how can there be an object when the devotee, too, is necessarily part of and one with the cosmic unity?

It seems, therefore, that we face a paradox; God is separate from the worshipper, and at the same time is the worshipper himself; the passionate element in Sufism (like that of the Hindu *bakhtis*) can only come from a

12

perceived duality that acts as a barrier between God and the worshipper. It is the barrier itself, however, that resolves this paradox: its resistance sets up precisely the intense devotional energy which the worshipper must develop in order to burst through it. Beyond lies that in which no paradox survives: the intense awareness of oneness, of the magnificent unity of the cosmos, absolute and indivisible. This perceived singularity, in which at one level one remains oneself, at another one totally loses oneself, is the Real, and it is with this Reality that Sufism is concerned. To reach it, to understand it, to see it clearly — in different words, to reach and understand God — is the object of its disciplines.

At the end of the Sufi path, therefore, as at the far limit of other spiritual or mystical processes, there seems to lie an all-devouring blaze in which duality and self both vanish. And the pathway is marked, both in general terms and with the special signposts of Sufism. Professor A. M. A. Shushtery in his *Outlines of Islamic Culture* tells us, 'A Sufi believes that it is by purifying his heart and not by observances of religious rituals, or prayer or fast, one can realize the truth . . . It is through self-discipline, devotion, virtue and intention that one can know his God. This stage is called *fana-fil-lah* or annihilation in God . . .' The route is by way of *maqam,* translated as 'stations', each of which corresponds to a particular spiritual attainment. Also on the way are experiences of ecstasy — *hal* or *ahwal,* meaning 'state' or 'states' — which, like the stations, have finally to be transcended. The stations are reached by a series of exercises prescribed by one's Teacher, but for the experience of *hal* there is no prescription. 'Hal', wrote Ali al-Hujwiri in the eleventh century, 'is something that descends into a man, without his being able to repel it when it comes, or to attract it when it goes . . .'

Yet in Sufism one often comes across mistrust not only of the stations as ends in themselves, but also of the ecstatic states. It is not that they are considered spurious; on the contrary, it is precisely the genuineness of the

13

divine energy that makes Sufi writers doubt the fitness of those minds that so abruptly and sometimes so catastrophically receive it. It is as though the Sufi path had on either side of it pleasant bowers, shady places, welcoming groves, and in each of these there was a group of people murmuring to each other, 'See? We have arrived'. Some repeat certain exercises, convinced that to continue in this way is the object of their journey. Others again stand with eyes rolled up, or whirl with widespread arms, or roll on the ground, a light froth upon their lips; they cry out the names of God and feel themselves filled with a divine response. Yet, faintly, perhaps through difficult country, perhaps up an ever-increasing slope, the path winds on and the traveller truly concerned to reach its end must leave these others behind, each of them comforted by apparent certainty, each of them deceived. It is he, stubborn in his quest and not disturbed by the passage of the years or the hardships of the journey, who has the only chance of reaching the true goal. Writing in his *Revelation of the Veiled*, Ali al-Hujwiri tells us, 'All the Sheikhs of the Path are agreed that when a man has escaped from the captivity of the "stations" and gets rid of the impurity of the "states" and is liberated from the abode of change and decay and becomes endowed with all praiseworthy qualities, he is disjoined from all qualities'. In other words, beyond *maqam*, beyond *hal*, there is another state, the condition of peace, of self-realization, partaking of the cosmic unity; that final state he calls *tamkin*. Seen by one in that stable condition, doubtless the followers of the exercises seem little better than apprentices, while those in the grip of ecstasy must appear simply unprepared, unready for the force that has entered them. Thus what in many other traditions would be taken as proof of a spiritual journey properly undertaken and joyfully completed, indicates to Sufis little more than that the journey is under way.

A bewildering array of sages, saints and self-styled masters moves towards us from the recesses of Asia, and we may be forgiven when in our minds their several

14

doctrines begin to merge into one ill-defined if attractive mish-mash of reach-me-down exoticism. Yet we should be careful: each tradition has been moulded by its own centuries, and by the society from which it has sprung. If we are to deal with the Hindu guru, for example, we must remember that reincarnation and the concept of *karma* are of the essence of his teaching. With the Sufis, as we have seen, it is Islam that provides the terminology and much of the ritual. The Buddhists of Tibet and those of the discipline we know as Zen wrap their teachings in the preconceptions and vocabulary of the lands where those teachings developed. Each tradition appeals in a different way, demands a different kind of discipline, suggests its goals in different terms. There is in the end, it seems, no 'Eastern philosophy', no 'Asiatic religion'.

The difference between one and another discipline may be crucial, either for an individual's own development or, possibly, for the development of the West as a whole. If it is true that the people of Europe, and those whose cultures stem from that of Europe, are now in a new condition of bewilderment and doubt; if it is true that Christianity, a religion of ethics and of revelation, cannot become again what it was before scientific materialism routed it; if it is true that more and more Westerners are embarked upon the search for an individual experience of the transcendent, and upon the self-discovery that must both precede and follow that experience; if all this is true, then the attitude that we take up now to this or that particular teaching may well have repercussions over many years. Our Western culture is changing and, threatened or excited by that possibility, we have begun to look beyond the borders of the West for guidance. It is necessary that we look clearly and learn to distinguish between the various solutions suggested by the cultures and traditions which we may examine.

Mircea Eliade in his essay *Experiences of the Mystic Light** writes 'In the course of human history there have

---

*Published in *The Two and the One,* London 1965.

15

been a thousand different ways of conceiving and evaluating the Spirit ... For all conceptualization is irremediably linked with language, and consequently with culture and history. One can say that the meaning of the supernatural light is directly conveyed to the soul of the man who experiences it — and yet its meaning can only come fully to his consciousness clothed in a pre-existent ideology'. It is the present dilemma of the West that it has no such pre-existent ideology; the politics of ecclesiastical domination and the essential dualism of Christianity have reduced the cultural impact of the monistic experience of the mystics to relative insignificance. The separation made by religion between Mankind and God, and by science between Mankind and Nature, has denied us a framework for any notion of cosmic unity, even for any real conception of an inner self not couched in the arid terms of psycho-analytical theory. If we are to pursue such a notion, such a conception, it seems to me we had better try to do so through disciplines that fit in as nearly as possible with those ideas, about society, about culture, about the spirit and about the cosmos, that we have developed.

It may be that an implication of the greatest significance to the West is contained in one of the names by which Sufis are known: *Ahl al ishara*, 'Those who learn by allusion'. For Sufi preceptors it is the effect of their teaching, and not the teaching itself, which is of the first importance. Not what is said or done, but what happens to the listener as a result of what is said or done, is the Teacher's primary concern. What a Sufi says or writes need not be factually true; it is an instrument intended to work upon the minds of those who come across it. Metaphor, hyperbole, joke or boredom, all these are tools that the Sufi Master may use to harmonize with his disciples. For this reason, quite apart from the prevailing priorities of Islamic and especially Persian culture, many of the great Sufi luminaries of the past have been poets. So often active at levels more numerous and deeper than we are conscious of, able at times to yield layer after layer

16

of meaning to our fascinated scrutiny, lingering in the mind with an echoing after-impact that sometimes lasts as long as memory itself, poetry is the ideal medium for those who want to move us as it were obliquely, through allusion.

As a result, those who follow the Sufi path soon begin to learn in a manner new to them. The process of learning itself, rather than anything factually learned, begins to alter them, to alter the way they think and the way they perceive the world. Long before the Sufi way turns into a purely mystical discipline therefore, it works at the level of the intellect and the imagination. Its first stages are intended to prepare one for the later experiences, in order that one should not mistake their nature. Properly directed by a teacher who understands his individual needs, the disciple will achieve the sought-after ecstasy central to mysticism only when completely ready for it. Then, far from overwhelming him, it will complete him.

It is not for nothing that Sufis, therefore, equate the Absolute with Reality. The process of learning is the process of discovering what really exists. In order to do this, the neophyte upon the path must be persuaded to use his senses, his intelligence and his imagination in a new fashion. He must be helped towards a new kind, as well as a new level, of consciousness. Here Sufism, like certain other similar disciplines, begins to link with present developments in psychology. As Professor Robert Ornstein has written in his *The Psychology of Consciousness,* 'We know . . . that our "normal" consciousness is not complete, but is an exquisitely evolved, selective personal construction whose primary purpose is to ensure biological survival. But this mode, although necessary for survival, is not necessarily the only one in which consciousness can operate . . . The automatization of ordinary consciousness is a trade-off: for the sake of survival, we lose much of the richness of experience . . . The deautomatization of consciousness is the key. It enables us personally to note factors which had previously escaped attention. It is here that the work of the

17

esoteric traditions is most fruitfully incorporated into Western science'. The many automatic responses we make to our environment, although necessary for sanity and efficiency, stand between us and the world's reality. To reach the real, we have to learn to respond to it; we have, in other words, to become real ourselves.

A way in which one may differentiate between various mystical traditions is to see what attitude they take to reality — the hard, intractable reality of the physical and social world we all inhabit. One view is that of Hinduism, which conceives of the undifferentiated unity glimpsed during the ecstatic experience as the only true reality; it therefore insists upon the illusory nature of the differentiated world available to ordinary sense-experience. The disciples of the spiritual guru are enjoined, as are in the course of time all orthodox Hindus, to withdraw from that illusory world and to base themselves upon the cosmic unity that is Brahman. If everything is finally one, then family attachments, relationships, activity in the world, all of which reflect subject-object dependencies, must be fundamentally misguided. The disciple therefore casts them off, removes himself to an *ashram,* and there attempts to match the singularity of the cosmos with his own. Withdrawal of a similar nature, to hermitage and cloister, marks the history of Christian mysticism; for reasons practical and political, as well as philosophical, it has largely been the preserve of the enclosed orders — or else, by definition of the Church, of heretics.

The whole burden of what such disciplines teach is that the serious person, the person dedicated to the search for ultimate reality, must turn away from the illusion of differentiated 'normality', as a Hindu might say, or from the temptations of the world, as a Christian might put it. Yet such withdrawal is not necessary in other traditions. Zen Buddhists, for example, while seeking *samadhi,* or the ecstatic annihilation of self, do not make this the end of their endeavours. On the contrary, writes Katsuki Sekida in *Zen Training,* 'if you want to

18

attain genuine enlightenment and emancipation, you must go completely through this condition . . .' In his maturity the student of Zen 'goes out into the actual world of routine and lets his mind work with no hindrance . . . If we accept that there is an object in Zen practice, then it is this freedom of the mind in actual living'. This is the fourth category of *samadhi,* the one that lies beyond mere ecstasy and, as we have seen, Sufi beliefs too accommodate such a condition in that level of consciousness called by Hujwiri *tamkin,* and elsewhere *baga.*

Although both Zen and Sufi teachings have led to the formation of monastic orders, within which those devoted to the ascetic life tend to their own spiritual development and, perhaps, learn in time to help others through the same process, many of the followers have always been laymen. The Sufi orders have through the centuries of their existence been surrounded by the non-monastics who were tied to them by vows and ceremonies of initiation. In Islam above all there can surely be no incompatibility between the secular and the mystical life, when the Prophet upon whose Message it stands was himself a merchant, a politician and a military leader as well as a religious philosopher and a mystic. Indeed the impact of Mohammed's life depends upon the contrast between his outer ordinariness and the blazing light of divinity with which he was filled. Thus it comes as no surprise to find a Sufi thinker, Abu Nasr Sarraj, pointing out as early as the 10th century that extreme asceticism could be as debilitating to the spirit as luxury, and doubting the value of the hermit's seclusion for the good reason that the sources of evil lie within the self. Human beings, whatever their spiritual condition, ought, he considered, to fulfil their obligations in the world; self-illumination would make them even better able to do so.

From the beginning, therefore, a large proportion of Sufis have maintained their connection with the 'ordinary' world, and in the list of Sufism's great men there stand many who by no stretch of the imagination could be considered ascetic or monastic. For them, the effects of what they knew, had seen and understood were brought into play in their dealings with the world about them. What they believed shone through what they wrote and did. They had prepared their minds for the mystical experience, and when it came, when it had filled them, they became, not frenzied, but infinitely richer. That wealth they then brought to bear on those around them, those who came to them, those who heard and read their treatises.

It was yet another 10th-century Sufi sage, Abu Bakr al-Kalabadhi, who wrote, 'If a man's ecstasy is weak, he exhibits ecstasy . . . If, however, his ecstasy is strong, he controls himself and is passive'. In that state of controlled ecstasy, calmed inwardly by the certainty that only enlightenment can bring, the Sufi is free to move about the world, to act in it, to take his place in it, and often to excel in it. He has achieved a new level of perception, a new kind of understanding, a new breadth of consciousness, he has experienced the cosmos as unity and so has understood his own significance: he is the enlightened man.

It is no wonder that the great luminaries of Islam, whose works no passing of the generations seems able to diminish, have in so many cases been Sufis. As we have seen, it is claimed even by the most orthodox doctors of religious law that the first Sufi was the Prophet himself. But the long line of the distinguished winds down the centuries of Islam as though by their brightness to mark out the path of their tradition. That is not to say that with each of them the tradition made a greater or lesser degree of 'progress', but rather that each lights that segment of the path where his illumination will be of the greatest use.

Nevertheless, Abu Hamid Mohammed el-Ghazali must stand as the figure, reconciliatory, scholarly, deeply philosophical and profoundly religious, with whom Sufism made a new beginning. It was he who gathered

20

together the doctrines and ideas of his Sufi predecessors, selected, synthesized, and finally reconciled his conclusions with the orthodoxies of Islam. But underlying his patient and creative scholasticism there burned a constant, mystic fire, and the life that he breathed into the academic clay, once he had gathered it and kneaded it into shape, was that of the Sufi certainties.

Born in north-eastern Persia in 1058, he was brought up and educated by a Sufi master. Before he was thirty-five he had been appointed to the Chair of Philosophy and Theology at Nizamiyya University, one of the great establishments that made Baghdad the centre of Islamic culture. Although el-Ghazali, the youngest of the university's professors, was instantly acclaimed, he turned his back on fame and success after only five years. It was not that he disliked praise, indeed, he confessed that he liked it too well, but rather that he had come to the end of what he might usefully arrive at through the techniques of scholasticism, had reached the limits, both as student and as teacher, of what in the academic world had value for him.

As he wrote later, 'I next turned with set purpose to the method of Sufism. I knew that the Sufi way includes both intellectual belief and practical activity . . . The intellectual belief was easier. But it became clear to me, however, that what is most distinctive of mysticism is something which cannot be apprehended by study, but only by immediate experience, by ecstasy and by moral change. I apprehended clearly that the mystics were men who had real experience, not men of words, and that I had already progressed as far as was possible by way of intellectual apprehension . . .'

In the work he was yet to do there would be, within the academic integument that gave it both form and legitimacy, an elusive other certainty baffling to scholars, a hint of secrets which, although by their nature no words can communicate them, he was taken wilfully to have left unrevealed. Nevertheless he was to write and speak a great deal, his works finally becoming among the

21

most influential ever published. After wandering for twelve years (the classical period of dervish training), during which he 'had no other objective than that of seeking solitariness, overcoming selfishness, fighting passions, trying to make clear my soul, to complete my character', he returned, changed but active, to the world. The work he did during his lifetime earned him the amazing title of The Authority of Islam; but after his death his work spread even wider than the religion's boundaries. He had woven into his philosophy the ideas of both Jewish and Christian mysticism, had adapted the transcendental world-scheme of Plotinus and the neo-Platonists; now his new synthesis, fruitfully translated, returned these theories and certainties, embellished and increased, to the cultures from which he had drawn them. In Hebrew and Latin his books spread through the academies and among the churchmen of Europe. That 13th century imperial genius, the Hohenstaufen Frederick II, as Holy Roman Emperor the ruler of Sicily (and happily engaged there in creating his own synthesis between Europe and the Middle East), had el-Ghazali's books translated into Latin. St. Thomas Aquinas, another great synthesizer, drew on his theories, as he did on those of the pagan Plotinus. El-Ghazali, known to the Schoolmen of the West as Algazel, became a figure central to the work of the universities of Padua and Bologna, and later of other Italian centres of learning. A few years on, Occam, whose 'razor' logicians still like to flourish, was basing much of his anti-scholastic views on el-Ghazali's treatises. The ascetic struggling in the arid depths of Syria with the problems of self-development had become, posthumously and perhaps despite his wishes, a world figure, and paradoxically one often beloved of the very academics who by their training were perhaps among the least able to understand him.

El-Ghazali's was a liberating effect upon Islamic thought. The increasingly narrow orthodoxies of the doctors of law were challenged and, indeed, superseded by the refreshing speculation he pioneered and endorsed.

22

His attitude to philosophy opened new approaches to religion, as well as to other facets of human spiritual and psychological existence. His belief that thought was natural and right was reinforced by his conviction that human will was free and that human beings had the God-given ability to choose between alternatives. However, he went beyond both philosophy and active choice in his certainty that the ultimate perceptions take place in the condition of ecstasy, and that the reality then perceived takes precedence over anything else mankind may know. For this reason, both theology and philosophy had to be finally subordinated to personal experience, through which a person may achieve revelations more piercing and direct than any truth arrived at by mere ratiocination. But in the end, like all great spiritual teachers, he was not his doctrines, but was in himself the truth he taught. What he knew with the very centre of himself no words could describe or pass to anyone else. In his *Revival of Religious Sciences* he wrote, 'The question of divine knowledge is so deep that it is really known only to those who have it. A child has no real knowledge of the attainments of an adult. An ordinary adult cannot understand the attainments of a learned man. In the same way, a learned man cannot understand the experiences of enlightened saints or Sufis'. One can only write what can be written; for the rest, one either *is* it — or one is not.

Jalaluddin Rumi, whom Sufis call 'The Master' and Professor Fatemi entitles The Light of Sufism, was born in Balkh, now in Afghanistan, in 1207. His father was a famous scholar and theologian, so that Rumi's early training was in the rigorously classical and logical modes. When he was twelve his family left Balkh and, after some time spent in travelling about the Middle East, finally settled in Konia, anciently Iconium, in what is now Turkey. Rumi married, was left a widower, married again; from both marriages he had children. He early became a teacher, but soon he was himself wandering through western Asia in the company of a Sufi master

23

named Burhan al-Din, his task now self-development. When after some years he returned to Konia, he resumed the teaching of theology, but added to it a new spiritual resonance through the guidance he was able to give. As a result, he quickly achieved a position of great religious — and thus, in Islam, social and even secular — importance. When he was at the height of this relatively conventional fame, he met the Sufi teacher, Shamsuddin of Tabriz.

This strange and powerful man, who seemed to some no more than a noisy, arrogant blusterer, at once dislocated Rumi's life. In the esoteric traditions of Asia, relying as they do on the transmission of a mystic essence from a teacher to a disciple, there occurs again and again that moment of recognition in which Master and student understand — wordlessly, at once — that they are destined to work together. Such a moment evidently occurred between Rumi and Shamsuddin; the revered theologican, seized with an intoxication that expressed itself at times in solitary dance, placed himself without reservation among the wandering Sufi's pupils. As his son wrote, 'The great professor became a beginner in self-perfection'. The orthodox criticized, bewailed the loss of their teacher or decided simply that Rumi was mad. Shamsuddin after fifteen months left Konia, but Rumi continued his inward, intensely devoted progress. Perhaps then, perhaps a little later, in 1248, Shamsuddin died, apparently in violence caused by the jealousies and antagonisms Rumi's 'strange' behaviour had provoked. Eventually, however, Rumi, who was no longer to be deflected, reconciled the increasing pressures of his inward search with the social demands of the people of Konia, or, more accurately, reconciled the people of Konia to the demands of his inward search, in part by guiding them in their own.

To understand the role that Shamsuddin — internalized by his pupil, his religious essence transferred — played thenceforth in the life of Rumi, one must understand the nature of the feeling that exists, in living

24

mystical traditions, between *murshid* and *murid, guru* and *shishya,* between teacher and taught. The Master becomes a living metaphor for the perfection of the Absolute. He seems for the disciple at once the stepping-stone to divinity and, as a self-realized man, divinity made flesh. At the same time there exists in both the conviction that between them the transmission of a quality, indefinable yet unmistakable, can take place, through which the disciple will be permanently altered. When this transmission has occurred, the disciple is in no doubt about what he has gained, nor will the departure or death of the Master diminish one iota of it: he has been flooded by a perception of the Absolute so clear that almost nothing he can do will make him lose it, especially since all he does is done only in its light. In him, therefore, the fact of the teacher and the fact of the divine merge into an inextricable whole, fusing with his own essence to produce a new level of being. Thus Rumi could write:

> When I go into the mine he is the carnelian and ruby;
> When I go into the sea he is the pearl.
> When I am on the plains he is the garden rose; when I
> come to the heavens he is the star . . .
> My master and my sheikh, my pain and my remedy;
> I declare these words openly, my Shams and my God.
> I have reached truth because of you, O my soul of truth.

These lines come from his *Divani Shamsi Tabriz;* he was now in the condition that Professor Arasteh has described in his *Rumi the Persian.* 'He was all love, all joy, all happiness. He had no grief, no anxiety. He was totally born, totally spontaneous . . .'

Rumi now felt able to set up a school of devotees of his own, and in it to guide others towards that state to which the fact of Shams had guided him. It was now, too, that he probably began to work on that six-volume compilation of fables, poems, tales, examples and speculations, the *Mathnavi,* through which, perhaps more than anywhere else in his work, he attempted to induce in the reader something of his own state of mind; as Idries Shah

25

puts it, 'a picture is built up by multiple impact to infuse into the mind the Sufi message'. In the 'Mevlevi Order' was later codified what had at times been his own practice of dancing, developing the steady whirling which is at one level a mechanical aid to the induction of trance, but is at another (I quote Shah again) 'designed to bring the Seeker into affinity with the mystical current, in order to be transformed by it'.

But for Rumi trance was, as it must be for a Sufi, no more than a stage in the process of self-development. Again and again, in the *Mathnavi*, in his *Fihi ma Fihi* and elsewhere, he refers to the condition beyond trance, beyond belief, beyond mere creed or doctrine.

> Cross and the churches, from end to end
> I surveyed; He was not on the cross.
> I went to the idol temple, to the ancient pagoda,
> No trace was visible there.
> I bent the reins of search to the Ka'ba,
> He was not in the resort of old and young.
> I gazed into my own heart;
> There I saw Him, He was nowhere else.

And, as he stated explicitly in the *Divani Shamsi Tabriz*, 'I have put duality away . . . One I seek, One I know, One I see, One I call'. This monism Rumi experienced directly, and he interpreted the experience as love. He is above all the poet of transcendent love; he saw it clearly and never made it an excuse for rhetoric, imprecise although exciting. He had very definite ideas about the nature of the human being, and the struggle needed to transcend the polarity between reason and instinct in order to reach, once again, the state of peaceful certainty beyond. In that final condition, an individual was able to integrate instinct and reason with intuitive perception and the love that would both keep him whole and permit him direct involvement with every aspect of the cosmos. Love, in other words, became at this level a medium for perceptions otherwise impossible to human beings. It is this vision of the person evolved that remains immediate and full of meaning. As we struggle earnestly to understand ourselves in a world where we seem, at precisely the same time and with precisely the same dedication, to be building endless barriers and creating endless pressures, Rumi's insights and oblique admonitions are more relevant than they have ever been.

Born into a Sufi family almost exactly a hundred years after El-Ghazali, almost exactly forty years before Rumi, Ibn el-Arabi, like them, displayed great gifts even in childhood. Brought up in the heyday of Arabic Spain (paradoxically, one of the most civilized societies in European history) he studied in Lisbon, Seville and Cordoba. All his life he wrote poetry; in it, he often returned to the theme of human love — deeply felt and magnificently described — used as a metaphor for the transcendent emotion that lies glittering at the core of all his work. Yet 'metaphor' does inadequate justice to the reality he evidently experienced at both levels; either reading, the sensual and the mystical, is a true reading. He was, indeed, frequently attacked for being no more than a writer of erotic poetry who sought to cover his indulgence by claiming a spiritual meaning for it. The fact is that among the various levels of perception and feeling experienced by the developed person some are not less real than others, nor does the last stage cancel all those that have gone before. Each is true in its own way. The error is to imagine any one of them the total reality. The divine is the only total reality, and that includes all aspects, all levels.

Thus for Ibn el-Arabi his sensual response to feminine beauty was real, not imagined; yet, precisely because of its reality, he saw that beauty as a metaphor for the world's beauty, the beauty of nature, just as he saw in the relation between men and women a metaphor for that between humanity and God. For if Genesis is true, then woman is made in man's image as man is in God's; thus, as God stands, in love and concern, to his creation, Nature, so man stands to woman. The feeling is real in its own terms, yet only becomes complete in the metaphysical dimension. Today we may reject Genesis

27

and thus the metaphor may lose some of its particular force, but it is at our peril that we reject this awareness of the multiplicity of the real.

Ibn el-Arabi made such ideas explicit in his prose treatises, for he was a scholar more complete even than his doctorial critics. His explanatory notes to his love poetry seem to have satisfied the most puritanical and rigorously orthodox theologians that he had nowhere deviated from the approved path of righteousness. Thus his encyclopaedic survey of Sufi ideas, *Futuhat-al-Makkiyya* and his dissertation on various aspects of Sufism, *Fusus-al-hikam*, like his other books of theory and speculation, passed to succeeding generations not as the outpourings of a heedless poet, but as the considered works of a scholar acknowledged to be among the greatest of his time.

As Rumi and other Sufis have, Ibn el-Arabi emphasized (for example in Chapter XXII of *Fusus-al-hikam*) that beyond *fana*, the mystical annihilation of self, there exists another state in which that experience is, as it were, stabilized, made permanent. It was because of his awareness of this ultimate condition that he was able to accept the structures of orthodoxy. He realized that within every such structure, perhaps almost snuffed out by its weight but certainly once ablaze, there could be found the flame of mysticism. All great teachers — Moses, Jesus, Mohammed and others — had embodied that flame, and though human perversity might distort faith in the divine, as in the case of self-punishing ascetics, yet any true religion might be the mystic's starting-point. It is no wonder that throughout his life doctrinaire scholars and theologians, like men in narrow valleys which they believe to be the world, condemned his breadth of understanding as the dangerous deviations of a heretic.

A near contemporary of Rumi, and as widely known wherever Persian poetry is remembered and recited, is Saadi of Shiraz. Born in 1184, he like el-Ghazali was educated at the Nizamiyya University in Baghdad,

28

studying there under the Sufi sage, Jilani. Thereafter he spent many years wandering, in the prescribed poverty of the dervish, through the Middle East, North Africa, Ethiopia and Asia Minor. It was typical of his troubled period that at one point he was captured by Crusaders, and had to be ransomed. The price paid for this incomparable poet, employed while captive as a trench-digger, was ten dinars.

Saadi's most famous works, his *Gulistan* and *Bustan*, 'Rose Garden' and 'Orchard', are rich mixtures of aphorisms, proverbs, love lyrics, erotic stories, descriptions of great rulers and, above all, pronouncements in prose and verse on morality and ethics, on the right role of rulers and the proper attitudes of their advisers, on tyranny and its consequences, on human cruelty, human frailty and human potential. All this he did in a style apparently straightforward, easily assimilable; the uncluttered affection that informs his writings has made them for seven centuries a source from which ordinary people have drawn advice, information and enjoyment. Yet in his lifetime the Mongols came crashing out of Central Asia, dismembering Persia and bringing to an end the great centuries of Baghdad's cultural supremacy. Seen against the circumstances of history, Saadi's urbanity, his humanity and, not least, his lightness of touch, seem superhuman.

Yet Saadi, too, for all his ease of manner, saw the truth as complex and many-layered. In him, this often expressed itself through paradox and contradiction. There is no facile consistency in the surface of his works; those wishing to refute him can often find the arguments they need elsewhere in his own writings. As a result of this, and of his word-play and wit, those who read or hear his works are constantly forced to become aware of the very act of understanding, and thus both of the works themselves and of their own responses. One cannot surrender to passive delight for long before some change of direction, some unexpected profundity, joke or reversal jolts one into intellectual activity. What this suggests is that the consistency in what Saadi wrote lies at another level and perhaps in another place, not in the works but in those who receive them. In their complexity they are, it seems, primers for self-development, instruments for the dynamic alteration of consciousness. He was a Sufi in his sense of the universality of religion, in his humanity, in his understanding of the links between flesh and spirit, but above all perhaps in this, that he knew that the value of what is taught lies in the minds of those whom it reaches.

The work of Hafiz, too, has its unsuspected levels, its complexities. Born some hundred years after Rumi, in Shiraz, he was during his early manhood installed in a school of his own, where he taught theology and expounded his theories of religion. He lost his father when a young child, and later both his wife and son. His poetry appears in the main a celebration of romantic love, modified by his awareness of himself as too old for such emotion. From this it has been inferred that the bulk of it was written when he was aged. Whether that is so or not, he was so acutely aware of the value of love that he detested those who, as it were, clouded its brightness: the censorious, the hypocritical, the sanctimonious, the pedantically orthodox. He believed in the liberty of the intellect and of the senses; no wonder that there were those who thought him both profligate and heretic.

He, too, in his works ran the gamut of modes and feelings, for his poems were licentious, mystical, humorous, satirical or epigrammatic by turns. At the centre of his writings, however, lie his cool, affectionate humanity marked by a dislike for fanaticism, for the trappings of power and wealth — and his mystical certainties. Addressing a man of property who had attempted to add to his secular riches the acclaim proper to one returning from pilgrimage to Mecca, Hafiz wrote, 'Boast not rashly of thy fortune. Thou hast visited the Temple — and I have seen the Lord of the temple'. This is the nub of the matter, and the certainty which that conviction gave to Hafiz sustained him in a world where, in the wake of the

30

Mongol assault, social and political structures were collapsing, religion had been coarsened and civilization weakened, apparently forever. It is the certainty of the mystic, and Hafiz shared it with all the great names of Sufism.

In that list there are many more, stretching from the 10th century ecstatic, Hallaj crucified by the orthodox, and the founders of Sufism in the centuries before, by way of philosophers and poets — the chemist, Fariduddin Attar, the polymath Omar Khayyam and many others — solitary saints, men in humble occupations hiding the secrets of their serenity, great leaders, heads of dervish orders, to the adepts of today. Yet for each neophyte setting forth on this difficult path, the only important person, eclipsing all the great, will be his chosen Teacher. It is the Teacher he must trust, the Teacher who must know the right sequence of his development, through the Teacher that he will discover the intellectual and emotional adjustments necessary to prepare him for the knowledge to come.

At first the knowledge will be short-lived, entering the student at will, and leaving even if bidden to stay. 'I staggered to my feet and looked about me and tried to remember what had until that instant been crowded in my brain and it was all gone, all the details, covered over by the present and my humanity as a flash-flood will cover the pebbles lying in the dry bottom of an ancient creek. It was all there, or at least some of it was there, for I could sense it lying there beneath the flash-flood of my humanity. And I wondered, vaguely, as I stood there, if this burial of the matters transmitted by my friend might not be for my own protection, if my mind, in a protective reflex action, had covered it and blanked it out in a fight for sanity'. But in the end, the altered self emerges into the sought-for state of readiness, and the ultimate certainty responds: 'It was all there again — all that I had known and felt, all that I had tried to recapture since and could not find again. All the glory and the wonder and some terror too, for in understanding there must be a

31

certain terror . . . There were many universes and many sentient levels and at certain time-space intervals they became apparent and each of them was real, as real as the many geologic levels that a geologist could count. Except that this was not a matter of counting; it was seeing and sensing and knowing they were there. Not knowing how, but filled with mystic faith, we . . . took the step out into the infinite knowing and were there'.

The quotations come from no mystic's reminiscences, but from a science-fiction novel, *Destiny Doll*, by Clifford Simak. Those who think this inappropriate have understood very little of what has gone before.

2/ii.

Sanai and Sufism in the 20th Century West

David Pendlebury

The following is the text of an address delivered in Kabul, Afghanistan, on October 22nd, 1977. The occasion was a seminar, attended by more than ninety scholars and writers from fifteen countries, to mark the 900th anniversary of the birth of the great Sufi poet Hakim Sanai of Ghazna.

Apart from a few initial words of apology in Persian, and the quotations from Hakim Sanai, the address was given in the English language, followed by a summary in Persian by Dr. Abdul Hakim Tabibi.

Appended to the text there is a brief discussion of the main points raised both formally and informally by various participants at the seminar.

It seems to me that the best way for me to begin would be to explain briefly how I come to be taking part in this seminar. The obvious answer is that certain gentlemen among you were kind enough to invite me; but that again begs the question 'Why?' Because it has come to your attention that a few years ago I wrote a short book — a *very* short book — on the *Hadiqa* of Hakim Sanai.[1] Yes, but how did *that* come about?

In 1964 I read a book called *The Sufis* by Sayed Idries Shah.[2] The very first words in this extraordinary book are a quotation, in English, from Hakim Sanai's *Hadiqat ul Haqiqat*, which I re-translate as follows:

> All mankind is asleep
> living in a desolate world;
> the desire to transcend this
> is mere habit and custom,
> not religion — idle fairy tales.
>
> Stop bragging in the presence
> of men of the path:
> better consume yourself
> like burning chaff.
>
> If you yourself
> are upside down in reality,
> then your wisdom and faith
> are bound to be topsy-turvy.
>
> Stop weaving a net about yourself;
> burst like a lion from the cage.

These lines and the ensuing pages of Shah's book made such an impression on me that I conceived a very strong wish to become more closely associated with this man and his work, and eventually opportunities began to present themselves. One avenue of approach seemed to be to try and follow the innumerable 'leads' which he indicated in *The Sufis* and in his brief but invaluable sequel to that book, *Special Problems in the Study of Sufi Ideas*.[3] From the latter I discovered that there existed an English translation of part of Sanai's *Hadiqa* and this I was eventually able to obtain.[4] I have already described my subsequent adventures with it in some detail in my own little book, so I shall not go into them here; however, I should like to amplify in this gathering how great was the encouragement I received from Idries Shah during the first embryonic stages of the book's existence.

When your invitation came I was of course highly flattered; but my first reaction was to refuse. The last thing I would claim to be is an orientalist, or *any* kind of scholar for that matter; and as for being a Sufi, however much I may sometimes wish I were one, reading a few lines of the *Hadiqa* is quite enough to remind me that I am not. So at first I was going to refuse, as I sensed that in more ways than one I should be out of my depth.

But on the other hand I do share with you a deep affection for the poet Hakim Sanai Ghaznawi, and to be able to pay homage to him in this way on the occasion of his 900th anniversary seemed an opportunity too good to be missed, especially as I am unlikely to be able to attend his thousandth anniversary. In the midst of these hesitations I got in touch with Idries Shah, and once again his encouragement gave further weight to my decision to come.

And so three factors seem to have brought me here: yourselves, Hakim Sanai and Idries Shah.

I wish it were Shah, and not myself, talking to you now and commemorating with you the monumental work of Hakim Sanai of Ghazna; for if I am neither scholar nor Sufi, he for his part is an almost unique blend of the two.[5] For those who know him, he is the living proof that the spirit which inspired Sanai is as active today as it was nine centuries ago; and in times as confused as these, that is surely cause for rejoicing.

But let me quote the first couplet translated in my little book, so that there can be no misunderstanding about what it is that is here being praised.

> The seeing soul perceives
> the folly of praising
> other than the creator.

It is not the man, be it Sanai or Shah, but the creative spirit visible in their work that we are celebrating here.

This current seminar, as far as its outward conception goes, seems to be focusing on Hakim Sanai primarily as an *Afghan* phenomenon, as possibly the greatest poet Afghanistan has ever known. This is thoroughly understandable and laudable; every country should be justly proud of its poets and philosophers, especially when they attain the eminence of Hakim Sanai. But, obviously, for an outsider, however well-disposed he may feel towards Afghanistan and the Afghans, this is unlikely to be central in his motivation to study Hakim Sanai. As I see it, Hakim's legacy is and should be for the *whole* of humanity, regardless of national groupings, or even religious groupings for that matter.

One of the amicable background disputes in which I have been involved at this seminar has been the question of whether or not Sufism is the sole prerogative of Islam. For my part I cannot accept that Islam, in the sense of an organized body of dogma and practices, has any exclusive property rights over the manifestations of Sufism; though, of course, in the basic sense of Islam as 'surrender to God' it may be regarded as identical with Sufism, as indeed may certain aspects of Christianity. For me *Tasawwuf*, 'the creed of love', is above and beyond any particular religious formulation and in case this notion should appear like a heretical innovation to you, let me remind you that Hakim Sanai was already saying something of the sort more than eight hundred years ago:

At His door, what is the difference
between Moslem and Christian,
virtuous and guilty?
At his door all are seekers
and He the sought.

It is true that during the past ten centuries Sufism has flourished visibly, and to an unprecedented degree within the bosom of the Islamic culture: but that in itself does not indicate to me, as it does to some of my colleagues here, that Sufism and the Islamic faith are inextricably intertwined. I can perfectly well imagine genuine Sufi activity taking root in non-Moslem countries, such as the one I myself come from. And I am not thinking of some kind of arbitrary grafting of exotic Eastern practices (like the whirling Dervishes of Baron's Court) but of a thoroughly indigenous phenomenon, specifically created to take into account the strengths and

35

weaknesses of the prevalent culture.

I say I can imagine it; but that is being less than honest: I have seen such a thing with my own eyes. To be true it is still in its infancy, and there are plenty of teething troubles; but I venture to state here that in the West a widespread community of people from all walks of life are slowly and methodically preparing themselves for the Sufi undertaking: the conscious evolution of humanity.

That sounds terribly dramatic: the day-to-day reality is much humbler; it is largely a matter of carrying on doing what one did before, perhaps a little more conscientiously, until the conditions of 'time, place and people (*zaman, makan, ikhwan*)', are exactly right for a step forward. The people I have in mind are familiar, to an extent that might surprise a number of my colleagues here, with the ideas of the great classical Sufis of the East, such as Sanai, Mevlana, Attar, etc., and many other lesser-known figures besides them; and I am sure they would wish me to say '*Ishq!*' to all of you gathered here who are students of these and other great men of the past. But you are not likely to find them rushing round Afghanistan in a frantic search for *Khanaqas, Pirs, Sheikhs* and *Wazifas* — not because they do not respect these things, but because they realize that any improvement in their situation can only come from grappling with it on the spot, not from running away from it to some totally alien situation.

When I was working in Afghanistan about four years ago, it used to sadden me to watch the thousands of young 'world-travellers' and 'hippies' who came pouring through usually on their way to India in search of DEEP KNOWLEDGE. It always reminded me of that famous Mulla Nasrudin story in which he loses his key, in the darkness of his own house, but insists on looking for it outside, 'Because', he says, 'there is more light there'. Sanai makes the same point:

> Why don't you seek what you lost
> where you lost it?

36

Over the past decades an intellectual and social climate has come into being in the West in which it is at last possible for the Sufi ideas of Sanai and other great teachers of the past to form the fulcrum for an entirely new movement in human history. Such ideas are no longer merely in the possession of a handful of scholars and travellers, but are rapidly becoming available to an ever-widening circle of informed people in every walk of life. Such ideas are no longer an exotic curiosity, a rare delicacy from distant places and distant times: they are weaving themselves into the very fabric of Western culture.

The mental framework of the society in which Sanai lived and wrote was essentially religious, and very strictly so. The mental framework of Western thought, as we all know, is a scientific and technological one. And yet such an intellectual climate stands just as much in need, as did the dogmatically religious one of Sanai's day, of the subtle, many-sided and many-levelled insights which are perhaps the most immediately obvious spin-off of Sufic activity.[6] There are abundant signs that this process of refinement is already making itself felt in the West, and not a moment too soon, when we consider the almost insoluble problems now confronting the world as a result of the somewhat insensitive application of technology in the past hundred years or so.

If there is to be any improvement in the general condition of mankind, two factors seem to me to be of essential importance, and both of these happen to be of a psychological nature. Firstly, there must be a ruthlessly realistic understanding of what man is and what his situation is. Practically all our problems in this world arise out of misconceptions concerning our own and other's natures. Secondly, there must be a realistic, credible vision of a better state of affairs for mankind, lest the very realization of our grim situation should drive us all to despair. Nowhere have I found these factors more clearly and forcefully expressed than in Hakim Sanai's *Hadiqa*; and it was for that reason that I attempted to

37

convey something of what I had found there to fellow English-speakers. It is for that reason, too, that I am happy to be able to express my gratitude to this great human being on the occasion of the 900th anniversary of his birth.

POSTSCRIPT

Owing to shortage of time, and other pressures, it was not possible at the seminar to discuss fully a number of points arising out of the above address. For the record I should like briefly to mention the most important of these now.

By far the most controversial aspect of the talk seemed to be the assertion that Sufism was not confined solely to the Islamic Religion. Practically the whole of the brief question period was given over to this point. Two closely related questions emerged:

(1) Please explain on what Sufism (*Tasawwuf*) is based, if it is not based on the Religion of Islam, as formulated in the *Qur'an*.

(2) In the minds of millions of Moslems, Sufism (*Tasawwuf*) is identified with a very specific form of activity within Islam: is it not then perverse to identify it with something else, which historically and geographically extends beyond the scope of Islam?

Although these questions are dealt with in the above text, further clarification might be useful. Nothing could be further from my intention than to belittle Islam, which in its essential conception I regard as the highest and purest form of religion the world has yet seen — and is ever likely to see, for that matter. But the evidence of Sufi activity both prior to the foundation of Islam and extending far beyond the sphere of Islamic influence is so abundant and widespread (see Shah, *op. cit.*), that it is impossible to regard Islam and Sufism as coterminous.

The assumption that Sufism is 'based' on something, for instance a religion, is in my view an inversion of the real situation. It is not that Sufism is based on Islam, or any other religion: it is much more a case of these

38

religions demonstrably being based on a common source: Sufism. As for what the foundation of the latter might be, that is a very large and daunting topic. Any brief and provincial answer one might attempt inevitably has about it the dissatisfying ring of a truism, cliché or half-truth. One might call the basis of Sufism 'love', 'conscience', 'the evolution of humanity', etc., etc.; but by themselves these are simply words.

As for the second question, there does not seem to be anything perverse in attempting to apply to a 20th century Western context the vast resources of wisdom and knowledge accumulated by Sufis in other places and times. Indeed there would be something perverse about *not* trying to make use of such resources, once one had stumbled across them.

But why call it *Sufism*? Why not call it something else? It is indeed unfortunate, but perhaps it cannot be helped, that people's notions of what Sufism is and can be, so easily degenerate into a sort of parochial totem pole. Sufism is *always* 'something else', and the wonder of it is that it is always the same. The question arises out of the old confusion between the contents and the container. It is rather like being told that what I am drinking is not wine because I am drinking it out of a disposable paper cup instead of a corroded old brass goblet.

We call it Sufism because that is exactly what it is: a work taken up in accordance with the needs of the present, but entirely in the spirit of the great Sufis of all times, using the knowledge, techniques, materials — and dare I say the *Baraka*? — bequeathed by them to humanity.

REFERENCES
1. Hakim Sanai, *The Walled Garden of Truth*, an abridged translation by D. L. Pendlebury. London 1974; New York 1976.
2. Idries Shah, *The Sufis*, London and New York 1964.
3. Idries Shah, *Special Problems in the Study of Sufi Ideas*, London 1965. The text of a lecture delivered at the

39

University of Sussex, this paper is now incorporated as a chapter in Shah's *The Way of the Sufi*, London 1968.

4. Hakim Sanai, *The First Book of the Hadiqat ul Haqiqat*, edited and translated by Major J. Stephenson, Calcutta 1910.

5.i. *Sufi Studies East and West*, Ed. L. Rushbrook Williams, New York 1973.

ii. Akhmet Azimovitch, 'Idries Shah in Modern Science', *The Voice of Islam*, Vol. XXI. No. 9, Karachi.

6. Among others, the work of Ornstein in the U.S.A. and de Bono in the U.K. come immediately to mind; but a comprehensive list of people in the West whose work has been significantly influenced by Sufi ideas would be exceedingly voluminous and quite beyond the scope of this paper.

2/iii.

Some Sufi Tales from Burton's Arabian Nights

My spirit urged me, once upon a time, to go forth into the country of the Infidels; and I strove with it and struggled to put away from me this inclination; but it would not be rejected. So I fared forth and journeyed about the land of the Unbelievers and traversed it in all its parts; for divine grace enveloped me and heavenly protection encompassed me, so that I met not a single Nazarene but he turned away his eyes and drew off from me, till I came to a certain great city at whose gate I found a gathering of black slaves, clad in armour and bearing iron maces in their hands. When they saw me they rose to their feet and asked me, 'Art thou a leach?' and I answered, 'Yes'. Quoth they, 'Come speak to our King', and carried me before their ruler, who was a handsome personage of majestic presence. When I stood

40

before him, he looked at me and said, 'Art a physician, thou?' 'Yes', quoth I; and quoth he to his officers, 'Carry him to her, and acquaint him with the condition before he enter'. So they took me out and said to me, 'Know that the King hath a daughter, and she is stricken with a sore disease, which no doctor hath been able to cure; and no leach goeth in to her and treateth without healing her but the King putteth him to death. So bethink thee what thou seest fitting to do'. I replied, 'The King drove me to her; so carry me to her'. Thereupon they brought me to her door and knocked; and, behold, I heard her cry out from within, saying, 'Admit to me the physician, lord of the wondrous secret!' And she began reciting:

Open the door! the leach now draweth near;
　And in my soul a wondrous secret speer:
How many of the near far distant are!*
　How many distant far are nearest near!
I was in strangerhood amidst you all:
　But willed the Truth** my solace should appear.
Joined us the potent bonds of Faith and Creed;
　We met as dearest fere greets dearest fere:
He sued for interview whenas pursued
　The spy, and blamed us envy's jibe and jeer.
Then leave your chiding and from blame desist,
　For fie upon you! not a word I'll hear.
I care for naught that disappears and fleets;
　My care's for Things nor fleet nor disappear.

And lo! a Shaykh, a very old man, opened the door in haste and said to me, 'Enter'. So I entered and found myself in a chamber strewn with sweet-scented herbs and with a curtain drawn across one corner, from behind which came a sound of groaning and grame, weak as from an emaciated frame. I sat down before the curtains and was about to offer my salám when I bethought me of his words (whom Allah save and assain!), 'Accost not a

---

*i.e. in spirit; the 'strangers yet' of poor dear Richard Monckton Milnes, Lord Houghton.
**Al Hakk = the Truth, one of the ninety-nine names of Allah.

41

Jew nor a Christian with the salám salutation*; and when ye meet them in the way constrain them to the straitest part thereof'. So I withheld my salutation, but she cried out from behind the curtain, saying, 'Where is the salutation of Unity and Indivisibility, O Khawwás?' I was astonished at her speech and asked, 'How knowest thou me?' whereto she answered, 'When the heart and thoughts are whole, the tongue speaketh eloquently from the secret recesses of the soul. I begged Him yesterday to send me one of His saints, at whose hands I might have deliverance, and behold, it was cried to me from the dark places of my house — Grieve not, for we soon will send thee Ibrahim the Basket-maker'. Then I asked her, 'What of thee?' and she answered, 'It is now four years since there appeared to me the Manifest Truth, and He is the Relator and the Ally, and the Uniter and the Sitter-by; whereupon my folk looked askance upon me with an evil eye and taxed me with insanity, and suspected me of depravity, and there came not in to me doctor but terrified me, nor visitor but confounded me'. Quoth I, 'And who led thee to the knowledge of what thou wottest?' Quoth she, 'The manifest signs and visible portents of Allah; and when the path is patent to thee, thou espiest with thine own eyes both proof and prover'. Now whilst we were talking, behold, in came the old man appointed to guard her, and said, 'What doth thy doctor?' and she replied, 'He knoweth the hurt and hath hit upon the healing' — And Shahrazad perceived the dawn of day and ceased to say her permitted say.

Now when it was the Four Hundred and Seventy-eighth Night, She said, It hath reached me, O auspicious King, that when the Shaykh, her guardian, went in to her

---

*The Moslem is still unwilling to address Salám (Peace be with you) to the Christian, as it is obligatory (Farz) to a Moslem (Koran, Chapt. iv and lxviii). He usually evades the difficulty by saluting the nearest Moslem or by a change of words, Allah Yahdi-k (Allah direct thee to the right way) or 'Peace be upon us and the righteous worshippers of Allah' (not you), or Al-Samm (for Salám) alayka = poison to thee. The idea is old: Alexander of Alexandria in his circular-letter describes the Arian heretics as men whom it is not lawful to salute or to bid 'God-speed'.

he said, 'What doth thy doctor?' and she replied, 'He knoweth the hurt and hath hit upon the healing'. Hereupon he manifested joy and gladness and accosted me with a cheerful countenance, then went and told the King, who enjoined to treat me with all honour and regard. So I visited her daily for seven days, at the end of which time she said to me, 'O Abú Ishák, when shall be our flight to the land of Al-Islam?' 'How canst thou go forth', replied I, 'and who would dare to aid thee?' Rejoined she, 'He who sent thee to me, driving thee as it were'; and I observed, 'Thou sayest sooth'. So when the morrow dawned, we fared forth by the city-gate and all eyes were veiled from us, by commandment of Him who when He desireth aught, saith to it, 'Be', and it becometh†; so that I journeyed with her in safety to Meccah, where she made a home hard by the Holy House of Allah and lived seven years; till the appointed day of her death. The earth of Meccah was her tomb, and never saw I any more steadfast in prayer and fasting than she.

Allah send down upon her His mercies and have compassion on him who saith:

When they to me had brought the leach (and surely
    showed* The signs of flowing tears and pining
    malady),
The face-veil he withdrew from me, and 'neath it naught*
    Save breath of one unsouled, unbodied, could he see.
Quoth he, 'This be a sickness, Love alone shall cure;*
    Love hath a secret from all guess of man wide free.'
Quoth they, 'An folk ignore what here there be with him*
    Nature of ill and eke its symptomology,
How then shall medicine work a cure?' At this quoth I,*
    'Leave me alone; I have no guessing speciality'.

---

†Koran, Chapt. xxxvi, 82. I have before noted that this famous phrase was borrowed from the Hebrews, who borrowed it from the Egyptians.

And they tell a tale of

THE PROPHET AND THE JUSTICE
OF PROVIDENCE

A certain Prophet* made his home for worship on a lofty
mountain, at whose foot was a spring of running water,
and he was wont to sit by day on the summit, that no
man might see him, calling upon the name of Allah the
Most Highest, and watching those who frequented the
spring. One day, as he sat looking upon the fountain,
behold, he espied a horseman who came up and dis-
mounted thereby, and taking a bag from his neck, set it
down beside him, after which he drank of the water and
rested awhile, then he rode away, leaving behind him the
bag which contained gold pieces. Presently up came
another man to drink of the spring, who saw the bag and
finding it full of money took it up; then, after satisfying
his thirst, he made off with it in safety. A little after came
a wood-cutter wight with a heavy load of fuel on his back,
and sat down by the spring to drink, when lo! back came
the first horseman in great trouble and asked him,
'Where is the bag which was here?' and when he
answered, 'I know nothing of it', the rider drew his sword
and smote him and slew him. Then he searched his
clothes, but found naught; so he left him and wended his
ways. Now when the Prophet saw this, he said, 'O Lord,
one man hath taken a thousand dinars and another man
hath been slain unjustly'. But Allah answered him,
saying, 'Busy thyself with thy devotions, for the or-
dinance of the universe is none of thine affair. The father
of this horseman had violently despoiled of a thousand
dinars the father of the second horseman; so I gave the

---

*The story of Moses and Khizr has been noticed before. See Koran,
Chapt. xviii, 64 *et seq.* It is also related, says Lane (ii. 642), by Al-
Kazwini in the Ajaib al-Makhlukát. This must be 'The Angel and
the Hermit' in the Gesta Romanorum, Tale lxxx, which possibly
gave rise to Parnell's Hermit; and Tale cxxvii, 'Of Justice and
Equity'.

44

son possession of his sire's money. As for the wood-cutter, he had slain the horseman's father, wherefore I enabled the son to obtain retribution for himself'. Then cried the Prophet, 'There is none other god than Thou! Glory be to Thee only! Verily, Thou art the Knower of Secrets'.† — And Shahrazad perceived the dawn of day and ceased saying her permitted say.

Now when it was the Four Hundred and Seventy-ninth Night, She said, It hath reached me, O auspicious King, that when the Prophet was bidden by inspiration of Allah to busy himself with his devotions and learned the truth of the case, he cried, 'There is none other god but Thou! Glory be to Thee only! Verily, Thou and Thou alone wottest hidden things'. Furthermore, one of the poets hath made these verses on the matter:

The Prophet saw whatever eyes could see,*
    And fain of other things enquirèd he;
And, when his eyes saw things misunderstood,*
    Quoth he, 'O Lord, this slain from sin was free.
This one hath won him wealth withouten work;*
    Albe appeared he garbed in penury.
And that in joy of life was slain, although*
    O man's Creator free of ain he be'.
God answered, ' 'Twas his father's good thou saw'st.*
    Him take; by heirship not by roguery;
Yon woodman too that horseman's sire had slain;*
    Whose son avenged him with just victory;
Put off, O slave of Me, this thought, for I*
    In men have set mysterious secrecy!
Bow to Our Law and humble thee, and learn*
    For good and evil issues Our decree'.††

And a certain pious man hath told us the tale of

THE FERRYMAN OF THE NILE AND THE HERMIT

I was once a ferryman on the Nile and used to ply

---

†Koran, Chapt. v, 108.
††The doggerel is phenomenal.

between the eastern and the western banks. Now one day, as I sat in my boat, there came up to me an old man of a bright and beaming countenance, who saluted me and I returned his greeting; and he said to me, 'Wilt thou ferry me over for the love of Allah Almighty?' I answered, 'Yes', and he continued, 'Wilt thou moreover give me food for Allah's sake?' to which again I answered, 'With all my heart'. So he entered the boat and I rowed him over to the eastern side, remarking that he was clad in a patched gown and carried a gourd-bottle and a staff. When he was about to land, he said to me, 'I desire to lay on thee a heavy trust'. Quoth I, 'What is it?' Quoth he, 'It hath been revealed to me that my end is nearhand, and that tomorrow about noon thou wilt come and find me dead under yonder tree. Wash me and wrap me in the shroud thou wilt see under my head and after thou hast prayed over me, bury me in this sandy ground and take my gown and gourd and staff, which do thou deliver to one who shall come and demand them of thee'. I marvelled at his words, and I slept there. On the morrow I awaited till noon the event he had announced, and then I forgot what he had said till near the hour of afternoon-prayer, when I remembered it and hastening to the appointed place, found him under the tree, dead, with a new shroud under his head, exhaling a fragrance of musk. So I washed him and shrouded him and prayed over him, then dug a hole in the sand and buried him, after I had taken his ragged gown and bottle and staff, with which I crossed the Nile to the western side and there nighted. As soon as morning dawned and the city-gate opened, I sighted a young man known to me as a loose fellow, clad in fine clothes, and his hands stained with Henna, who said to me, 'Art thou not such an one?' 'Yes', answered I; and he said, 'Give me the trust'.

Quoth I, 'What is that?' Quoth he, 'The gown, the gourd, and the staff'. I asked him, 'Who told thee of them?' and he answered, 'I know nothing, save that I spent yesternight at the wedding of one of my friends singing and carousing till daylight, when I lay me down

46

to sleep and take my rest; and, behold! there stood by me a personage who said, "Verily Allah Almighty hath taken such a saint to Himself and hath appointed thee to fill his place; so go thou to a certain person (naming the ferryman), and take of him the dead man's gown and bottle and staff, for he left them with him for thee".' So I brought them out and gave them to him; whereupon he doffed his clothes, and donning the gown went his way and left me.† And when the glooms closed around me, I fell a-weeping; but that night while sleeping I saw the Lord of Holiness (glorified and exalted be He!) in a dream saying, 'O my servant, is it grievous to thee that I have granted to one of My servants to return to Me? Indeed, this is of My bounty, that I vouchsafe to whom I will, for I over all things am Almighty'.

So I repeated these couplets:

> Lover with lovèd†† loseth will and aim;*
>> All choice (an couldst thou know) were sinful shame,
> Or grant He favour and with union grace*
>> Or from thee turn away, He hath no blame.
> An from such turning thou no joy enjoy*
>> Depart! the place for thee no place became.
> Or canst His near discern not from His far?*
>> Then Love's in vain and thou'rt a-rear and lame.
> If pine for Thee afflict my sprite, or men*
>> Hale me to death, the rein Thy hand shall claim!
> So turn Thee to or fro, to me 'tis one;*
>> What Thou ordainest none shall dare defame:
> My love hath naught of aim but Thine approof*
>> And if Thou say we part I say the same.

---

†He went in wonder and softened heart to see the miracle of saintly affection.

††In Sufistical parlance, the creature is the lover and the Creator the Beloved: worldly existence is Disunion, parting, severance, and the life to come is Reunion. The basis of the idea is the human soul being a divinae particula aurae, a disjoined molecule from the Great Spirit, imprisoned in a jail of flesh; and it is so far valuable that it has produced a grand and pathetic poetry.

And of the tales they tell is one concerning

THE ISLAND KING AND THE PIOUS ISRAELITE

There was once a notable of the Children of Israel, a man of wealth, who had a pious and blessed son. When his last hour drew nigh, his son sat down at his head and said to him, 'O my lord, give me an injunction'. Quoth the father, 'O dear son, I charge thee, swear not by Allah or truly or falsely'. Then he died, and certain lewd fellows of the Children of Israel heard of the charge he had laid on his son, and began coming to the latter and saying, 'Thy father had such and such moneys of mine, and thou knowest it; so give me what was entrusted to him or else make oath that there was no trust'. The good son would not disobey his sire's injunction, so gave them all they claimed; and they ceased not to deal thus with him till his wealth was spent and he fell into straitest predicament. Now the young man had a pious and blessed wife, who had borne him two little sons; so he said to her, 'The folk have multiplied their demands on me and, while I had the wherewithal to free myself of debt, I rendered it freely; but naught is now left us, and if others make demands upon me, we shall be in absolute distress, I and thou; our best way were to save ourselves by fleeing to some place, where none knoweth us, and earn our bread among the lower of the folk'. Accordingly, he took ship with her and his two children, knowing not whither he should wend; but, 'When Allah judgeth, there is none to reverse His judgment';† and quoth the tongue of the case:—

O flier from thy home when foes affright!*
　　Whom led to weal and happiness such flight,
Grudge not this exile when he flees abroad*
　　Where he on wealth and welfare may alight.
An pearls for ever did abide in shell,*
　　The kingly crown they ne'er had deckt and dight.

---

†Koran, Chapt. xiii, 41.

48

The ship was wrecked, yet the man saved himself on a plank and his wife and children also saved themselves, but on other planks. The waves separated them and the wife was cast up in one country and one of the boys in another. The second son was picked up by a ship, and the surges threw the father on a desert island, where he landed and made the Wuzu-ablution. Then he called the prayer-call — And Shahrazad perceived the dawn of day and ceased to say her permitted say.

Now when it was the Four Hundred and Eightieth Night, She said, It hath reached me, O auspicious King, that when the man landed upon the island, he made the Wuzu-ablution to free himself from the impurities of the sea and called the call to prayer and stood up to his devotions, when, behold, there came forth of the sea creatures of various kinds and prayed with him. When he had finished, he went up to a tree and stayed his hunger with its fruits; after which he found a spring of water and drank thereof and praised Allah, to whom be honour and glory! He abode thus three days, and whenever he stood up to pray the sea-creatures came out and prayed in the same manner as he prayed. Now after the third day, he heard a voice crying aloud and saying, 'O thou just man and pious, who didst so honour thy father and revere the decrees of thy Lord, grieve not, for Allah (be He extolled and exalted!) shall restore to thee all which left thy hand. In this isle are hoards and moneys, and things of price which the Almighty willeth thou shalt inherit, and they are in such a part of this place. So bring thou them to light; and verily, we will send ships unto thee; and do thou bestow charity on the folk and bid them to thee'. So he sought out that place, and the Lord discovered to him the treasures in question. Then ships began resorting to him, and he gave abundant largesse to the crews, saying to them, 'Be sure ye direct the folk unto me and I will give them such and such a thing and appoint to them this and that'. Accordingly, there came folk from all parts and places, nor had ten years passed over him ere the island was peopled and the man became its King.* No one came to him but he entreated him with munificence, and his name was noised abroad, throughout the length and breadth of the earth. Now his elder son had fallen into the hands of a man who reared him and taught him polite accomplishments; and, in like manner, the younger was adopted by one who gave him a good education and brought him up in the ways of merchants. The wife also happened upon a trader who entrusted to her his property and made a covenant with her that he would not deal dishonestly by her, but would aid her to obey Allah (to whom belong Majesty and Might!) and be used to make her the companion of his voyages and his travels. Now the elder son heard the report of the King and resolved to visit him, without knowing what he was; so he went to him and was well received by the King, who made him his secretary. Presently the other son heard of the King's piety and justice and was also taken into his service as a steward. When the brothers abode awhile, neither knowing the other, till it chanced that the merchant, in whose home was their mother, also hearing of the King's righteous and generous dealing with the lieges, freighted a ship with rich stuffs and other excellent produce of the land, and taking the woman with him, set sail for the island. He made it in due course and landing, presented himself with his gift before the King; who rejoiced therein with exceeding joy and ordered him a splendid return-present. Now there were among the gifts certain aromatic roots of which he would have the merchant acquaint him with the names and uses; so he said to him, 'Abide with us this night'. — And Shahrazad perceived the dawn of day and ceased saying her permitted say.

Now when it was the Four Hundred and Eighty-first Night, She said, It hath reached me, O auspicious King, that when the King said, 'Abide with us this night', the

---

*Robinson Crusoe, with a touch of Arab prayerfulness. Also the story of the Knight Placidus in the Gesta (cx), Boccaccio, etc.

50

merchant replied, 'We have in the ship one to whom I have promised to entrust the care of her to none save myself; and the same is a holy woman whose prayers have brought me weal, and I have felt the blessing of her counsels'. Rejoined the King, 'I will send her some trusty men, who shall pass the night in the ship and guard her and all that is with her'. The merchant agreed to this and abode with the King, who called his secretary and steward and said to them, 'Go and pass the night in this man's ship and keep it safe, Inshallah!' So they went up into the ship and seating themselves, this on the poop and that on the bow, passed a part of the night in repeating the names of Allah (to whom belong Majesty and Might!). Then quoth one to the other, 'Ho, Such-an-one! The King bade us keep watch and I fear lest sleep overtake us; so, come, let us discourse of stories of fortune and of the good we have seen and the trials of life'. Quoth the other, 'O my brother, as for my trials Fate parted me from my mother and a brother of mine, whose name was even as thine; and the cause of our parting was this. My father took ship with us from such a place, and the winds rose against us and were contrary, so that the ship was wrecked and Allah broke our fair companionship'. Hearing this the first asked, 'What was the name of thy mother, O my brother?' and the second answered, 'So-and-so'. Said the elder, 'And of thy father?' said the younger, 'So-and-so'. Thereat brother threw himself upon brother saying, 'By Allah, thou art my very brother!' And each fell to telling the other what had befallen him in his youth, whilst the mother heard all they said, but held her peace and in patience possessed her soul. Now when it was morning, one said to the other, 'Come, brother, let us go to my lodging and talk there'; and the other said, ' 'Tis well'. So they went away, and presently the merchant came back and finding the woman in great trouble, said to her, 'What hath befallen thee and why this concern?' Quoth she, 'Thou sentest to me yesternight men who tempted me to evil, and I have been in sore annoy with them'. At this he was wroth, and

51

repairing to the King, reported the conduct of his two trusty wights. The King summoned the twain forthwith, as he loved them for their fidelity and piety; and sending for the woman, that he might hear from her own lips what she had to say against them, thus bespake her, 'O woman, what hath betided thee from these two men in whom I trust?' She replied, 'O King, I conjure thee by the Almighty, the Bountiful One, the Lord of the Empyrean, bid them repeat the words they spoke yesternight'. So he said to them, 'Say what ye said and conceal naught thereof'. Accordingly, they repeated their talk, and lo! the King rising from his throne, gave a great cry and threw himself upon them, embracing them and saying, 'By Allah, ye are my very sons!' Therewith the woman unveiled her face and said, 'And by Allah, I am their very mother'. So they were united and abode in all solace of life and its delight till death parted them; and so glory be to Him who delivereth His servant when he resorteth to Him, and disappointeth not his hope in Him and his trust! And how well saith the poet on the subject:—

Each thing of things hath his appointed tide*
    When 'tis, O brother, granted or denied.
Repine not if affliction hit thee hard;*
    For woe and welfare aye conjoint abide:
How oft shall woman see all griefs surround*
    Yet feel a joyance thrill what lies inside!
How many a wretch, on whom the eyes of folk*
    Look down, shall grace exalt to pomp and pride!
This man is one long suffering grief and woe;*
    Whom change and chance of Time have sorely tried:
The World divided from what held he dearest,*
    After long union scattered far and wide;
But designed his Lord unite them all again,*
    And in the Lord is every good descried.
Glory to Him whose Providence rules all*
    Living, as surest proofs for us decide.
Near is the Near One; but no wisdom clearer*
    Shows him, nor distant wayfare brings Him nearer.

52

And this tale is told of

ABU AL-HASAN and ABU JA'AFAR
the Leper*

I had been many times to Meccah (Allah increase its honour!) and the folk used to follow me for my knowledge of the road and remembrance of the water-stations. It happened one year that I was minded to make the pilgrimage to the Holy House and visitation of the tomb of His Prophet (on whom be blessing and the Peace!), and I said in myself, 'I well know the way and will fare alone'. So I set out and journeyed till I came to Al-Kadisiyah** and entering the mosque there, saw a man suffering from black leprosy seated in the prayer-niche. Quoth he on seeing me, 'O Abu al-Hasan, I crave thy company to Meccah'. Quoth I to myself, 'I fled from all my companions, and how shall I company with lepers?' So I said to him, 'I will bear no man company'; and he was silent at my words. Next day I walked on alone, till I came to Al-Akabah,*** where I entered the mosque and found the leper seated in the prayer-niche. So I said to myself, 'Glory be to Allah! how hath this fellow preceded me hither?' But he raised his head to me

---

*Arabs note two kinds of leprosy, 'Bahak' or 'Baras', the common or white, and 'Jusam', the black leprosy, the leprosy of the joints, mal rouge. Both are attributed to undue diet as eating fish and drinking milk; and both are treated with tonics, especially arsenic. Leprosy is regarded by Moslems as a Scriptural malady on account of its prevalence amongst the Israelites, who, as Manetho tells us, were expelled from Egypt because they infected and polluted the population. In mediaeval Christendom an idea prevailed that the Saviour was a leper; hence the term 'morbus sacer'; the honours paid to the sufferers by certain Saints and the Papal address (Clement III, A.D. 1189) dilectis filiis leprosis. (Farrar's Life of Christ, i. 149.)
**A city in Irak; famous for the three days' battle which caused the death of Yezdegird, last Sassanian king.
***A mountain pass near Meccah famous for the 'First Fealty of the Steep' (Pilgrimage, ii. 126). The mosque was built to commemorate the event.

and said with a smile, 'O Abu al-Hasan, He doth for the weak that which surpriseth the strong!' I passed that night confounded at what I had seen; and, as soon as morning dawned, set out again by myself; but when I came to Arafat† and entered the mosque, behold! there was the leper seated in the niche! So I threw myself upon him and kissing his feet said, 'O my lord, I crave thy company'. But he answered, 'This may in no way be'. Then I began weeping and wailing at the loss of his converse, when he said, 'Spare thy tears which will avail thee naught!' — And Shahrazad perceived the dawn of day and ceased to say her permitted say.

Now when it was the Four Hundred and Eighty-second Night, She said, It hath reached me, O auspicious King, that Abu al-Hasan continued:— Now when I saw the leper man seated in the prayer-niche, I threw myself upon him and said, 'O my lord, I crave thy company'; and fell to kissing his feet. But he answered, 'This may in no way be!' Then I began weeping and wailing at the loss of his company when he said, 'Spare thy tears which will avail thee naught!' and he recited these couplets:

> Why dost thou weep when I depart and thou didst parting claim;* And cravest union when we ne'ever shall reunite the same?
> Thou lookest on nothing save my weakness and disease;* And saidst, 'Nor goes nor comes, or night or day, this sickly frame'.
> Seest not how Allah (glorified His glory ever bē!)* Deigneth to grant His slave's petition wherewithal he came.
> If I, to eyes of men be that and only that they see,* And this my body show itself so full of grief and grame,
> And I have naught of food that shall supply me to the place* Where crowds unto my Lord resort impelled by single aim,

---

†To my surprise I read in Mr. Redhouse's 'Mesnevi' (Trübner, 1881): 'Arafat, the mount where the victims are slaughtered by the pilgrims'. (p. 60) This ignorance is phenomenal. Did Mr. Redhouse never read Burckhardt or Burton?

54

I have a high Creating Lord whose mercies aye are hid;*
A Lord who hath none equal and no fear is known to
Him.
So fare thee safe and leave me lone in strangerhood to
woe* For He, the only One, consoles my loneliness so
lone.

Accordingly, I left him; but every station I came to, I
found he had foregone me, till I reached Al-Madinah,
where I lost sight of him and could hear no tidings of
him. Here I met Abu Yazid al-Bustámi and Abu Bakr al-
Shibli and a number of other Shaykhs and learned men,
to whom with many complaints I told my case, and they
said, 'Heaven forbid that thou shouldst gain his company
after this! He was Abu Ja'afar the leper, in whose name
folk at all times pray for rain and by whose blessing-
prayers their end attain'. When I heard their words, my
desire for his company redoubled and I implored the
Almighty to reunite me with him. Whilst I was standing
on Arafat,† one pulled me from behind, so I turned and
behold, it was my man. At this sight I cried out with a
loud cry and fell down in a fainting fit; but when I came
to myself he had disappeared from my sight. This increased my yearning for him and the ceremonies were
tedious to me, and I prayed Almighty Allah to give me
sight of him; nor was it but a few days after, when lo! one
pulled me from behind, and I turned and it was he again.
Thereupon he said, 'Come, I conjure thee and ask thy
want of me'. So I begged him to pray for me three
prayers; first, that Allah would make me love poverty;
secondly, that I might never lie down at night upon
provision assured to me; and thirdly, that He would
vouchsafe me to look upon His bountiful Face. So he
prayed for me as I wished, and departed from me. And
indeed Allah hath granted me what the devotee asked in
prayer; to begin with He hath made me so love poverty
that, by the Almighty! there is naught in the world
dearer to me than it, and secondly since such a year, I

---

†It is sad doggerel.

55

have never laid down to sleep upon assured provision; withal hath He never let me lack aught. As for the third prayer, I trust that He will vouchsafe me that also, even as He hath granted the two precedent, for right Bountiful and Beneficent is His Godhead, and Allah have mercy on him who said:*

> Garb of Fakir, renouncement, lowliness;
> His robe of tatters and of rags his dress;
> And pallor ornamenting brow as though
> 'Twere wanness such as waning crescents show.
> Wasted him prayer a-through the long-lived night,
> And flooding tears ne'er cease to dim his sight.
>
> Memory of Him shall cheer his lonely room;
> Th' Almighty nearest is in nightly gloom.
> The Refuge helpeth such Fakir in need;
> Help e'en the cattle and the winged breed:
> Allah for sake of him of wrath is fain,
> And for the grace of him shall fall the rain;
> And if he pray one day for plague to stay,
> 'Twill stay, and 'bate man's wrong and tyrants slay.
>
> While folk are sad, afflicted one and each,
> He in his mercy's rich, the generous leach:
> Bright shines his brow; as thou regard his face
> Thy heart illumined shines by light of grace.
> O thou who shunnest souls of worth innate,
> Departs thee (woe to thee!) of sins the weight.
>
> Thou thinkest to overtake them, while thou bearest
> Follies, which slay thee whatso way thou farest,
> Didst wot their worth thou hadst all honour showed,
> And tears in streamlets from thine eyes had flowed.
>
> To catarrh-troubled men flowers lack their smell;
> And brokers ken for how much clothes can sell;
> So haste and with thy Lord reunion sue,
> And haply fate shall lend thee aidance due,
> Rest from rejection and estrangement-stress,
> And Joy thy wish and will shall choicely bless.
> His court wide open for the suer is dight: –
> One, very God, the Lord, th' Almighty might.

56

2/iv.
In the World, not Of It
Doris Lessing

That East must ever be East and West must be West is not a belief which is subscribed to by Sufis, who claim that Sufism, in its reality, not necessarily under the name, is continuously in operation in every culture. Sometimes invisible, it is at times offered as openly as goods in a supermarket. When this happens, it is expected by them that there will be hostility from those academics who have made orientalism their property, and sometimes from literary or other authoritarian bodies. During well over 1,000 years of connected literary and psychological tradition, embracing Spain, North Africa, Central Asia and the Middle East, they have almost invariably clashed with narrow thinkers. Often the struggle between Sufis and the 'establishments' looks unpleasantly like what happened when the Nazis took a stand against something. Some past patterns are unfamiliar to us; others can still be instructive, for in one form or another they repeat themselves.

'Hallaj was dismembered in Baghdad, A.D. 922, for blasphemy. The evidence against him included the dread indictment that he was the grandson of a Zoroastrian, and that he was "ignorant of the Koran and its ancillary sciences of jurisprudence, traditions, etc. and of poetry and Arabic philology". Searches of the houses of some of his followers showed that they actually possessed books inscribed in gold on Chinese paper. In case you didn't know it, this was taken to suggest that the writings must be heretical, since Manichees used gold ink and Chinese paper . . .'*

Suhrawardi was killed in 1191, the charge including 'atheism heresy and believing in ancient philosophers'.

Ibn El Arabi of Spain was hauled before an inquisition of scholars in the 12th century, for immodesty in

---

*E. G. Browne, *Literary History of Persia* (1964).

57

pretending that love-poetry could be spiritual, when it was pornographic.

Sarmad was executed in India in 1563 for exposing his body; he was alleged to be a Jew or of Jewish origin.

Jalaluddin Rumi was accused of publishing trivial folk-tales in the guise of spiritual writings.

There were sometimes difficulties in attacking the Sufis, once they had established a name for literature, or could not be shown to be vicious. One such case is the frame-up of Nasimi. Unable to fault Nasimi in argument, certain scholars sent him a pair of shoes as a gift, from another country. Into the sole they had sewn a chapter from the Koran. Then they sent word to the Governor of Aleppo that Nasimi was defiling the Koran. The Governor had his shoe slit open. On the production of the paper Nasimi made no answer to the charge, knowing that he was going to be killed. He was flayed alive, reciting verses.

The charges are always the same. The academic scholars persecute, claim apostasy, ignorance, dubious parentage, desire for power over the people, danger to public order, self-advertisement and the circulation of spurious, superficial or irresponsible literature. But in spite of these accusations, in spite of persecution often followed by judicial murder, the Sufi teachers subsequently became major spiritual authorities to the Islamic world. Most of these Sufis were literary men, and all were marked by their inability to accept the dogmas of their current 'establishments'. Once safely dead, they could be unofficially canonised; but during their lifetimes many suffered grievously.

But perhaps this treatment was not surprising: people persecute or ignore what they do not understand. And there was something particularly provoking about the Sufis. What, for instance, could a medieval theologian make of a man who called himself a mystic, was interested in man's evolution to a higher level, was associated with scientific work?

It is against this sort of historical background that it

can be useful to view Sufi literature, which exists on many levels, from simple entertainment to truths that 'lie under the poet's tongue'. Codes and the cryptic had their practical, as well as their spiritual, uses.

Oriental studies even today are the Cinderella of the learned world. The reason for this is historical as well as the perennial difficulty that scholars who have cornered a market can refuse, or be unable, to recognize a real Sufi practitioner when one appears; even now our mental sets in the West exclude much factual information about the extent of the influence that Spain, the Arabs, the Moors — Islam — has had on our culture. This influence has been immense, if often not acknowledged at all. It is in this field that we can expect — it is already happening — startling results in academic research. But the block is there, and strong. Professor A. J. Arberry of Cambridge complains in a current book that someone trying to develop in this field 'should find himself on the defensive, that he should have to contend with cheap jibes, sometimes with active opposition'.*

The career of Idries Shah, who is the main current exponent of Sufi literature and teaching, has in the past few years shown a resemblance to some of the classical Sufis. The same signs and symptoms of opposition have been seen; but there has also been support, and from the highest levels. Late in 1970, for instance, no sooner had the expected handful of irritated scholars opposed him, than a large body of experts set about writing a *festschrift* (published by Cape). They include scholars from the West specialising in orientalism, and also many Orientals, covering between them the whole spectrum of oriental studies in which he works — Islamics, mysticism, Persian, Arabic, Turkish, Sufism, history. They include Arabs and Jews, and academics from both sides of the Iron Curtain, not to mention such people as diplomats, generals, a judge, and a Cabinet Minister who is also a

---

Oriental Essays (1960), p. 256.

Sufi authority in the Middle East.*

The need for this type of active support can be encapsulated in a tale from the Mulla Nasrudin corpus:

'Nasrudin found a falcon sitting on his windowsill. He had never seen a bird of this kind before. "You poor thing", he said, "how were you ever allowed to get into such a state?" He clipped the falcon's talons, cut its beak straight, and trimmed its feathers. "Now you look more like a bird", said Nasrudin'.**

There is also the problem that we are used to thinking of Eastern philosophies and their representatives through our Indian spectacles. 'Gurus' are teachers, are respected by the religious and scholarly establishments, are interviewed plentifully by journalists fascinated by their bizarre and obviously holy practices, are considered the more authentic the more they claim the things of this world are of no account. But Sufism does not resemble in any way what it considers to be a degeneration of a real tradition, and says that you cannot approach Sufism until you are able to think that a person quite ordinary in appearance and in life can experience higher states of mind. Sufism believes itself to be the substance of that current which can develop man to a higher stage in his evolution. It is not contemptuous of the world. 'Be in the world, but not of it', is the aim.

But the inability to believe in the combination of the mystic and the practical is not only of our time.

Roger Bacon, the Franciscan monk, lectured at Oxford from Sufi books in the 13th century: it was for his recommendation of Sufi practices that he got into trouble with the religious authorities. Lully of Majorca praised Sufi methodologies, was 'a devotee of Arabian mysticism' (Professor E. W. F. Tomlin). Today he finds a place in scientific literature as the inventor of a digital computer. Rumi, poet and mystic, stressed a theory of evolution

---

*Professor L. F. Rushbrook Williams (Ed.) *Sufi Studies: East and West*, 1973, 1974.
**Idries Shah, *The Exploits of the Incomparable Mulla Nasrudin*, p. 100 (Jonathan Cape, London).

eight hundred years before Darwin. Shabistari, a 13th century Persian Sufi, writes of the mystic way while emphasizing the unbelievable power which could be released from the atom. El Ghazali wrote of the collective unconscious in relation to medical and psychological techniques. Hujwiri of India, at the time of the Norman Conquest of England, was writing (in a book about Sufi saints) that time and space are identical. Jafar Sadiq and Jabir (Geber), the fathers of Western chemistry, were Sufis. Baba Farid had commercial interests and Rumi had to defend him for it — as probably would have to be done today. For claiming that human enlightenment must be achieved by working with the material world, innumerable Sufis were isolated from potential well-wishers, because of the inculcated thought that they must be superficial if they lived ordinary lives and were concerned with the practical welfare of man. It is to be hoped that this ancient bias will not be strong enough to keep people's minds closed against what Sufism is offering now.

But less than ten years have achieved a remarkable softening of prejudice. The first of Idries Shah's books, *The Sufis,* which becomes more extraordinary the more it is studied, because of its comprehensiveness, and because of what it is able to state openly about a subject which in its deeper reaches is by definition beyond verbalization, was accepted for review by the conventional literary establishment for the most part because of pressure from poets and other literary people; it was overlooked by academics in the field. Yet many people, on reading this book which nowhere stated that a 'school' was to start, that 'The Teaching' was being offered again, applied from all over the world to be students. This is a small example of the multi-sidedness of every Sufi activity and artefact. 'We are economical in our functioning', say the Sufis. 'If you like, even parsimonious: everything we say, each thing we do, has many different functions and results'. A book which will be pasture for academics, is material for esoteric study, but made as dramatic an appearance as a man walking on to stage to blow a trumpet.

A newer book, *The Magic Monastery*,* continues a theme. People who may ask: 'Right then, what *is* Sufism?' will find Sufism's 'taste' here. But it is also a textbook for students, if the word textbook is an appropriate word for activity which is not like anything that we have been taught to regard as study.

'Sufism is a study which is not scholastic. Its materials are taken from almost every form of human experience. Its books and pens are in the environment and resemble nothing that the scholastic or the enthusiast even dream about. It is because recitations, effort and books are included in this kind of study, and because Sufi teachers are called "Teacher", that the fact of a specialized communication has become confused with academic or imitative study. There is, therefore, "Sufi study" and "ordinary study" and the two are different. The position is as if "mouse" and "elephant" have both been given the same name. Up to a point (being quadrupeds, being grey, having tails) this inexactitude is of no moment. After that it is necessary to distinguish between the two. This distinguishing takes place in a Sufi Circle'.**

This book, like some previous ones, consists of pieces of various lengths, each illustrating points, or themes, on various levels. Some are anecdotes, some parables, some are practically informative. But the book differs from its predecessors (except for *Reflections,* Octagon Press, London) in that Shah includes pieces specially written by himself to complete the book 'as a course in non-linear thinking'. In previous collections the emphasis has been on tales illustrating the instructional methods employed by sages during the last thousand years, taken from written and oral sources.

The Magic Monastery is particularly and intriguingly informative about methods used by a Teacher in active operation, who cannot always behave according to the

---

*Idries Shah, *The Magic Monastery,* Jonathan Cape, London.
**Idries Shah, *The Way of the Sufi,* Jonathan Cape, London.

62

conventions of ordinary social usage and politeness: his actions may be sharply at variance with both.

As, for instance, this: a famous 19th century Sufi Teacher, Jan Fishan Khan, of Afghanistan, heard that a certain scholar was viciously attacking a neighbour. He invited both men to a feast, and, having asked the neighbour to react to nothing that might happen, when the feast was at its height he began to berate him as the scholar had done for iniquities and shortcomings of all sorts. The man kept silent, until the scholar cried, 'Please stop. I saw my own behaviour in you, and I cannot bear the sight'. Jan Fishan Khan said: 'In being here tonight we all took a chance. You that our friend here would not sit patiently but would attack you, I that you might be further inflamed by my vituperation instead of being shamed by it, and he that he might start to believe that I was really against him. Now we have solved the problem. The risk remains that the account of this interchange, passed from mouth to ear by those who do not know what we are doing, will represent our friend as weak, you as easily influenced, and me as easily angered'.

Such stuff is designed for, if you like, self-improvement; at least for self-observation. You don't have to be a formal student to make use of it. Nasrudin again: 'You have leather? You have thread and nails and dye and tools? Then why don't you make yourself a pair of shoes?'

A difficulty is that some people expect this material to be more sensational than it is; a Sufi would reply that our palates have been blunted; that we do not give gentle impacts a chance to operate; that people can put themselves at a remove from the Sufi operation by calling it 'banal'.

> 'The necessity for a social or emotional ingredient in a teaching situation is denied by the Sufis, in sharp contradiction of other persuasions, whose advocates invariably, in theory or in reality, strive to include as many subjective and community ingredients as possible in "teaching" contracts. An astonishing parallel to the Sufi

63

insistence on the relatively greater power of subtle communication to affect man, is found in scientific work which shows that all living things, including man, are "incredibly sensitive to waves of extraordinarily weak energy — when more robust influences are excluded".'*

Finally a piece from *The Magic Monastery* which illustrates the first approach of many people to Sufism:

'There is a story about a man who went to a dictionary-compiler and asked him why he was interested in money. The lexicographer was surprised and said: "Wherever did you get that idea?"

"From your own writings", said the visitor.

"But I have only written that one dictionary", said the author.

"I know, and that is the book which I have read", said the other man.

"But the book contains a hundred thousand words! And out of those I don't suppose that more than twenty or thirty are about money".

"What are you talking about all the other words for", said the visitor, "when *I* was asking you about the words for *money*?"'

---

*Idries Shah, *The Dermis Probe,* Notes, quoting M. Gauquelin's *The Cosmic Clocks,* which cites recent scientific work.

3 HUMOUR AND THE SUFI

3/i.
In a Naqshbandi Circle
Raoul Simac

It has truly been said that ancient traditional teachings which we — for want of a better term — call religious, especially in the East, can be projected in forms which many people would not recognize as 'religious' in our present-day sense at all.

Psychology, self-development, social adjustments, the cultivation of certain arts and modes of thinking: these all form parts of the Order of the Naqshbandi, whose members are found throughout the Arabic, Persian, Turkish, Indian and Malayan worlds. The order was founded in the 14th century in Bukhara, and its chief centres have generally been in Central Asia since that time.

While the Sufis, or Dervishes, are generally regarded as religious enthusiasts on the pattern of Western monastic communities, or else as individual poets or wanderers, this seems to be because only certain forms of their activities have become generally known.

I recently spent three months with a Naqshbandi circle in Pakistan, whose members refused to have any ideological contact with the overtly religious clerics, and entry to whose private deliberations and exercises was difficult.

An important part of the studies was the consideration of the Mullah-Nasreddin corpus of literature, generally regarded by people in Pakistan as a series of jokes.

The use to which the tales of Nasreddin are put in Sufi

65

circles, however, shows that the intention of the teachers is to develop in students a form of thinking which is different from customary patterns. The emphasis upon faith, discipline and ritual, generally regarded as essential in religious formulation in the world of Islam, 'is the concern of other specialists'. I was most impressed by these techniques. Whether or not they have any spiritual validity as a part of a way to universal truth, the application of this study-system has undeniable effects upon those taking part. They seem to suffer from little sectarian bias, and in fact insist that different religions are external shapes within which, from time to time, eternal truths have been preached and 'made to work within man'.

This outline is intended to describe some of the stories used in this system, and the interpretation put upon them by the teachers.

The first story is when Nasreddin falls from his roof on to a man in the street. The man's neck is broken, but the Mullah is not hurt. The teaching is: 'This goes against expected cause and effect. Similarly, there is a system of understanding in the world which you can attach yourself to when you can realize that cause and effect need not enter into it'.

In the second story of the series, Nasreddin is made to say: 'I *never* tell the truth'. The explanations include: 'If this is true, he is lying, if it is untrue, he does tell the truth. Note that by word-play we can arrive at anything, but this can never be truth'.

In the third story, the Mullah illustrates that man tries to improve on his knowledge, his techniques, his capacities in life, but he may lack other basic knowledge without which he is in fact doing harm. Nasreddin finds a hawk with a curved beak and talons. He has only seen pigeons before, so he thinks that this bird is deformed. He cuts its claws and beak until they are straight. 'This', goes the moral, 'is what you try to do with metaphysical teaching. You try to fit it into preconceptions. If you realize this, you will truly start to learn'.

66

Certain levels of human understanding cannot be attained, it is claimed, until the brain can work in more than one way. This is the equivalent of the result of what is in some systems a 'mystical illumination' process; but the Naqshbandis appear to hold that the brain is prepared by degrees without this illumination being as violent an experience as in other methods.

The problem of time and of justice and injustice is illustrated by the contention that, whereas ordinary man believes that reward and punishment follow actions, these Sufis hold that there is a different time-system at work concurrently. In other words, something that seems to follow something else may in fact precede it in another time-system which is in fact with us.

This principle is illustrated by the tale of the bath-house. Mullah Nasreddin visits a bath-house, where the man in charge treats him badly, getting a gold piece for his pains. On the next visit, the man waits on the Mullah hand and foot; but he only gets a copper coin. 'This coin', says the Mullah, 'is for the treatment which you gave me the first time. You have already had the gold coin which was payment for the second visit'.

These dervishes believe very strongly in this dogma: a man may be given great advantages, for instance, which he must regard as 'payment for something which he has to do'. The converse may also be true.

If the Naqshbandis seem to be projecting an image of a series of experiences of an invisible world parallel to ours, they also stress strongly the need to be aware of the real events in this time-system. In the story of the cloak, Nasreddin is admitted to a certain feast because the doorkeepers are impressed by the regal garb which he has assumed for the purpose. He comments upon this by feeding some of the food to his cloak: 'You got me in, here is your share', he says to it. The teaching underlying this is given thus: 'Make sure that you realize the true cause and effect situation when you are in one. Do not mistake one thing for another'.

Self-deception and unfounded assumptions are held by

67

this circle to prevent the attainment of higher knowledge. There is a tale which is used to illustrate this. Nasreddin says: 'The king addressed me'. Everyone is impressed, because they assume that something important must have been said. In fact, however, the king had only said: 'Get out of my way'. In this story the assumption is laid bare. So is the self-deception, because the listener deceives himself into thinking that something important must have happened. In real life, man does not carry his thinking through to a point where he will see that he deceives himself: in this case by feeling interested that he knows someone who has been spoken to by a king.

Things are actually happening in the world, and especially among the human race, which cannot be explained and which have to be experienced — so runs the Naqshbandi creed. One day, Mullah Nasreddin saw some people approaching. Fearing that they might be robbers, he ran away and lay down in an open grave nearby. The travellers, their curiosity aroused by this strange behaviour, crowded around him and asked him why he was there. His answer illustrates the impossibility of answering some questions: 'You are here because of me, and I am here because of you'.

But the Naqshbandis teach in many different ways, in addition to this Nasreddin-joke system. Whom they teach, and by what method, will depend upon factors which they say have to be decided by the teacher. For this reason they are often accused of not sticking to one formula: they have no dogmas, 'only objectives', as one teacher put it.

When I enquired into this aspect of the teaching, which was quite new to me, I was told this joke as an answer: Nasreddin went into a shop. He said to the shopkeeper: 'Have you flour?'
'Yes'. 'And milk, and sugar, and honey?' 'Yes'.
'Then, for Heaven's sake, why don't you make sweetmeats?'

The moral, of course, was that a man may have certain things and may need certain other things. But what each

68

man has and what he needs will vary, according to his individuality and other factors.

3/ii.
Forty-five Adventures of Mulla Nasrudin

HOW FAR TO SAMARKAND?

Someone said to Nasrudin:
'How far is it to Samarkand?'
'Well,' said the Mulla, 'it used to be three days' march from here. What with the changes going on these days, I expect it is about four days' march by now'.

HOW TO LEARN

'How is it that you have learned so much, Mulla?'
'By talking a lot. I string together all the words I can think of. When I get interesting, I can see the respect on other people's faces. When that happens, I start making mental notes of what I have said'.

THE DRUNK

Mulla Nasrudin went up to a drunken man and started to try to help him walk. The man said a few words to the Mulla, and Nasrudin walked away, nodding.

Some spectators asked: 'Why did you not help him, Mulla?'

'Oh', said Nasrudin, 'he explained everything to me. The houses are going around and around. As soon as he sees his own house appear, he will leap in at the door. In that way he won't have to walk home'.

One Thing at a Time

Nasrudin was digging a pit in the garden.

'What are you doing?' his wife asked him.

'I want to get rid of this pile of earth I have left over from digging in the turnips'.

'But what will you do with the soil left over from the disposal pit?'

'If you were at my level of understanding you would realize that I am above such minor points'.

Lost Property

Nasrudin's wife suffered from bouts of ill-temper. When this happened, people usually became very frightened.

One day some neighbours came running to the tea-house. 'Quickly, Nasrudin!' they cried, 'your wife has lost her wits!'

'Lost property is the concern of the police', said Nasrudin; 'and, for my part, I shall testify, if suspected, that I never knew that she had any'.

Man of Truth

Nasrudin was about to be sworn-in during a court case.

The clerk of the Court objected to him as a witness, saying:

'We cannot allow a perjurer as a witness. One of the famous claims of Nasrudin is: "Truth is something which I never speak".'

'The matter is quite simple', said the Mulla, 'I know dozens of people who are thoroughly reliable in this sense. All you have to do is to swear *them* in instead'.

70

The Well and the Water

One man bought a well from another. When, however, the buyer wanted to draw water from the well, the crafty original owner said: 'You have bought the well, not the water'.

The case came to Nasrudin to judge.

As soon as the details of the case had been read out, everyone in court craned forward to see how the Mulla would deal with this one.

Without a moment's hesitation, Mulla Nasrudin said:

'The well has been sold, without water. Of course the seller has no right to store his water in someone else's well. He will immediately remove all the water from it, or else forfeit all claim to the water'.

Men and Women

'I have been in places', Nasrudin was informing the people in the teahouse, 'where it is so hot that nobody can bear clothes next to the skin'.

'Then how do they tell men from women, Mulla?' asked one of the patrons.

'Well . . . they can't, not in that country'.

Snakebite

'Why do you want snakebite treatment, Mulla?'

'Well, I picked up a stick I thought was a snake'.

'But that wouldn't bite you!'

'But what about the real snake I picked up to hit the stick with?'

As I Thought . . .

Nasrudin was convinced that Hamza was the greediest man in the world.

Someone had told him that Hamza simply couldn't stop taking things. 'He does it all the time. You'll never see our Hamza when he isn't eating or taking something . . .'

One day the Mulla saw Hamza walking along the road.

'What are you up to now, Hamza?' he called.

'I'm only taking the air . . .'

'Good Heavens!' shouted Mulla Nasrudin, 'can't you leave *anything* alone?'

STAND-IN

A schoolmaster owed Nasrudin some money, and the Mulla went to collect it.

'I have the money at home, Mulla, but I cannot give it to you now, I have to teach the class'.

The Mulla watched the lesson for a few minutes, then he said:

'I have the solution, schoolmaster. I'll stay here and nod and shake my head on your behalf, while you slip home for the money'.

WHAT CREAM-CAKES ARE FOR

Nasrudin was starving, when he came across a shop full of delicious cream-cakes.

He was just stretching out his hand to touch one when the baker stopped him.

'Are they yours?' asked the Mulla.

'Yes, they are, all of them', said the baker.

'Then why, why for the sake of Providence, why don't you eat them?'

THE BRAIN IS SAFE

Nasrudin had joined the army. He was wounded in

72

battle, by a slash in his head. He was carried to a doctor.

Before the doctor could say anything, Nasrudin cried out: 'At least we can be sure that it has not harmed the brain!'

'We cannot know that' said the doctor, 'until I have made my examination'.

'Oh, yes we can!' said Nasrudin. 'If my head had not been solid bone I would not have been such a fool as to volunteer for all this!'

NASRUDIN IN THE LAND OF FOOLS

When Mulla Nasrudin was on his travels, he chanced to stray into the Land of Fools. The people asked him what his work was, and when he said 'I am a judge', they made him a judge there.

One day a couple of men came before him to have a particularly tricky case tried.

The first man said:

'I am the plaintiff. This man asked me to help him cross a river ford. I said: "What will you give me if I help you?" He answered: "Nothing". On that basis I helped him. But when we got to the other side of the river, he said he could not give me what I had been promised'.

'That is so', said the other man, 'I admit I spoke rather without thinking. When I promised him "nothing", I did not realize that I hadn't got any of it'.

'Oh, that's all right', said the Mulla, 'we have a fund of the very stuff here for the settlement of matters like this. Now, Plaintiff, just take up the corner of that carpet, will you?'

The man rolled back the carpet.

'What do you see underneath?'

'Nothing'.

'Splendid! It's all yours. Take as much as is your due and go home, both of you, there's good fellows'.

STRAIGHT LINE

'What is the shortest route to the Palace, Mulla?'

'The very shortest?'

'Yes, I want to go there'.

'If you want to go there, the very shortest is no good to you'.

'Why not?'

'The very shortest route is getting yourself born into the right family'.

LET'S LEAVE IT AT THAT

Once a neighbour asked Mulla Nasrudin to look after a jar for him.

The Mulla could not restrain his curiosity and opened it. At first taking just a lick, he had eaten all the honey in a few days.

When the neighbour came and found his jar empty, he angrily asked where the honey had gone.

'If you didn't ask me, I wouldn't have to explain to you', said Nasrudin. 'Couldn't we leave it at that?'

LUCKY IT'S MINE

The Mulla's little boy was naughty.

Nasrudin threw some water over him.

His wife furiously upbraided him for losing his temper with a child.

'He is lucky he is my own', said Mulla Nasrudin, 'because if he had been someone else's, I don't know what I would have done'.

HONEY

Nasrudin said to his wife:

'Honey is delicious, curative, precious, beautiful, quite

74

my favourite thing'.

His wife said:

'What about it?'

Nasrudin started again:

'Just a moment, I haven't finished . . . Honey is bad for you, causes disease, is made by insects and is therefore unwholesome!'

'How can you have two conflicting opinions about the same thing?'

'I have only one of these opinions. I'll tell you which one it is as soon as you have told me whether there is any honey in the house'.

NASRUDIN'S BROTHER

'They say', said the timid traveller, 'that if you speak against certain dervishes, something terrible happens to you'.

'That is nonsense', said Mulla Nasrudin, 'and I can prove it'.

He took out a matchbox. Inside was a small frog.

'This is my brother. He doesn't look quite the same since he criticised a dervish — but he is in the very best of health, and he needs to eat much less.

'In fact, they say that frogs live for a hundred years, so he is that much better off'.

LIGHT

'Surely the Sun is the greatest of all things', said a Sun-worshipper, 'for it makes everything visible. What can we not see by the light of the Sun?'

'Simple', said the Mulla, 'one of the most extensive of all things is invisible in sunlight'.

'And what is that?'

'Darkness'.

HIS PORTERAGE

Nasrudin hired a porter to carry home some baskets from the market.

When they were in the maze of alley-ways of the town, the porter took to his heels and disappeared.

The Mulla told all his friends. One day, weeks later, he and a friend were in the market when Nasrudin said: 'Quick, let us hide — there is the porter'.

'But why don't you ask him for your goods?'

'I might get my goods from him, but supposing he asked for several weeks' porterage?'

THE WELL

Nasrudin met a friend on the road.

'Will you do something for me?' ·

'Certainly, Mulla, what is it?'

'There is a man who has fallen into a well over there. I am going to get him a rope. Please go and tell him not to go away until I get back'.

WOOL AND SAND

Nasrudin was leading his donkey, heavily laden, along a road.

A traveller asked him: 'What have you in those saddle-bags?'

'One has wool, the other sand to balance the first'.

'But you could lighten your load by throwing away the sand and dividing the wool into equal weights to balance each other'.

'You must be a genius', said Nasrudin, and he did as the man suggested.

They continued on their journey.

After a little time the Mulla looked at his companion and said, 'You are poorly dressed. Surely this must be from choice, since you are so clever?'

'No, it is not'.

'Then you are a king, or a mystic sage — perhaps you have been bewitched by some magician?'

'No'.

'Then you *are* a poor man?'

'Yes, of course I am'.

Nasrudin started to put all his wool back into one saddlebag.

'Fill this other sack again with sand from the roadside', he said, 'because if your knowledge has put you into poorer clothes than even *I* have, I'd be better off with my old ways'.

POISON

The sweetmeat-vendor was urgently called away from his stall in the market, and there was nobody to look after it.

He saw Nasrudin hovering nearby. So he quickly scribbled a notice: 'Danger — I have poisoned everything here'.

Nasrudin came closer and read the sign.

'They have curious habits in this market-place', he thought, 'but, after all, has it not been said, "In a country, follow the customs of the country"?'

He made a small purchase of arsenic powder, tipped it over the sweetmeats, and added a line: 'So have I'.

WHY THE MULLA NEVER HAD HALWA

In the teahouse the subject of *halwa* cropped up. Everyone gave his own recipe, and several people spoke of great halwas they had tasted.

Nasrudin said nothing.

Someone asked: 'What have your experiences been with halwa, Mulla? They must be memorable'.

77

'Memorable they are', said Nasrudin, 'for I have never had any.'

'But how could that happen? Everyone has had halwa. Haven't you ever made it at home?'

'When I have been at home, we never had butter, flour and sugar all at the same time'.

'Surely there is nowhere that does not at some time have all three?'

'Yes, there must have been some such times in my home, but I was never at home on those occasions'.

STORAGE PROBLEM

A local gossip sought out the Mulla.

'Can you keep a secret, Nasrudin?'

'I am afraid that I have no space for any at the moment', said the Mulla. 'You see, one has to protect oneself against other people's storage problems'.

NO DRUNKS

Mulla Nasrudin said one day to the king:

'I have never seen a drunk in my life'.

'Then perhaps you keep off the streets at night and drink alone?'

'No, I am always in company'.

'Then how can it come about that you never see anyone drunk?'

'I am always the first to pass out'.

OUT WITH THE LIGHT

The midwife was called to Mulla Nasrudin's wife.

She hurried into the house, went into the bedroom, and soon afterwards, as night was falling, put her head around the door to command the anxious Mulla to 'bring a candle at once'.

78

Nasrudin took her a lighted candle.

In a very few minutes the midwife called out:

'It's a boy!'

Nasrudin was delighted.

Five minutes later, to his surprise came the cry:

'Mulla, another boy!'

'Excellent', shouted the Mulla.

A few moments afterwards the voice of the midwife came again:

'Now a girl, Nasrudin!'

Mulla Nasrudin rushed into the room and blew out the candle.

'Why on earth are you doing that?'

'Midwife, surely the candle has done its duty — and now it doesn't know where to stop'.

IN THE CELLAR

The Mulla went down into his cellar, forgetting that he had left all sorts of bits and pieces there.

As soon as his foot touched the floor in the gloom, a large sieve bounced up and hit him on the head.

The more he tried to fight it off, the more it seemed to bounce back at him.

Nasrudin bounded back up the cellar stairs and shouted down:

'You are brave enough in the dark — but come up here, into broad daylight, bringing all the sieves on earth, and see whether you can prevail over me, Mulla Nasrudin!'

HOW TO PAY DEBTS

A pressing creditor came to the Mulla for his money.

'I cannot pay the debt yet', said Nasrudin.

The man became angry.

'Why do you borrow money if you can't repay it?'

79

'It is a matter of the thorn thickets I am working on, you see'.

'What have thorn thickets got to do with paying me back?'

'Simple. I am going to plant them on both sides of this street'.

'Are you mad as well as everything else?' The man was really enraged now.

'No, it is to get money to pay you back'.

'From thorns?'

'No, but when sheep pass, some of their wool will stick to the thorns. I will collect it, and sell it, and then I'll be able to pay you back'.

At this absurd idea the creditor started to laugh.

'Yes', said Mulla Nasrudin, 'you begin to be in a better humour now, don't you, when you feel the certitude of money in the offing'.

ACCIDENT

Mulla Nasrudin, trying to spring onto the back of a horse which he saw as he passed a field, fell heavily.

'People must have seen me', he thought, and before looking up he shouted: 'Accidents can happen to anyone!'

Then he saw that he was alone.

'All right', said the Mulla to the horse, 'I admit I cannot ride, but don't you tell anyone'.

KNOWN IT LONG ENOUGH

Once a large earthenware pot was stolen from Nasrudin's neighbour.

The Mulla was called to court to confirm that it really did belong to the owner.

'I can identify this pot quite positively', he said, 'for have I not known it since it was only a little bowl?'

80

Books and Rabbits

'Most of the things that people do are just the same as animals do, only they think they are different', pronounced Nasrudin in the teahouse.

'That is ridiculous', snorted a visiting monk; 'if you were right, rabbits would be writing books'.

'I am firmly persuaded', said Nasrudin calmly, 'that rabbits would write books if only they would forget, from time to time, the pressing desire to eat lettuce'.

Stolen: One Rusty Coin

The Mulla found a rusty coin by the roadside. He took it to the market, where a jeweller said: 'This is a valuable antique', and gave him five silver pieces for it.

'I'll invest this in cloth', thought Nasrudin.

A merchant, anxious to get rid of some surplus material, sold him his entire stock of rough felt for five silver pieces.

As soon as it was his, the buying agents of a certain king, about to start a military campaign and needing uniform fabric, bought it for a thousand silver pieces.

While Nasrudin was counting his money, a silver-smith, who had a special order to complete in a hurry, gave him five hundred gold pieces for the silver — far in excess of the value of the coins.

Nasrudin took his gold and started homeward.

Just at the gate of his house a robber held him up and took the bag of gold.

His wife came rushing to the door:

'What was the extent of your loss, Mulla?'

Nasrudin shrugged:

'A rusty coin I picked up this morning'.

81

MIRACULOUS REMEDY

Ill in bed and coughing incessantly, Nasrudin called a physician.

The doctor prescribed a bronchial mixture: 'That will put you right, Mulla'.

'But will it make me normal?'

'Certainly'.

'Doctor, when I have taken the medicine will I be able to sing in tune?'

'Of course'.

'Why did I not meet you before — I have never been able to sing a note all my life!'

HOT AND COLD

Nasrudin's wife told him to go to the Turkish Baths one day. The baths were very hot, and the Mulla roasted. On the way home he was soaked in freezing rain.

When he was almost home, he met a friend.

'Mulla', said the other man, 'my wife has just told me to go to buy some meat'.

'Never do what women say', said Nasrudin, 'if you don't want to be burnt and then frozen, that's my experience'.

THEN AND NOW . . .

It is said that Mulla Nasrudin lived for five hundred years before he started to become ancient.

He used to sit at a crossroads, nodding himself to sleep and jerking awake again.

One day a countryman passing by said:

'What have you seen, Mulla?'

'I saw hundreds of invaders swarm up that valley yonder, sword in hand, they were. I had to rush down to repulse them'.

'Why did you not call me for help?'
'Who would have heard me? It was a hundred and forty years ago'.

WHAT I NEED

'I am going to the shops, Mulla. Is there anything you need?'
'Yes'.
'What is it?'
'A haircut'.

GROUND WHEAT

'Once', said Mulla Nasrudin, 'I had a marvellous idea'.
'What was that?'
'Well, it was to eat ground wheat. But it only had one snag'.
'What was that?'
'I didn't like the taste of it'.

QUANTITY AND QUALITY

Nasrudin was taking a donkey-load of grapes to market.
Groups of small children kept begging grapes: but he only gave them a very small handful each.
'You are mean, Nasrudin!' they shouted.
'Not at all', said the Mulla; 'I am doing this to illustrate the silliness of children. All these grapes taste the same. Once you have had some you know what all the rest are like. So it doesn't matter whether you have many or just a few'.

BAD ENVIRONMENT

Once Nasrudin's calf was bitten by a mosquito. It started to run and kick.

The Mulla at once began to beat the bull.

'Why do that?' one of his neighbours asked.

'People learn bad conduct from their associates', said Mulla Nasrudin.

HE WON'T LISTEN

Mulla Nasrudin was always quarrelling with the mayor of his village.

When the mayor was very ill, the people called the Mulla to say a prayer over him.

'Sorry', said Nasrudin, 'I would like to do so, but I can't. Get someone else: he is always angry with me, so he won't listen'.

PUSSY CAT

Strange to relate, Mulla Nasrudin had never seen a cat in his life when he found one on the road into town one day.

'Aha!' he thought, 'this may be a rare animal — it is pretty enough — I will try to sell it'.

The first man he met said:

'What a pretty pussy!'

Nasrudin said: 'Do you want to buy it?'

'No, thank you', said the man.

'I know what they are called, anyway', said Nasrudin.

Presently another man came past.

'It is scarcely more than a kitten', he said.

'Do you want to buy it?' asked the Mulla.

'No, I don't', said the man.

'They have more than one name', observed Nasrudin to himself.

Then, when he reached town, someone else came up to him.

'What a beautiful Persian', he said.

'Do you want to buy it?' asked the Mulla.

'No', said the man.

'Everyone is ignorant of the true name of these animals, that is obvious', said Nasrudin to himself, 'and they cover up by inventing names for them. Therefore they must be exceedingly rare'.

He spent the whole of the day trying to find a buyer, and spent half a silver coin on meat for the animal.

Then he found himself in front of a pet shop.

'How much will you give me for this one?' he asked the owner.

'It's only a tabby, and not worth a single copper', said the man.

Nasrudin let the cat jump down. 'A day's work, half a *dirham*, and nothing! You may have plenty of names, but you are not worth much when it comes down to facts, are you?'

FLOG HIM

When Nasrudin was a magistrate, a man was brought before him for being drunk and disorderly. The Mulla said:

'Give him forty lashes if he is ever found drunk again'.

The verdict was duly entered in the books.

'You will suffer for this', fumed the drunk, 'for I am a high official of the Government, and if I am flogged I'll have you flayed!'

'According to law', said Nasrudin, 'we cannot alter a court decision. But we can *add* something. Amend that sentence to read: "And also give three hundred lashes to anyone who brings this man in for punishment".'

THE HOLES OF MOLES

'When you see moles' holes, don't you ever wonder what they do with the earth that they dig out, leaving nothing visible outside?'

'No I do not'.

'Why not, Mulla?'

'Because I know that they start at the other end, in the middle of the earth, and fill up the hole as they go along'.

'But how do they get into the middle of the earth in the first place?'

'I regret to inform you that today is my day for answering only one question at a time'.

4. SUFISM IN EASTERN RELIGION

4/i.
Indian Thought and the Sufis
Dr Tara Chand

In this paper I wish to examine the inner springs of our civilization — the ideas upon which it was founded, the goals towards which it moved, its world outlook.

Now, culture is an extremely complex phenomenon. It has been defined as the sum-total of ways of living built up by a group of human beings, transmitted from one generation to another. It has reference to innumerable relations which exist between individuals, groups, associations and the social whole. It includes their manners, customs, and institutions as well as thoughts, sentiments and aspirations, expressed or unexpressed, held consciously or felt dimly, embodied in their systems of philosophy and religion, or uttered through their art, poetry and music. It also embraces all material structures, all products of social or economic activity, all articles which satisfy human wants.

Obviously, it is a task of great difficulty to extricate the essential principles of a civilization during a particular period of a people's history. When we realize that culture is a changeful phenomenon, that it is not uniform in all the strata of a society and that it is composed of differing and sometimes contradictory strands, the immense complexity of the task becomes even more palpable. Change is in the nature of things. No society can remain static for any length of time. Evidently, every new generation brings into the old moulds of society new temperaments, attitudes and emphases, which sometimes gradually and sometimes rapidly alter the character of that civilization.

Developments arise in the inner workings of a society as a result of changing moods of the individuals, modifications in the disposition of groups, variations in environment. Developments take place in response to the impact of external factors — immigration of ideas and artifacts, in the wake of peaceful contacts or forceful intrusions. All these causes of change have operated in all societies. Yet a society may maintain for long periods the taste and flavour of its particular brand of civilization, accepting change in a measure which does not altogether alter its essential character. It also happens that the nature of the change is sometimes violent and revolutionary, resulting in the overthrow of the old and the appearance of an altogether different society and culture.

The examples of the two kinds of change are numerous. In England the changes which occurred after the Norman Conquest are an illustration of the first type. On the other hand, the changes which resulted from the occupation of England by the Anglo-Saxons were of the second kind. In Greece when the Ionians, Achaeans and Dorians migrated southwards and destroyed the ancient Mycenaean-Minoan civilizations, the second type of change occurred. But the development of civilization from the settlement of the Hellenes in the peninsula till its occupation by the Gothic tribes did not alter the fundamental character of civilization. This happened in the fourth century A.D. as a consequence of the migrations of the Goths.

In India there was a continuity of cultural change which was brought about by internal developments like the spread of Jainism and Buddhism, the rise to power of the Mauryas, the Guptas and the Rajput clans, the teachings of the great Acharyas like Sankara and Ramanuja. But external impacts, too, exercised influences on society and culture; for example, the Iranian contact, the invasion of the Greeks, and later the rule of

88

the Muslims. But none of these affected the basic principles of Indian culture. So that through the long vista of change spread over three thousand years, it is possible to trace the fundamental identity of Indian culture. The reason appears to be that whatever was received from abroad was assimilated by India to her own genius. Where it failed to do so completely — as in the case of Islam — its failure was only partial, as there was *rapprochement* in a number of cultural features, and, in some, complete fusion.

From the earliest times two trends are visible in the working of the Indian mind. One trend finds expression in the Vedas and Brahmanas and the other in the Upanishads. In one case the gaze is turned outward, man aspires for perfection in action, in worship of God to win His approval, in faith, in prayer, and in rites whereby one is sanctified. In the other, the aim is withdrawal from objective reality, abstraction from the outgoing tendencies of the mind, in order to realize the difference between the self that knows and the world that is known, in order that the self in its aloneness may be at one with itself, so that the not-self may cease to press, besiege and imprison the mind.

The two tendencies have been present in every epoch of our history; sometimes the one and at other times the other has dominated. From time to time attempts have been made to strike a compromise between them. But throughout, there has been an endeavour to recognize the claims of the infinite, not forgetting to give what is due to the finite in the total scheme of things.

It is interesting that in the Middle Ages the higher class, Apollonian in its attitude, was on the whole the follower of the path of ritualistic worship. The middle class preferred the way of the mystic, of Dionysian worship, and of self-abandonment. But the vast mass of people, unfortunately, was steeped in deep ignorance and crass superstition. Yet their weird forms of worship cast shadows upon the belief and conduct of the whole society.

India then was not one people but many peoples. Each people formed a linguistic entity, possessing some faint consciousness of unity. But within each linguistic region there were religious groups and communities corresponding to similar groups and communities in other regions. But through the multiplicity of societies, groups, and communities, the same tendencies operated, so that Hindu societies of different regions, and Hindus and Muslims all over India, possessed similar attitudes and outlook. The spectrum of languages, religions, arts and customs was suffused with a uniqueness which distinguished the cultures of India from other cultures of the world.

Babar, who had the supercilious disregard of the conqueror for things Indian and who was impressed only by the wealth and population of this vast country, was struck with 'the Hindustani way' of India, which differed from the ways of life known to him in Central Asia and Afghanistan.

In many ways religion is the preserver of the cultural values of a people, and it most clearly indicates the character of their culture. Changes in the spirit, meaning, and outer forms of worship in a religion are signs of cultural change. Therefore, an examination of the religious situation is important for the understanding of the culture of the later Middle Ages.

There were two main religions professed by the people of India — Hinduism and Islam. In both we can distinguish the presence of the two tendencies mentioned before. The Hindus and the Muslims both had their traditionists — the orthodox who stuck to the letter of the law. They tried to conform to the injunctions of their sacred scriptures, to observe that which is commanded and abstain from that which is forbidden (*Vidhi, Nishedha; amr, nihi*). They followed in their conduct the law as laid down by the law-givers (*dharma; shariat*). For both the laws comprehended not only the personal life of the individual, but his entire public life in social, economic and political spheres. They believed that such a

90

disciplined life led to the realization of the highest good — perfection here and eternal bliss hereafter. There were many sects and sub-divisions among them. But whatever their differences, they agreed upon their emphasis regarding established doctrine and ritual.

Then, both among the Hindus and the Muslims there were groups of persons for whom the spirit of religion was more important than its letter. They laid stress upon inner discipline, upon the purification of mind, upon the disentanglement of the soul from the meshes of worldly attractions, upon unification with the Divine. They looked upon the attainment of the ineffable vision as the true goal of all human endeavour. Salvation (*moksha; najat*) from pain and sorrow, liberation from bondage to the transient and the contingent. This was the right way (*supatha; sirat-ul-mustaqim*). The traveller along this path has to pass through a number of stages, to undergo emotional crises, cultivate appropriate attitudes, apply severe restraints and practise physiological and mental disciplines, before he is able to reach the destination. The journey is for the strong of will and firm in faith. To this group belonged many orders and denominations.

Although the approach of the followers of Hinduism and Islam belonging to the first group was similar, that similarity itself created a wide gulf between them. Each of them depended upon and derived inspiration from scriptures embodying widely differing religious experiences and attitudes. The Hindu sacred books were in Sanskrit and those of the Muslims in Arabic. The pillars of orthodoxy were the learned of the two communities. Among the Hindus learning was confined to the Brahman caste whose function was study and teaching. There was no positive rule regarding the acquisition of learning among the Muslims. But in India of the Middle Ages the Saiyids had come to monopolize the study of the sacred lore.

Between the Pandits and Shastris on the one side, and the Maulavis and Ulama on the other, there was, unfortunately, little give and take. It is true that a few Muslim learned men acquired a knowledge of Sanskrit and a number of Sanskrit works were translated into Persian, also that the Mughal emperors were enlightened patrons of Sanskrit scholars. Yet this knowledge remained confined to the few. Mention of some examples of each will not be out of place here.

Of the Musalmans who learnt Sanskrit, Albiruni is the most celebrated. His Arabic work *Tarikhal Hind* is a compendium of Hindu sciences, philosophies and religions. Abu Saleh bin Shuaib and Abu Hasan Ali Jili were the translators of the *Mahabharata* into Persian. Mulla Ahmad Kashmiri, who lived in the reign of Zainal Abidin, rendered the famous *Rajataringini* of Kalhana into Persian. Mulla Abdul Qadir Badayuni — a narrow-minded theologian and a calumniator of Akbar — was entrusted by the Emperor with the translating of the *Mahabharata* and *Simhasana Dvatriansat* from Sanskrit. Masihi Panipati rendered Valmiki's *Ramayana* into Persian. Dara Shukoh translated fifty *Upanishads* into Persian. His letter in Sanskrit addressed to Goswami Nrisimha Swami shows his complete mastery of the language. It starts thus:

'Power which cannot be taken away or withstood; generosity, sweetness of words that have to be honoured in matters to be executed, that deserve to be borne on the head, that cannot be deceived in the world, that deserve to be swallowed by the gods, that cannot be pierced through by scholars, that are brothers to nectar; bravery, majesty, heroism capable of discharging important duties; beauty, abundance of the highest dexterity which has attained to blissfulness and from which admixture of caste is taken away; adroitness — may it be well with thee who is the abode of crowds of virtues beginning with these'.

Shayasta Khan, Dara's maternal uncle, too, was well-versed in Sanskrit and composed verses in this language. Mirza Roshan Zamir (died 1667 A.D.) translated *Parijataka*, a book on music, from Sanskrit into Persian. Wali rendered Krishna Misra's drama *Prabodha Chandrodaya* into Persian. In Bilgram there were great Arab scholars

92

like Mir Ghulam Ali Azad, who had made a comparative study of Sanskrit Bhasha, Arabic and Persian rhetoric and *ars poetica*.

Of the Sanskrit works which were translated into Persian there is a long list which includes the *Atharva Veda*, the *Upanishads*, the *Puranas*, the *Mahabharata*, the *Ramayana*, the *Bhagwata, Bhagwad Gita*, and a host of others including books on medicine and astronomy. The patronage of Sanskrit scholars goes back to the Muslim monarchs of the pre-Mughal days. Bhanukara mentions Sher Shah in his verse:

'Nothing is lost to us — the leaders of thought and wisdom and authors of innumerable works — if destructive criticism is hurled at a minor half-verse, or half of it composed by us, by malicious people who have not understood the (real) sense. Similarly, if among the millions of horses of Sher Shah, which in speed excel the wind, a few (five or six) happen to be either one-eyed or lame, what does it matter?'

Govind Bhatta who assumed the pen-name of Kalidasa and added the adjective 'Akbariya' to please the great Emperor, refers to him in a verse as Jallala Kshonipala, or the protector of the earth. He describes Akbar thus:

'You are a tiger in regard to your forearm; a fleshy intoxicated elephant in regard to your shoulder; as regards your two arms a noble elephant; as regards voice a cloud; a lion in regard to your waist; your sword blade is jet black like a braid; your mind is the ocean: your eyebrows the staff of death; O scion of the family of Humayun, it is true that you are more terrible than the terrible one (*Yama*).'

Then there was the celebrated Jagannatha Panditaraja who belonged to the reigns of Jahangir and Shah Jahan — on both of whom he has showered encomiums. He apostrophized Jahangir thus:

'Why is your sacred thread black? On account of its contact with ink. Wherefrom has that come? From the waters of the Narbada. How did its water become collyrium? On account of its union with the rivers from

93

all round originating in the ceaseless flow of lac-tears from beautiful ladies with long eyelashes belonging to the hostile court of the wrathful King Nuruddin'.

Shah Jahan he compared with the Lord of the universe, in his well-known verse:

'It is the Lord of Delhi or the Lord of the universe who is capable of fulfilling desires. The other rulers are able to give either a vegetable or salt'.

He also composed the *Asaf Vilas* in honour of Asaf Khan, brother of Nur Jahan.

Dara Shukoh was taught Sanskrit by Kavindracharya, who helped him also in the translation of the *Upanishads*.

Abdul Fazl gives a list of the learned men of Akbar's court among whom 26 are Sanskrit scholars, nine of them belonging to the first class, in their understanding and the breadth of their views, 'who have received their spiritual power from the throne of His Majesty'. Their names are Madhu Saraswati, Madhu Sudan, Narayan Ashrama, Hariji Sur, Damodar Bhatta, Ramtirtha, Narsimha, Paramendra, Aditya.

Notwithstanding these efforts towards encouraging Sanskrit and spreading the knowledge of Hindu philosophy and religion among the Persian knowing people, the unfortunate fact remains that the vast majority of the learned of both communities showed little appreciation of each other's thought. A heavy curtain continued to hang between the two which did not permit them to come closer and exchange their views. Thus it was that though both the Pandits and the Ulama lived in the same country, breathed the same air, and shared many things in common, particularly their spoken languages, their minds did not meet.

So far as the Pandits were concerned, for them the world had hardly moved since the days when Sanskrit ceased to be the state language. The intervening thousand years hardly existed. They were held below the threshold of consciousness. The scholars were busy in chewing and re-chewing the cud of ancient lore — writing subtly learned commentaries, excursuses and

94

annotations of the works of original authors — law-givers, philosophers, scientists, etc. In such a subject as the science of war they were expounding even in the eighteenth century the tactics based on the use of bows and arrows, elephants and chariots. They did not care to acquaint themselves with the knowledge of warfare which the Muslims had brought from outside, and disdained to pay any attention to their philosophy, or theology, or science. The Muslim state was an undeniable reality, otherwise the world of the strangers within the gates was nothing more than a shadow.

The Ulama's world, on the other hand, was not so abstract. A number of them were indeed foreigners or their descendants. They had no roots in the country and for them India's past was a blank. They were unlike the Iranians who had accepted the Muslim faith, but who had not broken with their past which remained alive in their memories. It was thus natural in the circumstances for a Firdausi to sing of the exploits of Iran's ancient heroes — Sohrab and Rustum — and to take pride in their achievements in spite of the difference of religion. But no Firdausi arose among the Indian Muslims to sing of the glorious deeds of Asoka, Chandragupta Vikramaditya or Harsha. India was their home, but their spirit dwelt apart. The reason obviously was that all the Muslim ruling dynasties and most of their courtiers, officers, savants and seers hailed from Central Asia or Iran.

Again, although the Iranians were steeped in Islamic lore, and were in the front rank of Arabic scholarship — indeed they contributed more to the development of Arabic literature, Muslim theology and philosophy than did the Arabs themselves — yet they never lost their identity and individuality. On the other hand, India's Muslim scholars and divines were just the camp-followers of the Arab and Iranian thinkers and writers. They showed little independence of thought or courage, to devise their own system of theology.

In the circumstances, two streams of learning and

95

thinking continued to flow parallel to each other. The differences between them were many and radical. Take, for example, their conception of God. Now, the Hindus from the Vedic age had been familiar with the idea of the oneness of God. The Vedic verse which gives expression to the idea is quite well known.

'The real is one, the learned speak of him in many ways'.

Yet this is a peculiar type of oneness, for it identifies such diverse gods as Agni, Indra, Varuna, etc. It is not an exclusive unity, but a oneness which is the synthesis of the many.

When in later times the Vedic gods receded into the background and Brahma, Vishnu and Shiva acquired prominence, the same tendency to identify them reappeared in the concept of Trimurti, the triune god. In spite of a certain friendly competition between the followers of Shiva and Vishnu, the images of both were installed in numerous temples and the Harihara was the joint epithet for the combination. No embarrassment was felt even in coupling a goddess with a god, and so the figure of the 'arddhanarishvara' did not seem to excite surprise. It was possible for an absolute monist like Shakara, who taught that besides Brahman nothing is real, to write beautiful hymns in praise of Vishnu, Shiva and Shakti. Evidently the Hindu mind did not function in terms of limits, clear-cut distinctions, precisely defined concepts. Hence the Hindu idea of God is of a reality which is both transcendent and immanent, outside the universe of existence and yet within it, beyond being and not-being. The essence of this Reality lies in indeterminateness, it is undifferentiated (*abhishoma*), all-pervading (*sarvatravastha*), pure (*shuddha*), known to man in the immediacy of the experience of self (*atma*).

On the other hand, Islam conceives of a God who cannot make any other god a sharer in His divinity. The Muslim creed is 'there is no god save Allah' (*la ilaha illa allah*). He is the one, the only Reality, self-sufficient, all-powerful, all-knowing, all-encompassing, eternal. In

96

relation to the universe He is the absolute creator, sustainer and destroyer, and in relation to man He is compassionate and merciful, both loving (*Wudud*) and reckoning (*Hasib*), both generous (*Karim*) and powerful (*Qahhar*). God is so exalted that human understanding is bewildered in trying to apprehend His nature. Men, therefore, should not trust their intellect and should accept what the Prophet has taught. It is an absurdity to employ reason on things divine. This rigorous assertion of the unity of God and His absolute transcendence, which the conservatives upheld, had serious consequences. Whoever associated other gods with the one God was regarded as a reprobate (*mushrik*), who in his own interest should be forced to abandon a doctrine which was likely to condemn him to eternal disgrace and suffering. In this form of belief, there is involved a determinateness of conception and a consciousness of unlimited distance between God the Supreme Lord and man His abject slave.

In the circumstances the learned of the two groups did not show any inclination to come together. Each considered his religion, philosophy and way of life to be determined by divine ordination revealed in the sacred books. This absolutist attitude could not admit of any compromise.

I must, however, hasten to state that the ritualist, scripture-minded, literalist Pandit, and the dogmatic stickler for words, the assimilator (*mushabbihite*) Alim, were not the only representatives of their faiths in the India of the Mughals. There is no denying that the influence of the Pandits on the minds of the people in general and of the upper class Hindus in particular, was large. It is equally amply confirmed by history that the Ulama exercised considerable power during the reigns of certain monarchs. Yet it would be untrue to facts to exaggerate their authority.

Among both the communities, however, there were religious leaders of other views, common to whom was a less rigid adherence to the word of the sacred books and a more liberal interpretation of their meaning. Most of them had a mystic's approach to those important matters which concerned man's destiny; but some tried to reconcile religious law with mystic vision and others subordinated law to knowledge in varying degrees. Again, some regarded the discipline of the mind as a means of enlightenment, others considered ecstatic exaltation induced by emotional abandonment as an easy way to reach the goal.

Hinduism can lay claim to a long and highly interesting history of mystic speculation and practice. In fact, the deep insight, the systematic exploration of the mental processes, the understanding of the conditions and methods of spiritual discipline, and the knowledge of the experiences of the different states of consciousness which the Indian mystical treatises show, is unequalled in the religious literature of the world.

The story begins with the Upanishads, whose teachings have continued to inspire the religious life of the Indian people throughout the ages. From that perennial spring started a stream whose beneficence has not been limited to the peoples of India. The ideas and practices of Hindu mysticism of Vedanta spread East and West with the propagation of Buddhism and Hinduism in the distant countries of Asia and Europe.

Islamic mysticism originated and grew in two regions of the Muslim world — ancient Khorasan in the East, and Mesopotamia in the West. In both these regions seekers of truth and enlightenment among the Muslims came into close contact with Indian mystics. All Khorasan was studded with Buddhist monasteries and Hindu temples at the time of the Muslim conquest, as is testified by Hiuen Tsiang who had passed through these lands barely seventy years earlier. In Mesopotamia, Junda Shapur, Damascus, and Baghdad were centres of learning where Hindu scholars taught Indian sciences and Hindu ascetics (*yogis*) had debates with Muslim scholars. The Pramukhas of the Nava Vihara of Transoxiana became the prime ministers (*Baramakas*) of the

98

Abbasid Caliphs and they invited Hindu doctors, astronomers and scientists to Baghdad and encouraged the translation of Sanskrit treatises into Arabic. Thus it was that the philosophy of pantheism and the practical discipline of Yoga passed into the Sufi circles of the Middle East. No doubt the current of Tasawwuf was fed by another source too, namely, the Neo-Platonism of Egypt, but it must not be forgotten that the theosophistic thought of Egypt which was developed by such thinkers as Plotinus, Porphyry, Philostratus and others, owes not a little to the Hindu colony which flourished there till the beginning of the third century, when Caracalla, the Roman Emperor, wiped them out.

It was, perhaps, this foreign element in Tasawwuf which was partly responsible for the opposition it encountered from the orthodox. In any case, obstruction and persecution could not stop its onward course. Its martyrs' list is long, but their blood became the seed of a widespread fellowship.

The impact of Islam on India was disturbing, especially because in the early days of the Muslim advent Hindu religious life was confused. Buddhism was in decline, sectarianism was spreading, antinomian cults and deadening ritual were sapping the vitality of society. Krishna Misra, of the court of the Chandella King Kirtivarman, has drawn a picture of the religious situation in the eleventh century in his drama *Prabodha Chandrodaya*. He shows how the unholy alliance of corrupt and degraded Buddhist and Jaina monks, depraved Charvaka materialists, unscrupulous Mimansakas, and immoral Kapalikas, flourishing under the regime of falsehood and vice, oppressed truth and virtue.

The movement of Bhakti (love and devotion) began in the South and extended over the whole country. Ramanuja was the pioneer. He was succeeded by Madhvacharya, Vishnusvami, Nimbarka, and Vallabhacharya, who interpreted the doctrines of Vedanta from their distinct standpoints and founded sects of their own. As they wrote their works in Sanskrit,

99

their direct disciples were largely among the educated who belonged to the upper class.

But along with them marched a goodly company of saintly men who addressed themselves to the common people. They spoke the common people's dialects and in the main imparted their message through word of mouth. Many of them were endowed with the gift of poetry and their homely memorable verse went direct into the heart of their listeners. Their avoidance of the learned jargon, their simple teachings stressing the love of God and of man, their denunciation of idolatry and caste, of hypocrisy, inequality and the externalia of religion, their sincerity, purity and dedicated life, appealed to wide circles among the masses.

Their utterances gave shape to the modern Indian languages. Their enthusiasm stirred the springs of life and moved men to high endeavour and unselfish behaviour. There is a strange exaltation in society in every region during the fifteenth, sixteenth and seventeenth centuries, which cannot be accounted for without taking into consideration this sudden outburst of spiritual energy. These centuries are filled with voices — at once warning and encouraging — of truly noble and large-hearted men in surprisingly large numbers. Yet most of them were of humble origin and they destroyed the myth of aristocracy based on birth.

The spirit of Bhakti moved across the country from one end to the other. As Priyadas points out in his *Bhaktirasabodhini*, 'the tree of Bhakti was once but a sapling . . . now it hath climbed to the sky with its glory spread over the earth . . . Once but a feeble thing; now contentedly sways the mighty elephants of the passions'.

The men and women who propagated the movement of Bhakti may be divided into two groups. One group was the advocate of a devotional faith centred on a personal God — Rama or Krishna. The other selected for their object of adoration the Absolute, which is impersonal, is without attributes, without form or colour, beyond time and space.

100

The first group was affiliated to the sect established by Ramanuja, the Shri Sampradaya, which was divided into two schools — the Tengalai or the Southern school and the Vadgalai or the Northern school. This bifurcation took place in the fifteenth century when Pillai Lokacharya and Manavala Mahamuni started teaching in Tamil, gave up Sanskrit, and took *Nalayiram* as their scripture.

Ramananda, who belonged to the Shri Sampradaya, came to the North and his teachings became the source of inspiration for the devotees of Rama on the one side and of Nirakara Niranjana on the other. The first had their greatest exponent in Tulasidas whose *Ramcharit Manas* is the Bible of Ram Bhakti.

Madhva, Nimbarka and Vallabha were all devotees of Krishna. Vallabha settled down in Gokul and under his inspiration the worship of Krishna spread in northern India. His son's disciples were the Ashtachhap or the eight seals, among whom Surdas was the most eminent.

Tulasi and Sur are the two most brilliant stars of Hindi literature. Their works contain some of the finest poetry that India has produced, valuable from the point of view of art, and prized as inspiring and elevating hymnology.

Not even the briefest account of these movements can leave out the name of Chaitanya — the Krishna-intoxicated devotee — who thrilled northern India with his exciting appeal to tender emotions. He roused the passionate love of God through congregational hymn singing (*kirtana*), to the accompaniment of musical instruments and dancing. His new methods of worship spread the cult through Bengal like wildfire.

It was in these schools of Rama and Krishna Bhakti that the doctrines of mystic practices were developed. The differentiation of the stages of progress towards unification with God and of the emotions which accompanied them, and the causes that excited and enhanced the emotional states and the psychic conditions which followed them, were expounded. The five stages or *bhavas*

101

were resignation (*prashanta*), obedience (*dasya*), friendship (*sakhya*), tenderness (*vatsalya*) and love (*rati*). The two *vibhavas* (developing conditions) were *alambana* and *uddipana* (creation and stimulation); the *anubhavas* (psychic conditions) included the feelings excited by the *bhavas* and their expression.

The process of training in devotion implied worship for the Adorable One, sorrow for one's sins, doubt of all objects other than He, celebration of His praise, living for His sake, assigning everything to Him, resignation to His will, seeing Him in all things, renouncing anger, envy, greed and impure thoughts.

These states, emotions and processes bear comparison with what the Muslim Sufis taught in regard to *hal* and *maqam* (states of rapture and stages of ecstasy). For instance, Abu Nasr al Sarraj, the author of the oldest treatise on Sufism, recounts the seven stages, viz., (1) Repentance, (2) Abstinence, (3) Renunciation, (4) Poverty, (5) Patience, (6) Trust in God, and (7) Satisfaction; and the ten psychic states, namely (1) Meditation, (2) Nearness to God, (3) Love, (4) Fear, (5) Hope, (6) Longing, (7) Intimacy, (8) Tranquillity, (9) Contemplation, and (10) Certainty.

Apart from the founders of the four Sampradayas, Ramanuja, Madhva, Vishnuswami and Nimbaditya, who composed their religious treatises in Sanskrit, and the propagators of Vishnuite Bhakti of the schools of Rama and Krishna, who appealed to the conservative minded among the general public, there was the third group of mystics who employed the language of the people to preach their radical creeds. They mostly belonged to the lower castes and their movement represents the urge of the unprivileged masses to uplift themselves. Some of them were persecuted by governments, some incurred social opprobrium, and others were not regarded as worthy of notice. But they were held in high esteem among the humbler classes who followed their simple teachings with eagerness and understanding. They laid stress upon the dignity of man,

102

for they taught that every individual would reach the highest goal of human life by his own effort. They rejected the claim to special sanctity of priests (Pandits and Maulavis), of books (scriptures of Hindus and Muslims), of temples and pilgrimages, of rites and ceremonies, and encouraged the establishment of direct relation between man and God. The movement arose in the fifteenth century and continued till the middle of the seventeenth, but then it declined and gradually lost its momentum.

The leaders of this group hailed from all parts of India, but their teachings manifest distinct influences of Islam on their beliefs. In the Hindi-speaking region, the most notable reformer was Kabir, who was a most powerful exponent of devotional faith centred in an impersonal, transcendental God, and a most fearless denunciator of Hindu and Muslim hypocritical and superstitious practices. Love of God and man was his religion, and he accepted whatever he thought true in Hinduism and Islam.

There were a number of teachers whose point of view was similar to that of Kabir and who founded their orders in different parts of the country. Among them were Malukdas, Dadu Dayal, Virbhan, Prannath, Babalal and others.

In the Panjab, Guru Nanak founded the Sikh religion which was nourished by his nine successors. The last of them, Guru Govind Singh, transformed Sikhism into a military mission.

In Maharashtra, Namdeo, Eknath, Tukaram and Ramdas were noted saints who were hostile to idol worship, indifferent towards external acts of religion such as vows, fasts, austerities, pilgrimages, etc. They worshipped Vithal the one God who conferred tranquillity, and prayed for release from the snares of the illusory world. They condemned caste distinctions and sought to reconcile Hindu and Muslim faiths.

Bengal had the good fortune to produce Chaitanya, who was a devotee of Krishna but at the same time opposed the Brahmanical system of ritualism and caste.

Among his disciples was Thakur Haridas, a Muslim. But there were sects in Bengal which went far beyond Chaitanya in their criticism of Hindu orthodoxy, for example, the Kartabhajas.

The Vira Saivas or Lingayats of the Kannadadesha were a sect which came into existence in the twelfth century but rapidly spread in Mysore and the neighbouring districts. Their belief in one God who cannot be represented by images or propitiated by sacrifices, and their rejection of caste show their independence from the conservative religious ways. The Lingayats hold that love is the first creation of God, and faithful devotion the means of attaining the goal of human life, which implies sharing the joys of blissful union with God and recognizing Him in one's own self and in everything else. They did not approve of sacrifices, fasts, feasts and pilgrimages, nor recognize distinctions based on birth. A Pariah and a Brahman were equal as members of the sect. 'All men are holy in proportion as they are temples of the great spirit'.

The teachings of the Lingayats seemed to have inspired Chakradhar, who lived in the thirteenth century. He founded the Manbhau sect which spread heterodox doctrines among the Marathi-speaking people.

In the deep South the Tamil Siddhars, whom their latter-day detractors hold up to execration, were theists, the goal of whose search was the Eternal Light which they worshipped by the name of Siva, but they rejected the theory of transmigration and the authority of the Shastras. They held that God and love are the same and desired mankind to live in peace considering love as God.

This brief description shows how a powerful religious impulse, which drew its inspiration from Hindu as well as Muslim sources, spread all over India and sought to bring together the masses into the communion of a faith which transcended social, intellectual and communal barriers. Rising above empty formalism and narrow ritualism, it drew the hearts of men towards a pure life and loving fellowship of the human and the divine.

104

The stirring in the Hindu society had its parallel in the Muslim community. We have seen that Sufism even before its arrival in India had absorbed the main features of Vedanta – for instance the philosophy of absolute monism. The Indian *Advaita* had become the Muslim *Wahdat al Wujud*. If the Vendantist asserts *So ham asmi*, the Sufi exclaims *Analhaq*, 'I am He, I am the Truth'. In the *Upanishads* the divine reality is spoken of as *Jyotisham Jyoti*, and in the terminology of Tasawwuf as *Nurun ala nur* (the Light of Lights). God is both being and not-being (*Sad* and *asad*), and Attar says 'Oh! Thy manifestation is as much as Thy non-appearance.' He is indescribable, *neti, neti* (not this, not this), and Maghribi asks 'But then who is He, who is this also and that also?' The *Bhagavad Gita* calls him *Vettasi Veda cha* (knower and known), and Attar says:

'He is Himself His own seer and His own seen. He is Himself the show and Himself the show-maker'.

But the absolute is unknowable through human eyes. Says Rumi:

'He cannot be perceived by signs nor by eyes, nor does anyone have His knowledge or indication'.

And the *Upanishads* call Him *anirvachaniya*, 'where neither eye goes, nor speech, nor mind'.

The universe is His revelation. The *Veda* says, *Ekam veda vibabhuya sarvam*, and the Gita, *tvaya tatam vishvam ananta rupam*.

The Sufi renders the idea thus:

'Whatever you see of non-living and living, of beasts and birds and all creatures; all this is the essence of Pure God, who makes this manifestation in these ways'.

If according to Shankara the world is *maya*, unreal, Rumi is of the same view; says he:

'We and all our existences are non-entities. Thou art the absolute being whose appearance is transitory'.

And again:

'Thou showed the pleasure of existence to the non-existent. Thou had made non-existent Thy lover'.

In Hindu philosophy the identity of the self and the Supreme is asserted. *Atma is Paramatma, Atma vai Brahma*;

105

similarly in Tasawwuf:

'There is unity without condition and without measure between the Lord of men and the soul of men'.

Man is truly light, *manomayo yam purshah bha satyam*.

Rumi says:

'Soul is likewise light; Man's soul is like the sun'.

Then the creation of the universe and of man are explained in terms of emanation in both mystic systems. For the Hindu, Brahman is the supreme and absolute reality which is the necessary ground and substratum of all being. By its free choice it becomes the creating principle, a capacity for appearance, a possibility of duality. The next step is the immanence of the creating principle in the world, which finally appears in the multiplicity of the universe — the meeting place of the real and the unreal, of the soul and the body. Ibn el-Arabi, the great master of Islamic mysticism, affirms that God is one and the universe is His appearance. Creation is a process of emanation of which the three steps are (1) the stage of absolute unity (*ahdiat*), (2) the stage of latent or potential multiplicity (*wahdat*), and (3) the stage of apparent or actual multiplicity (*wahidiat*). The multiplicity expresses itself in souls (*Ruh*), forms (*Mithal*), and bodies (*Jism*).

The soul which is in essence one with the divine reality forgets its nature in association with the unreal world; it becomes hidden behind veils. In order that it may know the self, the veils must be removed. The removal involves a discipline, a journey from self to self. The stages of the journey are four. They are indicated by the words *Jagrata* (waking), *Swapna* (sleep), *Sushupti* (dreamless sleep), and *Turiya* (the fourth state), also by the terms *Vaisvanara, Taijasa, Prajna* and *Chaturtha*. The Muslim mystic gives these stages the names *Nasut, Jabrut, Malakut* and *Lahut*.

For both there is a common discipline. It includes purification of self, mastering of passions and desires, filling of the mind exclusively with the thought of God, obtaining control over bodily functions and mental processes, till the objective world ceases to distract consciousness, till man passes away (*fana, nirvana*) from

106

phenomenal existence and attains union with the divine. The soul stands self-enlightened, unperturbed by temptations and apprehensions.

The members of the Sufistic orders were the bearers of such doctrines and practitioners of this discipline (*yoga, dhikr*). Four of these orders were well known in India — Chishtiya, Suhravardiya, Naqshbandiya and Qadiriya. Among them all there appeared, from time to time, men who by their piety, other-worldliness, asceticism, human kindliness, and abundant love, attracted numerous disciples belonging to all classes and communities. The Chishtiya order which was established in India by Muinal Din Chishti and counted among its luminaries Qutbal Din Bakhtiar Kaki, Faridal Din Ganjshakar, Nizamal Din Aulia, Shaikh Nasiral Din Chiragh, Saiyid Banda Nawaz Gesu Daraz and later Shaikh Salim Chishti, were the upholders of the philosophy of absolute monism. They refused to accept any favours from the Delhi Kings and extended the hand of friendship towards both Muslims and Hindus.

Respect for the susceptibilities of others was an article of faith with the Sufis, for love was their religion. Dard, the Indian mystic poet, says:

'Love is the treasury of divine secrets, love is the music of the divine instrument; love peoples the abode, love makes the slave free; love is the harvest of our existence, love is our adornment and decoration'.

Abu Said Abul Khair says:

'Faith is one thing, and religion of love another, the prophet of love is neither from Iran nor from Arabia'.

And said Maulana Rumi:

'The people of love are different from all the world; the religion and society of lovers is God'.

Then said Attar:

'What is humanity?' And answered himself: 'To feel pain at the sorrows of our neighbours, to feel humiliated at the humiliation of fellow-beings'.

They looked upon the rites of religion not as formalities but as practices of devotion. Again Attar explains:

107

'Then what is lustration? The purification of the heart. What is purification of the heart? Cleaning of whatever is alien. Fasting is the protection of the heart from its agitations, and then breaking the fast after gaining the vision. What is pilgrimage to Mecca? Going away from self. Going where? Towards the Creator'.

It followed that all religions pointed to the same goal. Sanai holds:

'Unbelief and belief are both marching on His road, while both are saying, "He is one and He has no associates".'

And Amir Khusrau warned:

'O thou that throwest taunts at the Hindu, learn as well from him the way of worship'.

And Mir Dard declared:

'Neither do I lay the foundation of a mosque or a school, nor do I draw the plan of a cloister or a temple. I advise a purpose which is different from unbelief and belief. I rebuild what has fallen to my lot; heart is the abode which I people'.

Other poets in India support them. Faizi, who was the poet laureate of Akbar's court, dreams of a new *Kaaba* and of an edifice without fault. Says he:

'Come let us turn our faces towards the altar of light, let us lay the foundation of a new Kaaba with stones from Mount Sinai. The walls of the Kaaba have fallen and the foundations of Qibla have given way. Let us lay the foundation of a faultless edifice'.

Then says Naziri:

'Infidelity of faith are not necessary conditions in love. O Naziri, I can show to thee an infidel who possesses the highest degree of saintliness'.

And Maghribi says:

'I am in wonder why there is enmity between infidelity and belief, both Kaaba and temple are lighted by the same lamp'.

And lastly says Akbar:

'I am neither in the ranks of unbelievers nor of Musalmans. I am neither fit for hell nor for heaven. What am I to do?'

The mutual give and take, which is the marked

characteristic of Hindu and Muslim mystic religion, manifests itself in the fields of language and literature also. The beginning of the modern Indo-Aryan languages coincides with the establishment of Muslim rule in India, and hence it was inevitable that all of them should have absorbed elements from Persian — the language of the Muslims who settled in India. Even Sanskrit had not evaded the infection. In the earlier days when astronomical works from the Muslim schools of Central Asia came to India a number of technical terms were borrowed. The same thing happened when under Raja Jai Singh the *Al-Majest* was rendered into Sanskrit from Arabic. Words passed into literature too. Lakshmipati, a Sanskrit poet of the early eighteenth century, makes use of the following words:

zahr, gunah, dil, kambakht, sher, jawab, wazir, dushman, mushtari, sharah, pil, khabar, mahtab, ghusl, halal, asman, faramushi, bardasht, dalil.

Hindi, Bengali, Marathi, Panjabi and other northern Indian languages received with open arms numerous Persian words. In the South, Telugu, and less so the other Dravidian languages, accepted a great many loan words. In other ways, too, the languages were influenced — in grammar, in the formation of compounds, in syntax, also in phonetics. Perhaps the use of rhyming verse which is not known to Sanskrit came with Arabic poetry.

The influence on the literatures of Indian languages is quite unmistakable.

What is remarkable about the Indian languages is the variety and wealth of literature produced in these times. Much the greater proportion of this literature owed its inspiration to religion, and naturally some of the greatest names in literature are those of religious devotees and reformers who belonged to the sixteenth and seventeenth centuries. There were, as we have already noticed, a number of religious streams flowing among the people in this age. Each sect had its high priest who was also an inspired poet. For instance, the greatest advocate of

Krishna Bhakti was Surdas, probably a Bhat, whose name is mentioned by Abul Fazl in the *Ain-i-Akbari* as a great singer. Next to him were the eight seals, Ashtachhap, of whom Krishnadas, a Sudra and an eminent poet and scholar, and Nandadas, only second to Surdas as a poet, are justly famous. Outside this group but in no way inferior to them in devotion to Krishna was Ras Khan, a Muslim, whose songs express a love and passion amazing in its depth. There were others, too, but none of them reached the standard of Sur, Nand and Ras Khan.

Among the promulgators of Ram Bhakti, Tulasidas stands foremost. His life span extends between 1532 and 1623. In his line there were not many outstanding poets. Only Nabhadas and Senapati are mentioned as eminent.

The third branch of devotees is headed by Kabir who died at the beginning of the sixteenth century. He was not only a reformer and a saint but also a high-class poet. Among those who followed him in this type of devotion to God as the formless spirit was Raidas, a cobbler.

There was again a didactic school of poetry which followed both in form and content the example of Sanskrit poetry of this genre. Bhartrihari was their model. Among Hindi moralists Rahim, who was a Muslim, occupies the highest position. Others include Vrind, Giridhar and Ghagh.

Another interesting literary tradition was embodied in the romances created by Muslim poets like Malik Muhammad Jayasi, whose story of *Padamavat* is a fusion of Hindu and Muslim doctrines and ideas. Similar in intent were Manjhan's *Madhumalati*, Usman's *Chitravali*, Kasin Shah's *Hams Jawahar*, etc.

There is a ring of sincerity in these poet-saints. They seem to be genuinely concerned in the solution of the problem that their world presented to them. In the preceding age the great Acharyas were occupied with the inner conflicts of the individual belonging to the privileged leisured class. They tried to solve this conflict intellectually by means of complicated arguments involv-

110

ing fine distinctions, razor-sharp logic, and subtle metaphysics. But how were the doubts of the merchant, the artisan, the labourer, the government official, the common solider, who had neither the time nor the capacity to understand this highbrow philosophy, to be removed? Was conviction a matter of mere intellectual hair-splitting? Were not belief and conviction hard to attain without the involvement of emotion and will? So these godly men abandoned the language and the methods of the learned, reduced to the minimum their physical needs which entangle the mind in sorrow-producing and unsatisfying pursuits, and filled the space emptied of trash with the wealth of ineffable experience. So they garnered a joy and created a love which increased and grew by sharing. They sang of it, and of their trials and tribulations and their victory over the flesh. The affirmation of their faith found an echo in the hearts of their listeners.

But with the turn of the seventeenth century the mood began to pass away. The high moral tone receded; instead the solicitations of the world, the pleasures of sense, and the carnal love of woman, laid siege to the mind. Hindi poetry entered the domain of *Riti* and turned to exploit passion. The *sringar rasa*, the *nakh sikh* delineation, the amorous dalliance varying with seasons, and the virtuoso skill in play upon words unrelated to reality, engaged the attention of art.

Of this technique the supreme exponents were Biharilal, Matiram, Bhushan, Dev, and Rahim. But soon the high tide of their artistry ebbed.

This summary review shows how fecund the later Middle Age was in Hindi literature, how it was built up by the genius of both Hindus and Muslims, how in the very front rank stood Muslim writers and poets — Malik Muhammad Jayasi, Ras Khan, Rahim and Raslin. This is more or less true of the other languages of India also. Panjabi exhibits the same tendencies. The Sikh Gurus' hymns gave expression to the devotional faith in the one, unseen and formless God. Narrative poems of romantic

111

type were written in abundance, some borrowing their themes from Islamic countries, others from old Indian stories, e.g. Yusuf Zulaikha, Shirin Farhad, Laila Majnun, Sulaiman Bilqis, Sasi Punnu, Hir Ranjha, Gopichand, Chander Bhaga, Padmini, Urvase, Tilottama, Sohini, Mahiwal, Madhavanal, Kamkandala, Chandrabadan Mihyar, Nal Damayanti, Puran Bhagat, etc.

Among the poets and writers were Warris Shah Muqbil, Hamid, Abdul Hakim, Ahmad Yar, Hashim, as well as Damodar, Budh Singh, Waliram, etc.

Bengali owes much to the enlightened patronage of Muslim rulers for its emergence as a literary language and many Muslim poets contributed to its treasury. Their poetry is racy of the soil. It demonstrates their identification with Indian traditions. They sing of India's broad and swift rivers, of her multicoloured scented flowers, of her twittering birds. The heroes and heroines are Radha and Krishna, Rama and Sita, Arjuna and Draupadi rather than the famous characters of Arab and Persian tales. Some of them have written Vaishnava songs in which Hindu and Muslim ideas have been fused. On the whole their creations are inspired with that common culture which the Middle Age was striving to achieve. Shaikh Faizulla was the author of *Gorakh Vijaya*, which set the fashion for similar biographies including Maladhar Basu's *Srikrishna Vijaya* and Abdushshakur Mahmud's *Gopichander Sannyas*.

In the seventeenth century Qazi Daulat and Saiyid Alaul composed the romances of *Sati Mayano o Lor Chandrani* and *Padamavat*. They also wrote *Barahmasa* (seasons). Saiyid Murtaza's *Pad Kalptaru* is an anthology of Vaishnava songs, in which Sufism is combined with Tantrism. His poem *Murali* illustrates his attitude:

'How full of mirth is your flute, O Dark One! No sooner it starts its piercing note than women in every home get ready (to rush out) like a million moons fallen (from the sky).

Hidden in your heart lies a jewel of untold value: (take

care) the milkmaids may steal in and carry it away.
In the guise of Nanda's pampered son you caper about in public pretending innocence: you have your secret sports under cover of the Kadamb trees.
Little did you reck of (our) matronly shame and had your will (of us). Stranded do we now lie clasping the river-brim.
"A stranger can never be won over", says Saiyid Murtaza, "You have only filled the world with the story of your disgrace!"'

Similarly Ali Raja's *Gyan Sagar* is filled with mystic lore and the Sufi's devotion to the religion of love. Says he:

'There is neither success nor salvation without a training in (the technique of) love'.

Every Indian language was a common vehicle for all cultural groups. Each regional language was used by all the inhabitants of the region — Hindus as well as Muslims. Even so a new literary medium for cultural exchange between the communities had also grown up in the heart-land of the empire. Out of the Shaurseni Apabhramsha of the midlands, a new Indo-Aryan dialect designated Khari Boli had emerged in and around Delhi. When the Sultanat of Delhi became firmly established and the strangers from the West had become acclimatized, the association of the Persian-speaking foreigners and Khari Boli-speaking Indians produced a new style of speech which was known as Hindvi or Hindustani, and later christened Urdu, or the language of the royal entourage.

Born in Delhi, founded upon the grammar, phonetical system and idiom of Hindi, Urdu borrowed extensively from Persian words, phrases, poetical forms and themes. But within its broad bosom it gave ample accommodation to Hindu and Muslim traditions, and counted among its votaries persons of all communities. It spread all over India. In the North its centres were in the Panjab, Uttar Pradesh, Bihar, Bengal and Gujarat. In the Deccan, it flourished in Aurangabad and Hyderabad, and in the far South in Karnatak and

113

Madras. It had acquired in every sense an all-India character.

Its literature first developed in the Deccan, and its pioneers were the Sufis who sought to reach the mind of the people through their own language — such were Khwaja Banda Nawaz Gesudaraz, Shah Aligamdhani, Shah Miranji Shamsul Ushshaq, Shah Burhanuddin Janam and others. Aminuddin Ala (died 1675) wrote in verse as well as prose. His treatise *Risala Mazhabul Salikin* on comparative religion demonstrates the unity of godhead in all religions. Later numerous poets enriched the literature in Golkanda, Bijapur, Aurangabad and other places. Among them were the crowned Sultans of the Qutub Shahi and Adil Shahi dynasties.

Muhammad Quli Qutub Shah (1580–1611) was a great linguist. He knew Arabic, Persian, Marathi, Kannad and Telugu. He was master of Urdu in which he composed Ghazals, Qasidas, Masnawis, Rubais and Marsias.

In the court of these rulers numerous Urdu poets flourished. What distinguishes the literature that they produced is its dominantly Indian flavour, its naturalness, its simple diction, and its optimistic mood.

From the Deccan the impulses came to the North, and when about the end of the seventeenth century the Deccan Sultanates were extinguished by Aurangzeb, poets migrated, and Delhi welcomed with warmth its child which had by now grown into a lusty youth. The progress of Urdu was rapid, but the times were unpropitious — the Mughal empire was bleeding to death.

In an atmosphere surcharged with despair, frustration, and gloom, and in circumstances threatening the doom of old institutions and ways of life, poetry became the utterance of afflicted hearts and anguished souls. But those who poured out their pain and suffering in Urdu verse were men of genius. So it was that in the sky of murky twilight there shone above the horizon brilliant stars of great magnitude. In this galaxy were Mir Taqi

114

Mir, Mirza Muhammad Rafi Sauda, and Khwaja Mir Dard. Hindus also made a valuable contribution to these developments. Among them Chandrabhan Brahman, Waliram Wali, Jaswant Rai Munshi, Nawal Rai Wafa, Dayaram Pandit, Sarab Singh Divana, Khub Chand Zaka and Bindraban Raquim, have left their impress upon Urdu poetry.

The description of the literature of those times would remain incomplete if I did not say a word about Persian, which was the language of the state for more than five hundred years. Though a foreign tongue, Persian borrowed many words from the Indian languages and Persian poets expressed a deep attachment to their adopted country. Here is a list of words occurring in Persian poetry:

jhakkar (Urfi), ram rangi (Talib Amuli), mahajan, tamboli, dhobi, pathani, champa, maulsiri, kanwal, keora, bira, pan, kathal, rupiah, lakh, tal, hat, darshan, sagar, ban, jamdhar, jagraj (Kalim), paisa, boti, dakchauki, dagla, tel, bahal, kachehri, bans, palki, dupatta, patka, jogi (Tughra).

The list could be multiplied almost indefinitely.

The poets wrote about Indian flowers, fruits, animals, birds, customs and festivals.

In Persian, too, Hindu poets and authors showed high skill and great scholarship. Among them Mirza Manohar Tausini, Chandrabhan, Brahman, Mathuradas Hindu, Banwalidas Wali, Wamaq, Diwana, Begham, Amanat and Bedar were poets; Bhagwant Das, Hiraman, Bindraban Das, Sujan Bir, Narain Kaul Ajiz, Bhim Sain, Lachmi Narain Shafaq, Birbal Kachru, Khushal Chand, and Rai Chatarman were historians; Har Karan, Madho Ram, Malikzada Munshi and Munshi Uderaj were letter-writers; Rai Anand Ram Mukhlis, Sialkoti Mal Warasta and Tek Chand Bahar were lexicographers.

The arts are the mirror of the culture of a people. Like poetry — painting, architecture and music express the varying moods, longings and hopes of a society. In works

115

of art one finds reflected man's attitudes towards life and towards the world, his vision of reality, his insight into the deepest secrets of his mysterious world, his beliefs regarding the destiny of man and man's relation to the seen and unseen forces which are responsible for the order and chaos prevailing in all creation. Through art which is the highest manifestation of creative power, man seeks to bring into existence a world of imagination, beauty and truth which rivals the world of everyday experience, and seeks to transform it near to his heart's desire.

The arts of India of the Middle Ages were the products of a peculiar co-operation of the higher and the lower orders of society. Take for example painting. Most of the Mughal emperors were deeply interested in it. They were both patrons and critics, encouraging talent and guiding skill. They invited to their courts great masters from Central Asia and Persia. They gathered the humble but competent practitioners of India. The two worked together, and one was influenced by the other. The result was a style of wondrous beauty. Their miniatures depict equally the gorgeous splendour, the magnificent pageantry of the court with all its solemnity, dignity and power, as well as the simplicity, asceticism and serene content of the hermit. They are equally at home in painting scenes of war, chase and sport, as in the pictures of princes and princesses dallying in marble palaces and enchanting gardens or watching beautiful damsels dancing or celebrating colourful festivals like Holi, or in painting pictures of women visiting a Sadhu, or of men gathered to hear a religious discourse, and of a thousand other activities of the high and the low.

But whatever the subject, the picture is always bathed in clear light, every detail is rendered with immense care, the ground is carpeted with green and the trees are in bloom. The mien of the human dwellers in these scenes is one of good cheer, the hearts are elated, heads are held high, and the eyes look straight.

The technique is a combination of realism and

abstraction. Firm but supple lines individualize every figure. They do not admit of overlapping and confusion. But there is no truck with nature. There is hardly any perspective. Objects appear mostly in the flat, two-dimensional; faces are full, three-quarters, or in profile, and although full of character and vivacity, they are set over bodies altogether static and mechanically draped and stanced. Line only defines, but colour gives substance to the picture. Thus although form is abstract the content is as variegated as the many-hued world. Painting thus reflects the attitude of mind which seeks changelessness in change, abiding joy in the sensuous transience of the space and time continuum. If yoga leads to the integration of personality, art points to the unity which lies behind the multiplicity of nature.

It may not be out of place to name some of the painters who evolved the style at the Mughal court which became the prototype of the schools at the courts of provincial governors, and of the Hindu Rajas of Rajasthan and the hill states in the Himalayas. Humayun brought with him two pupils of Bihzad, namely Mir Saiyid Ali and Khwaja Abdus Samad. Akbar invited Farrukh Qalmaq and Aqa Raza. But among his artists there were many Hindu painters of great ability like Basavan, Daswant and Kesho. They were entrusted with the illustration of works like *Shah Namah, Khamsa-i-Nizami, Babar Namah, Timur Namah,* etc., as well as *Mahabharata, Ramayana, Nal Damayanti, Panchtantra,* etc.

Jahangir carried the art to perfection. He was himself a great connoisseur of art. He has stated in his *Tuzuk* that he could distinguish between the style of all living and dead painters and could say who the painter of a particular picture was. He could even differentiate and recognize the line of every painter, and if it was a work of a number of artists he could declare what part had been drawn by which artist. One of his painters was Mansur who was an expert in painting birds and flowers. Abul Hasan was given the title of Nadiruz Zaman. Bishandas excelled in portrait painting and Murad and Manohar

117

were unequalled in drawing.

Shah Jahan maintained the high traditions of his father. The great painters of his reign were Muhammad Nadir Samarquandi, Faqirullah Khan, Mir Hashim, Bishandas and Bichittar.

Though the art continued under Aurangzeb, it began to decline rapidly after him. But in the provinces and in the Hindu states, for instance, in Jaipur, Kangra, Chamba and Basohli, it continued to flourish vigorously.

Painting is the delicate plant and architecture the stately tree that adorns the arbour of culture. The Mughal emperors, endowed with an extremely refined taste in the arts, nurtured both with loving care. Babar laid out beautiful gardens with running water, cascading fountains, and marble pavilions. Humayun erected a seven-chambered palace in which each hall was dedicated to one of the seven planets. Akbar created Fatepur-Sikri with its residential palaces, the Panch Mahal, the hall of worship supported on a central pillar with a thousand-petalled lotus capital and the great mosque whose gateway, Buland Darwaza, is unique in the world. Jahangir directed the completion of Akbar's tomb at Sikandara and the Jahangiri Mahal in Agra, and Nur Jahan was responsible for the tomb of her father Itmadud Daulah in Agra. Shah Jahan's contribution to India's architectural monuments is well known. The Red Fort in Delhi with its numerous halls, mansions and mosque, the Jamia Masjid in red standstone led up to by a magnificent staircase, and above all the incomparable Taj Mahal, are immortal witnesses of his taste.

The three types of buildings in which the Mughals were mainly interested were palaces, mausoleums and mosques. The first two give monumental expression to their love of life, the palaces to the zest of living a full life in flesh and blood, and the mausoleums to perpetuate themselves in surroundings whose beauty is everlasting.

The mosques were, however, the embodiment of reverence and worship in stone. Islam's religious consciousness was moulded in Arabia, and because the

118

deepest convictions of man are embedded in emotions fed by history, tradition, and environment, the Arab experience found its own peculiar forms to express itself. For the Arab the universe is a great expanse peopled scantily at intervals but otherwise a void. He looks upwards and the heavens spread to infinity and the sky is cloudless. As he looks below, the earth as far as the eye can reach is a plain with a few scattered palm trees breaking the vast immensity of glittering particles of sand. God dwells in this universe and beyond. If a tabernacle has to be built which will remind man of the exaltation and majesty of the Lord of Creation, surely a dome whose circular surface is boundless and whose curves represent the limitless vault of heavens is the most appropriate form.

This pure aesthetic consciousness of the Arab was diluted when Islam spread to countries of Asia, and the Muslims who came to India had their minds formed under different conditions. Thus the mosques they built in India were a compromise or an amalgam of two art traditions – one Hindu and the other Iranian Muslim.

The Hindu tradition was founded upon the Hindu attitude towards the cosmic problem. Its basic formula was *atma vai Brahma* — the human soul is the absolute. It lays emphasis upon the identity of the individual with the world soul. It admits of no intermediate identity. The individual consciousness is not the national soul nor the human soul. It is the supreme soul. Man is alone with his master. He must commune with God in isolation. Man must, therefore, create a symbol of this relation, a replica of Brahmanda. This he does in his temple, which has two distinct aspects, one inner represented by the *garbha griha* into which light does not penetrate and all forms suggestive of multiplicity are blotted out. In this dark mysterious chamber dwells the spirit, and the worshipper may meditate upon Him alone and without distraction. The other aspect of the temple is its exterior which protects the precious sanctum. But the exterior is the universe, and therefore the temple outside revels in

119

multitudinous form; the platform, the walls, the pillars, the doors and the *Shikhara* (spire) are a riot of sculpture and moulding, a veritable forest crowded with life.

The Hindu abundance and richness met the Islamic consciousness of unfilled space and the result was the Indian mosque with roofs provided with bunches of domes and cupolas, pairs of turrets and towers, gates within recessed gates, rows of niches in the walls, multicusped arches, stalactites and squinches, stately pillars and capitals, and the effusion of colour through white, black and multi-coloured marble and red stone, and flowing inscriptions engraved on walls and doorways.

On the other side, the buildings created during these times show how the Hindu sense of form had absorbed the elements of Muslim architecture. Of this change the palaces of Man Singh in Gwalior, the temples of Govind Deva and Madan Mohan at Brindaban, the temple of Hamirdeva at Govardhan, the Jain temples of Sonagarh in Bundelkhand, the palaces and pavilions built in Vijayanagar, Chandragiri, Madura, Tanjore and Rajputana by Hindu rulers, are some illustrations.

Unfortunately, the line of these enlightened, large-hearted, generous humanists began to shrivel as the seventeenth century advanced towards it close. The *élan vital* which had sustained the extraordinary efflorescence of genius, began to wane. Reaction, fed by growing forces of confusion and anarchy, raised its ugly head; devotional faith receded into the background; blind bigotry, chilling frustration, and dark pessimism laid hold of the minds of men. The eighteenth century saw a divided and unhappy India move towards the climacteric of its downfall. Plassey set the seal upon that phase of our culture which had grown and developed during the later Middle Ages. With the British conquest of Bengal a new chapter in Indian history began.

120

4/ii.
Sufi Influence on the Formation of Sikhism
Frederic Pincott, M.R.A.S.

The literature and traditions of Sikhism present a strange intermingling of Hindu and Muhammadan ideas and superficial enquirers have been led to conclude that Nanak intended his creed to be a compromise between those two great religions. Dr Trumpp, the translator of the *Adi Granth* (the sacred book of the Sikhs) is, however, distinctly of the opinion that Sikhism has only an accidental relationship with Muhammadanism. In his Introduction (p. ci) he says:

'It is a mistake if Nanak is represented as having endeavoured to unite the Hindu and Muhammadan ideas about God. Nanak remained a thorough Hindu, according to all his views; and if many Mussulmans became his disciples, it was owing to the fact that Sufism, which all these Muhammadans professed, was in reality nothing but a Pantheism, derived directly from Hindu sources and only outwardly adapted to the forms of Islam. Hindu and Muslim Pantheists could well unite together, as they entertained essentially the same ideas about the Supreme'.

In fact the balance of evidence is heavily on the other side. A careful study of early Sikh traditions points strongly to the conclusion that the religion of Nanak was really intended as a compromise between Hinduism and Muhammadanism. Because very little seems to be known as to the views of the early Sikh teachers, it is necessary to establish the relationship which actually existed between the two faiths. The information given in this article is taken chiefly from original Punjabi books and from manuscripts in the India Office Library, and it is supported by the authority of the *Adi Granth*, which is the sacred canon of the Sikhs.

The *Janam-Sakhis*, or biographical sketches of Nanak and his associates, contain a profusion of curious tradi-

121

tions which throw considerable light on the origin and development of the Sikh religion. From these old books we learn that in early life Nanak, although a Hindu by birth, came under Sufi influence and was strangely attracted by the saintly demeanour of the *faqirs*, who were thickly scattered over Northern India and swarmed in the Punjab. Sufism is not derived from Hindu pantheism; it arose in the very earliest days of Muhammadanism and is almost certainly due to the influence of Persian Zoroastrianism on the rude faith of Arab Islam. Persian has ever been the stronghold of Sufistic doctrine, and the leading writers who have illustrated that form of Muhammadanism have been the Persian poets Firdusi, Nizami, Sa'di, Jalaludin Rumi, Hafiz and Jami.

Hafiz, the prince of Sufi poets, boldly declares: 'I am a disciple of the old Magians: be not angry with me, O Sheikh! For thou gavest me a promise; he hath brought me the reality'. Although this stanza alludes directly to two persons known to Hafiz, its almost obvious meaning is: 'I, a Persian, adhere to the faith of my ancestors. Do not blame me, O Arab conqueror, that my faith is more sublime than thine.'

That Hafiz meant his readers to take his words in a general sense may be inferred from the stanza in which he says: 'I am the servant of the old man of the Tavern (i.e. the Magian); because his beneficence is lasting: on the other hand, the beneficence of the Shaikh and of the Saiyid at times is, and at times is not'. Indeed, Hafiz was fully conscious of the fact that Sufism was due to the influence of the faith of his ancestors; for, in another ode, he plainly says: 'Make fresh again the essence of the creed of Zoroaster, now that the tulip has kindled the fire of Nimrod'. And Nizami, also, was aware that his ideas were perilously akin to heterodoxy; for, he says in his *Khusru wa Shirin*: 'See not in me the guide to the temple of the Fire-worshippers; see only the hidden meaning which cleaveth to the allegory'. These quotations, which could be indefinitely multiplied, sufficiently indicate the

122

Zoroastrian origin of the refined spirituality of the Sufis. The sublimity of the Persian faith lay in its conception of the unity of Eternal Spirit, and the intimate association of the Divine with all that is manifest. Arab Muhammadans believe in the unity of a personal God; but mankind and the world were, to them, mere objects upon which the will of God was exercised. The Sufis approached nearer to the Christian sentiment embodied in the phrase, 'Christ in us'.

The Persian conquerors of Hindustan carried with them the mysticism and spirituality of the Islamo-Magian creed. It was through Persia that India received its flood of Muhammadanism; and the mysticism and asceticism of the Persian form of Islam found congenial soil for development among the speculative ascetics of northern India. It is, therefore, only reasonable to suppose that any Hindu affected by Muhammadanism would show some traces of Sufi influence. As a fact we find that the doctrines preached by the Sikh Gurus were distinctly Sufistic; and, indeed, the early Gurus openly assumed the manners and dress of faqirs, thus plainly announcing their connection with the Sufistic side of Muhammadanism. In pictures they are represented with small rosaries in their hands, quite in Muhammadan fashion, as though ready to perform *zikr*. Guru Arjun, who was fifth in succession from Nanak, was the first to lay aside the dress of a faqir. The doctrines, however, still held their position; for we find the last Guru dying while making an open confession of Sufism. His words are: 'The Smritis, the Sastras, and the Vedas, all speak in various ways: I do not acknowledge one (of them). O possessor of happiness, bestow they mercy (on me). I do not say, "I", I recognize all as "Thee".' (*Sikhan de Raj di Vithia* p. 81.) Here we have not only the ideas, but the very language of Sufis, implying a pantheistic denial of all else than Deity. The same manner of expression is found in the *Adi Granth* itself, e.g. 'Thou art I; I am thou. Of what kind is the difference?' (*Translation*, p. 130); and again, 'In all the One dwells, the One is contained' (p.

123

41). Indeed, throughout the whole *Adi Granth* a favourite name for Deity is the 'True One', that is, that which is truly one — the Absolute Unity. It is hardly possible to find a more complete correspondence of ideas than that furnished by the following sentences, taken from the *Yusuf wa Zulaikha* of Jami, the Persian Sufi; and the others, from the *Jap-ji* and the *Adi Granth*. Jami says:

'Dismiss every vain fancy, and abandon every doubt;
Blend into one every spirit, and form, and place;
See One — know One — speak of One —
Desire One — chant of One — and seek One'.

In *Jap-ji*, a formula familiar to every Sikh household, we find:

'The Guru is Isar (Siva), the Guru is Gorakh (Vishnu),
Brahma, the Guru is the mother Parbati.
I should know, would I not tell? The story cannot be told.
O Guru, let me know the One; that the One liberal patron of all living beings may not be forgotten by me'.

In the *Adi Granth*, we read:

'Thou recitest the One; thou placest the One
in (thy) mind; thou recognizest the One.
The One (is) in eye, in word, in mouth;
thou knowest the One in both places (i.e. worlds).
In sleeping, the One; in waking, the One;
in the One thou art absorbed'.

(*India Office* MS., No. 2484, fol. 568.)

It is not only with respect to the idea of the unity of God that this identity of expression is descernible; for other technical terms of Sufism are, also, reproduced in Sikhism. Thus the Sufi Faridu'd Din Shakrganj calls Deity 'the *light* of life', and Jalu'd-Din speaks of '*flashes* of His love', while Jami represents the 'light' of the Lord of Angels as animating all parts of the universe; and Nizami exclaims, 'Then fell a *light*, as of a lamp, into the garden (of my heart)', when he feels that a ray of the Divine has entered into his soul. It is not difficult to collect many such instances from the works of Persian Sufis. Turning to Sikhism, we find that the *Adi Granth* is full of similar expressions. It is enough to cite the following exclama-

124

tion of Nanak himself: 'In all (is) light. He (is) light. From His light, there is light in all'. (*India Office* MS., No. 2484, fol. 35.) And in another place he says: 'The Luminous One is the mingler of light (with himself)'. (fol. 186.) On fol. 51 we find: 'There death enters not; light is absorbed in the Luminous One'.

Another favourite metaphor of Sufis for the Deity is 'the Beloved'; for example, when Hafiz says: 'Be thankful that the Assembly is lighted up by the presence of the Beloved'. This term is well recognized in Sikhism; thus in the *Adi Granth*, 'If thou call thyself the servant of the Beloved, do not speak despitefully (of Him)'. (*India Office* MS., No. 2484, fol. 564.) 'Love to the Beloved naturally puts joy into the heart. I long to meet the Lord (*Prabhu*); therefore why should I be slothful?' (*India Office* MS., No. 2484, fol. 177.) Also, 'In my soul and body are excessive pangs of separation, how shall the Beloved come to my house and meet (with me)?' And again: 'The Beloved has become my physician'. (*India Office* MS., No. 1728, fol. 87.) The words used in Punjabi texts are *piria, pritam*, and *piri*, 'a lover', or 'beloved one'.

Another remarkable proof of Persian influence is found in the form of the *Adi Granth* itself. It consists of a collection of short poems, in many of which all the verses composing the poem rhyme together, in singular conformity with the principle regulating the construction of the Persian *ghazal*. This resemblance is rendered more striking by the fact that the name of Nanak is worked into the composition of the last line of each of the poems. This last characteristic is too persistent to be considered the result of accident; and while it is altogether foreign to the practice of Hindu verse, it is in precise accord with the rule of the correct composition of the *ghazal*.

The foregoing facts seem conclusive as to the influence of Persian Sufism on the origin of the Sikh religion. Dr Trumpp, when discussing the philosophy of the *Adi Granth*, admits the intimate connection between Sikhism and Sufism in the following words:

'We can distinguish in the *Granth* a grosser and a finer

125

kind of Pantheism . . . In this finer shade of Pantheism, creation assumes the form of *emanation* from the Supreme (as in the system of the Sufis), the atomic matter is either likewise considered co-eternal with the Absolute and immanent in it, becoming moulded into various, distinct forms by the energizing vigour of the absolute *joti* (light); or, the reality of matter is more or less denied (as by the Sufis), so that the Divine *joti* is the only real essence in all'. (Introduction to *Translation of the Adi Granth*, pp. cci.)

Any doubt that may remain on the question seems to be set at rest by the express statement in the life of Guru Arjun, who was urged by his followers to reduce to writing the genuine utterances of Nanak, because 'by reciting the numerous verses and speeches *uttered by other Sufis*, which have received the name of Baba Nanak, pride and worldly wisdom are springing up in the hearts of men'. (*Sikhan de Raj di Vithia*, p. 29.) And in the *Adi Granth* itself, we find the following remarkable verses ascribed to Nanak:

'A ball of intoxication, of delusion, is given by the Giver.
The intoxicated forget death, they enjoy themselves four days
The True One is found *by the Sofis*, who keep fast his Court'.

(*Translation*, p.23.)

Here we have not only a plain claim of kinship with the Sufis, but the incorporation of several of their favourite terms.

The traditions of Nanak preserved in the *Janam-Sakhi*, are full of evidences of his alliance with Muhammadanism. He was a Hindu by birth, of the Bedi Khattri caste; and was the son of the *patwari*, or village accountant, of the place now called Nankana, in the neighbourhood of Lahore. In his very early days, he sought the society of faqirs; and used both fair and unfair means of doing them service, more especially in the bestowal of alms. At fifteen years of age, he mis-appropriated the money which his father had given him for trade; and this induced his parents to send him to a relative at Sultanpur, in order that he might be weaned

126

from his affection for faqirs (*India Office* MS., No. 1728, fol. 29). His first act in his new home was to join the service of a Muhammadan Nawab, named Daulat Khan Lodi; and, while serving him, he continued to give to faqirs all his salary, except the bare subsistence he reserved for himself. While in the service of the Muhammadan, Nanak received the ecstatic exaltation which he felt to be Divine inspiration. It is stated in the tradition of his life that Nanak went to the river to perform his ablutions, and that whilst so engaged, he was translated bodily to the gates of Paradise. 'Then a goblet of *amrita* (the water of life) was given (to him) by command (of God). The command was: "This *amrita* is the goblet of my name; drink thou it". Then the Guru Nanak made salutation, and drank the goblet. The Lord (*Sahib*) had mercy (and said): "Nanak, I am with thee; I have made thee happy, and whoever shall take thy name they all shall be rendered happy by me. Go thou, repeat my name, and cause other people to repeat it. Remain uncontaminated from the world. Continue (steadfast) in the name, in alms-giving, in ablutions, in service, and in the remembrance (of me). I have given to thee my own name: do thou this work".' (fol. 33.) Here we have notions closely akin to those of the Sufis, who lay much stress on the repetition of the name of God, which they term *zikr*, on religious ablutions (*wazu*), and on meditating on the unity of God (*wahdaniya*). No sooner had Nanak recovered from his trance than he uttered the key-note of his future system in the celebrated phrase, 'There is no Hindu, there is no Mussulman'. (fol. 36.) The *Janam-Sakhi* then goes on to say that 'The people went to the Khan (his former employer) and said, "Baba Nanak is saying, 'There is no Hindu, there is no Mussulman'." The Khan replied, "Do not regard his statement; he is a faqir". A Qazi sitting near said: "O Khan! it is surprising that he is saying there is no Hindu and no Mussulman". The Khan then told an attendant to call Nanak; but the Guru Nanak said: "What have I to do with thy Khan?" Then the people said: "This idiot is

127

become mad"... Then the Baba (Nanak) was silent. When he said anything, he repeated only this statement: "There is no Hindu, there is no Mussulman". The Qazi then said: "Khan, is it right that he should say, 'There is no Hindu, there is no Mussulman'?" Then the Khan said: "Go fetch him". The attendant went, and said: "Sir, the Khan is calling (you). The Khan says: 'For God's sake give me an interview; I want to see thee".' The Guru Nanak arose and went, saying: "Now the summons of my Lord (Sahib) is come, I will go". He placed a staff upon his neck and went. The Khan said: "Nanak, for God's sake take the staff from off thy neck, gird up thy waist; thou art a good faqir". The Guru Nanak took the staff from off (his) neck, and girded up his loins. The Khan said: "O Nanak, it is a misfortune to me that a steward such as thou shouldst become a faqir". Then the Khan seated the Guru Nanak near himself and said: "Qazi, if thou desirest to ask anything, ask now; otherwise this one will not again utter a word". The Qazi becoming friendly, smiled and said: "Nanak, what dost thou mean by saying, 'There is no Hindu, there is no Mussulman'?" Nanak replied: "To be called a Mussulman is difficult; when one (becomes it) then he may be called a Mussulman. First of all, having made religion (*din*) sweet, he clears away Mussulman wealth. Having become firm, religion (*din*) in this way brings to an end the revolution of dying and living".' (*India Office MS.*, No. 2484, fol. 84.) 'When Nanak had uttered this verse, the Qazi became amazed. The Khan said: "Qazi, is not the questioning of him a mistake"? The time of afternoon prayer had come. All arose and went (to the mosque) to prayers, and the Baba (Nanak) also went with them'. Nanak then demonstrated his supernatural power by reading the thoughts of the Qazi. 'Then the Qazi came and fell down at his feet, exclaiming, "Wonderful, wonderful! On this one is the favour of God".' Then the Qazi believed, and Nanak uttered this stanza: "A (real) Mussulman clears away self; (he possesses) sincerity, patience, purity of speech: (what is)

128

erect he does not annoy: (what) lies (dead) he does not eat. O Nanak! that Mussulman goes to heaven (bihisht)". When the Baba had uttered this stanza, the Saiyids, the sons of the Shaikhs, the Qazi, the Mufti, the Khan, the chiefs and leaders were amazed. The Khan said: "Qazi, Nanak has reached the truth; the additional questioning is a mistake". Wherever the Baba looked, there all were saluting him. After the Baba had recited a few stanzas, the Khan came and fell down at his feet. Then the people, Hindus and Mussulmans, began to say to the Khan that God (*Khuda*) was speaking in Nanak'. (*India Office* MS., No. 1728, fol. 36–41.)

The foregoing anecdotes are taken from the *India Office* MS., No. 1728; but the ordinary *Janam-Sakhis* current in the Punjab vary the account somewhat by saying that when the Khan reproved Nanak for not coming to him when sent for, the latter replied: "'Hear, O Nawab, when I was thy servant I came before thee; now I am not thy servant; now I am become the servant of Khuda (God)". The Nawab said: "Sir, (if) you have become such, then come with me and say prayers (*niwaj*). It is Friday". Nanak said: "Go, Sir". The Nawab, with the Qazi and Nanak, and a great concourse of people, went into the Jami Masjid and stood there. All the people who came into the Masjid began to say, "Today Nanak has entered this sect". There was a commotion among the respectable Hindus in Sultanpur; and Jairam, being much grieved, returned home. Nanaki perceiving that her husband came home dejected, rose up and said, "Why is it that you are today so grieved?" Jairam replied, "Listen, O servant of Paramesur (God), what has they brother Nanak done? He has gone, with the Nawab, into the Jami Masjid to pray; and, in the city, there is an outcry among the Hindus and Mussulmans that Nanak has become a Turk (*Muslim*) today".' (*India Office* MS., No. 2885, fol. 39.)

From the foregoing it is perfectly clear that the immediate successors of Nanak believed that he went very close to Muhammadanism; and we can scarcely

129

doubt the accuracy of their view of the matter, when we consider the almost contemporaneous character of the record, from which extracts have been given, and the numerous confirmatory evidences contained in the religion itself. It is particularly worthy of remark that a 'cup of *amrita*' (i.e., immortality) is considered the symbol of inspiration; just as Hafiz exclaims, 'Art thou searching O Hafiz, to find the waters of eternal life?' And the same poet expresses his own ecstasy in a way almost identical with the reception accorded to Nanak at the gate of Paradise. His words are: 'Then he gave into my hand a cup which flashed back the splendour of Heaven so gloriously, that Zuhrah broke out into dancing and the lute-player exclaimed, "Drink!".' The staff (*muttaka*) that is mentioned is, also, that of a faqir, on which a devotee supports himself while in meditation. Another significant fact is that when Nanak speaks of himself as the servant of God, he employs the word *Khuda*, a Persian Muhammadan term; but when his brother-in-law Jairam speaks of God, he uses the Hindu word *Paramesur*. It will, also, be noticed that Muhammadans are affected by the logic and piety of Nanak; and to them he shows himself so partial that he openly accompanies them to the mosque, and thereby causes his Hindu neighbours and friends to believe that he is actually converted to the faith of Islam. But, of course, the most remarkable expression of all is the emphatic and repeated announcement that 'There is no Hindu; there is no Mussulman'. This can mean nothing else than that it was Nanak's settled intention to do away with the differences between those two forms of belief, by instituting a third course which should supersede both of them.

Nanak's employer, in consequence of the foregoing manifestations of wisdom, became his devoted admirer. After this, Nanak undertook a missionary tour; and it is noticeable that the first person he went to and converted was Shaikh Sajan, who showed himself to be a pious Muhammadan. Nanak then proceeded to Panipat, and was met by a certain Shaikh Tatihar, who accosted him with the Muhammadan greeting, 'Peace be on thee, O Darvesh!' (*Salam-aleka Darves*); to which Nanak immediately replied, 'And upon you be peace, O servant of the Pir!' (*aleka us salamu, ho Pir ke dasta-pes*). (*India Office* MS., No. 1728, fol. 48.) Here we find Nanak both receiving and giving the Muhammadan salutation; and also the acknowledgment that he was recognized as a *darvesh*. The Punjabi form of the Arabic salutation is given lest it might be thought that the special character of the words is due to the translation. The disciple then called his master, the Pir Shaikh Sharaf, who repeated the salutation of peace, and after a long conversation acknowledged the Divine mission of Nanak, kissed his hands and feet, and left him. (fol. 52.) After the departure of this Pir, the Guru Nanak wandered on to Delhi, where he was introduced to Sultan Ibrahim Lodi, who also called him a *darvesh*. The previous conversations and acts are found to have awakened the curiosity of Nanak's attendant Mardana, who asked in surprise: 'Is God, then, one?' To which Nanak firmly replied: 'God (*Khuda*) is one'. (fol. 55.) This was intended to satisfy Mardana that there is no difference between the Muhammadan and the Hindu God.

Nanak is next said to have proceeded to the holy city of Benares, and there he met with a Pandit named Satrudas. The MS. No. 1728 (fol. 56) says: 'He came to this Nanak, and cried, "Ram! Ram!" Seeing his (Nanak's) disguise (*bhekhu*), he sat down and said to him, "O devotee (*bhaqat*), thou has no *sallgram*; no necklace of *tulsi*; no rosary; no *tika* of white clay; and thou callest (thyself) a devotee! What devotion has thou obtained?".' In other words, the Pandit is made to challenge his piety; because he has none of the marks of a Hindu upon him. Nanak explains his peculiar position and views: and is reported to have converted the Hindu Pandit to his own way of thinking. This anecdote, also, shows that the immediate successors of Nanak were aware that their great Guru occupied an intermediate position between Muhammadanism and Hinduism; for we see that he is made to convert Muhammadans on the one hand, and Hindus on the other. After this primary attack on Hinduism, Nanak is said to have converted some Jogis, Khattris, Thags, necromancers, witches, and even the personified Kaliyug, or present age of the world. These conquests over imaginary Hindus are obviously allegorical; though they clearly point to a well-recognized distinction between the teaching of Nanak and that of orthodox Hinduism.

The most significant associate Nanak found was, undoubtedly, Shaikh Farid. He was a famous Muhammadan Pir, and a strict Sufi, who attracted much attention by his piety, and formed a school of devotees of his own. Shaikh Farid must have gained considerable notoriety in his day; for his special disciples are still to be found in the Punjab, who go by the name of Shaikh Farid's faqirs. This strict Muhammadan became the confidential friend and companion of Nanak; and if all other traditions had failed, this alone would have been enough to establish the eclectic character of early Sikhism. The first greeting of these famous men is significant enough. Shaikh Farid exclaimed, 'Allah, Allah, O Darvesh'; to which Nanak replied, 'Allah is the object of my efforts, O Farid! Come, Shaikh Farid! Allah, Allah (only) is ever my object'. The words in the original being *Allah, Farid, juhdi; hamesa au, Sekh Farid, juhdi Allah Allah.* (*India Office* MS., No. 1728. fol. 86.) The use of the Arabic term *juhd* implies the energy of the purpose with which he sought for Allah; and the whole phrase is forcibly Muhammadan in tone.

An intimacy at once sprang up between these two remarkable men; and Shaikh Farid accompanied Nanak in all his wanderings for the next twelve years. The intended compromise between Hinduism and Islam is shown not only in the fact of this friendship, but in the important circumstance that no less than 142 stanzas composed by Shaikh Farid are admitted into the *Adi Granth* itself. An examination of these verses still further proves the mingling of the two religions which Nanak

132

effected. They are distinctly Sufistic in tone, containing such lines as: 'Youth is passing, I am not afraid, if love of the Beloved does not pass'; and still more pointedly, 'Full of sins I wander about; the world calls me a Darvesh'; while, between those declarations of steady adherence to Islam, comes the remarkable Hindu line, 'As by fire the metal becomes purified, so the fear of Hari removes the filth of folly.' The fact that the compositions of a genuine Sufi should have been admitted into the canonical book of the Sikhs, and that they should contain such a clear admixture of Hindu and Muhammadan ideas, is conclusive evidence that Nanak, and his immediate successors, saw no incongruity in the mixture.

As soon as Nanak and his friend Shaikh Farid began to travel in company, it is related that they reached a place called Bisiar, where people applied cow-dung to every spot on which they had stood, as soon as they departed. (*India Office* MS., No. 1728, fol. 94.) The obvious meaning of this is that orthodox Hindus considered every spot polluted which Nanak and his companion had visited. This could never have been related of Nanak had he remained a Hindu by religion.

In his next journey Nanak is said to have visited Patan, and there he met with Shaikh Ibrahim, who saluted him as a Muslim, and had a conversation with him on the Unity of God. Nanak expressed his views in the following openly Sufistic manner: 'Thou thyself (art) the wooden tablet; thou (art) the pen; thou (art) also the writing upon (it). O Nanak, why should the One be called a second?' (*India Office* MS., No. 1728, fol. 117.) The Pir asks an explanation of this verse in these words: 'Thou sayest, "There is One, why a second?" but there is one Lord (*Sahib*), and two traditions. Which shall I accept, and which reject? Thou sayest, "The only One, he alone is one"; but the Hindus are saying that in (their) faith there is certainty; and the Mussulmans are saying that only in (their) faith there is certainty. Tell me, in which of them is the truth, and in which is there falsity?' Nanak replied, 'There is only one Lord (*Sahib*), and only one tradition'. (fol. 119.) This anecdote serves still further to illustrate the intermediate position between the two religions ascribed to Nanak by his immediate followers.

Shortly after the foregoing episode, Nanak was captured among the prisoners taken by the Emperor Babar, who seems to have been attracted by the Guru's piety, and to have shown him some attentions. The chronicler informs us that 'all the people, both Hindus and Mussulmans, began to salute (Nanak)'. (fol. 137.) After his release, Nanak recommenced his missionary work, and is described as meeting a Muhammadan named Miyan Mitha, who called upon him for the *Kalimah*, or Muhammadan confession of faith (fol. 143); which leads to a long conversation, in which Nanak lays emphasis on the Sufi doctrine of the Unity of God. In this conversation Nanak is made to say, 'The book of the Qur'an should be practised'. (fol. 144.) He also acknowledged that 'justice is the Qur'an'. (fol. 148.) When the Miyan asked him what is the one great name, Nanak took him aside and whispered in his ear, 'Allah'. Immediately the great name is uttered, Miyan Mitha is consumed to ashes; but a celestial voice again utters the word 'Allah!' and the Miyan regains life, and falls at the feet of Nanak. (fol. 147.)

In precise conformity with this deduction is the tradition of Nanak's pilgrimage to Makkah. The particulars of his visit to that holy place are fully given, in all accounts of Nanak's life; and although, as Dr Trumpp reasonably concludes, the whole story is a fabrication, yet the mere invention of the tale is enough to prove that those who most intimately knew Nanak considered his relationship to Muhammadanism sufficiently close to warrant the belief in such a pilgrimage. In the course of his teaching in Makkah, Nanak is made to say: 'Though men, they are like women, who do not obey the Sunnat, and Divine commandment, nor the order of the book (i.e., the Qur'an)'. (*India Office* MS., No. 1728, fol. 212.) He also admitted the intercession of Muhammad, denounced the drinking of bhang, wine, etc.,

134

acknowledged the existence of hell, the punishment of the wicked, and the resurrection of mankind, in fact, the words here ascribed to Nanak contain a full confession of Islam. These tenets are, of course, due to the narrator of the tale; and are only useful as showing how far Nanak's followers thought it possible for him to go.

A curious incident is next related to the effect that Makhdum Baha'u'd-Din, the Pir of Multan, feeling his end approaching, said to his disciples, 'O friends, from this time the faith of no one will remain firm, all will become faithless (be-iman)'. His disciples asked for an explanation; and in reply he delivered himself of an oracular statement, 'O friends, when one Hindu shall come to Heaven (bihisht), there will be brilliancy (ujala) in Heaven'. To this strange announcement his disciples replied: 'Learned people say that Heaven is not decreed for the Hindu; what is this that you have said?' (India Office MS., No. 1728, fol. 224.) The Pir told them that he was alluding to Nanak; and sent one of his disciples to ask Nanak if he, also, had received an intimation of his approaching death.

In this anecdote we have the extraordinary admission from a Muhammadan that Nanak would succeed in breaking up the faith of Islam. It is in consequence of a Hindu's having conquered Heaven itself, and vindicated his right to a place in the paradise of Muhammad, that those who were then in the faith of the Prophet would lose confidence in his teaching. Here again the words employed are useful; for the Pir is made to say that Muslims will become be-iman, the Arabic term specially applicable to the 'faith' of Islam; and Heaven is called in the Punjabi story bhisat, that is bihisht, the Paradise of Muhammadans; for had the Hindu heaven been intended, some such word as swarg, or paralok, or Brahmalok would have been used.

The final incident in the life of this enlightened teacher is in precise accord with all that has been said of his former career. Nanak came to the bank of the Ravi to die — in conformity with Hindu custom — by the side of a

135

natural stream of water. It is expressly said that both Hindus and Muslims accompanied him. He then seated himself at the foot of a Sarih tree, and his Assembly of the faithful (*Sangat*) stood around him. His sons asked him what their position was to be; and he told them to subordinate themselves to the Guru Angad whom he had appointed as his successor. They were to succeed to no power or dignity merely on the ground of relationship; no hereditary claim was to be recognized; on the contrary, the sons were frankly told to consider themselves non-entities. The words are: 'Sons, even the dogs of the Guru are not in want; bread and clothes will be plentiful; and should you mutter "Guru! Guru!" (your) life will be (properly) adjusted'. (*India Office* MS., No. 1728, fol. 238.) The anecdote then proceeds in the following remarkable manner: 'Then the Hindus and Mussulmans who were firm in the name (of God), began to express themselves (thus): the Mussulmans said, "We will bury (him)", and the Hindus said, "We will burn (him)". Then the Baba said, "Place flowers on both sides; on the right side those of the Hindus, on the left side those of the Mussulmans, (that we may perceive) whose will continue green tomorrow. If those of the Hindus keep green, then burn (me); and if those of the Mussulmans keep green, then bury (me)". Then the Baba ordered the Assembly to repeat the praises (of God); and the Assembly began to repeat the praises accordingly. (After a few verses had been recited) he laid down his head. When the sheet (which had been stretched over him) was raised, there was nothing (under it); and the flowers of both (sides) remained green. The Hindus took away theirs; and the Mussulmans took away theirs. The entire Assembly fell to their feet'. (*India Office* MS., No. 1728, fol. 239, 240.)

The mixture of Hinduism and Muhammadanism is evident in this tradition. It is obviously intended to summarize the life of Nanak and the object of his teaching. He is not represented as an outcast and a failure; on the other hand, his purposes are held to have

136

been fully accomplished. The great triumph was the establishment of a common basis of religious truth for both Muhammadan and Hindu; and this he is shown to have accomplished with such dexterity that at his death no one could say whether he was more inclined to Hinduism or to Muhammadanism. His friends stood around him at the last moment quite uncertain as to whether they should dispose of his remains as those of a Muhammadan, or as those of a Hindu. And Nanak is represented as taking care that the matter should ever remain a moot point. The final miraculous disappearance of the corpse is obviously intended to convey the idea that Nanak belonged specially neither to one party nor to the other; while the green and flourishing appearance of the flowers of both parties conveys the lesson that it was his wish that both should live together in harmony and union. The narrator of the life clearly wishes his history to substantiate the prophetic statement recorded at the commencement of his book (*India Office* MS., No. 1728, fol. 7) that, at Nanak's birth, 'The Hindus said, "The manifestation of some God (*Devata*) has been produced", and the Mussulmans said, "Some holy man (*sadiq*) of God (*Khuda*) has been born".'

The most potent cause of the uncertainty as to Nanak's true position in the religious world arises from the initial fact that he was born a Hindu, and necessarily brought up in that form of belief. He was a perfectly uneducated man, there being no reason to suppose that he could either read or write, or perform any other literary feat, beyond the composition of extemporaneous verses in his mother tongue. Guru Arjun, the fourth successor of Nanak, appears to have been the first chieftain of the fraternity who could read and write. The necessary result of Nanak's early associations was that all his ideas throughout life were substantially Hindu, his mode of thought and expression was Hindu, his illustrations were taken from Hindu sources, and his system was based on Hindu models. It must be borne in mind that Nanak never openly seceded from Hinduism, or ever con-

137

templated doing so. Thus in the *Sakhi of Miyan Mitha* it is related that towards the end of Nanak's life a Muhammadan named Shah Abdu'r-Rahman acknowledged the great advantages he had derived from the teaching of Nanak, and sent his friend Miyan Mitha to the Guru so that he might derive similar benefit. 'Then Miyan Mitha said, "What is his name? Is he a Hindu, or is he a Mussulman?" Shah Abdu'r-Rahman replied, "He is a Hindu, and his name is Nanak".' (*Sikhan de Raj di Vithia*, p. 258.) He struck a heavy blow at Hinduism by his rejection of caste distinctions; and on this point there can be no doubt, for his very words, preserved in the *Adi Granth*, are: 'Thou (O Lord) acknowledgest the Light (the ray of the Divine in man), and dost not ask after caste. In the other world there is no caste'. (*Translation of the Adi Granth*, p. 494.) In consequence of this opinion Nanak admitted to his fraternity men of all castes; his constant companions being spoken of as Saiyids and Sikhs, that is, Muhammadan and Hindu pupils. Sikhs have ever before them the intermediate character of their religion from the stanza (21) of the *Jap-Ji* which says, 'Pandits do not know that time, though written in a Purana; Qazis do not know that time, though written in the Qur'an'. Hindu scholars are told in the *Adi Granth* that they miss the true meaning of their religion through delusion. 'Reading and reading the Pandit explains the Veda, (but) the infatuation of Maya (Delusion personified) lulls him to sleep. By reason of dual affection the name of Hari (i.e., God) is forgotten'. (*Translation*, p. 117.) In the same way Nanak turns to the Mussulman and says:

'Thou must die, O Mulla! Thou must die!
   Remain in the fear of the Creator!
Then thou art a Mulla, then thou art a Qazi,
   if thou knowest the name of God (*Khuda*).
None, though he be very learned, will remain,
   he hurries onwards.
He is a Qazi by whom his own self is abandoned,
   and the One Name is made his support.

He is, and will be, He will not be destroyed,
> true is the creator.
Five times he prays (*niwaj gujarhi*), he
> reads the book of the Qur'an.'

(*Translation*, p. 37.)

Nanak does not seem to have been particular as to the name under which he recognized the Deity, he was more concerned with impressing on his companions a correct understanding of what Deity was. The names Hari, Ram, Govind, Brahma, Parameswar, Khuda, Allah, etc., are used with perfect freedom, and are even mixed up in the same poem. The most common name for God in the *Adi Granth* is certainly Hari; but that does not seem to have shocked the Muslim friends of Nanak. Thus, in a poem addressed to Hari as 'the invisible, inaccessible, and infinite', we are told that, 'Pirs, prophets, saliks, sadiqs, martyrs, shaikhs, mullas, and darveshes; a great blessing has come upon them, who continually recite his salvation'. (*Translation*, p.75.)

The chief point of Nanak's teaching was un-questionably the Unity of God. He set himself firmly against the idea of associating any other being with the Absolute Supreme. This exalted idea of Divine Majesty enabled Nanak to treat with indifference the crowd of Hindu deities. To such a mind as that of Nanak it would have been sheer waste of time to argue, with any earnestness, about the attributes, powers, or jurisdic-tions, of a class of beings, the whole of whom were subor-dinate to one great, almighty, and incomprehensible Ruler. Without any overt attack on the Hindu pantheon, he caused the whole cluster of deities to subside into a condition similar to that of angels in modern Christianity; whose existence and operations may be the subject of conversation, but the whole of whom sink into utter insignificance compared with the central idea of the Divine Majesty. The One God, in Nanak's opinion (and, it may be added, in the opinion of all Sufis), was the creator of plurality of form, not the creator of matter out of nothing. The phenomenal world is the manifestation

139

of Deity, and it is owing to pure illusion that the idea of separateness exists. In the *Adi Granth* we read:

'The cause of causes is the Creator.
In His hand are the order and reflection.
As He looks upon, so it becomes.
He Himself, Himself is the Lord.
Whatever is made (is) according to His
    own pleasure.
He is far from all, and with all.
He comprehends, sees, and makes discrimination.
He Himself is One, and He Himself is many.
He does not die nor perish. He neither comes nor goes.
Nanak says: He is always contained (in all)'.

(Translation, p.400.)

Notwithstanding this conception that the Supreme One comprehends both spirit and matter, and therefore *is* what is; He is nevertheless spoken of as in some way different from the creatures He has formed, and has been endowed with moral and intellectual qualities. Thus we find in the *Adi Granth:*

'Whose body the universe is, His is not in it,
    the Creator is not in it.
Who is putting (the things) together, He is
    always aloof (from them), in what
can He be said (to be contained)?'
(Translation, p.474.)

The soul of man is held to be a ray of light from the Light Divine; and it necessarily follows that, in its natural state, the soul of man is sinless. The impurity, which is only too apparent in man, is accounted for by the operation of what is called Maya, or Delusion; and it is this Maya which deludes creatures into egotism and duality, that is, into self-consciousness or conceit, and into the idea that there can be existence apart from the Divine. This delusion prevents the pure soul from freeing itself from matter, and hence the spirit passes from one combination of matter to another, in a long chain of births and deaths, until the delusion is removed, and the entrammelled ray returns to the Divine Light whence it originally emanated. The belief in metempsychosis is

140

thus seen to be the necessary complement of pantheism; and it is essential to the creed of a Hindu, a Buddhist, and a Sufi.

In Sikhism, as in Buddhism, the prime object of attainment is not Paradise, but the total cessation of individual existence. The method by which this release from transmigration is to be accomplished is by the perfect recognition of identity with the Supreme. When the soul fully realizes what is summed up in the formula *so ham*, 'I am that,' i.e., 'I am one with that which was, and is, and will be,' then emancipation from the bondage of existence is secured. This is declared by Nanak himself in the *Adi Granth* in these words:

'Should one know his own self as the *so ham*, he believes
in the esoteric mystery.
Should the disciple (*Gur-mukhi*) know his own self,
what more can he do, or cause to be done?'
(*India Office* MS., No. 2484 fol. 53.)

The principles of early Sikhism given above are obviously too recondite for acceptance among masses of men; accordingly we find that the pantheistic idea of Absolute Substance became gradually changed into the more readily apprehended notion of a self-conscious Supreme Being, the Creator and Governor of the universe. Here Dr. Trumpp himself admits the influence of Muhammadanism, when he says: 'It is not improbable that Islam had a great share in working silently these changes, which are directly opposed to the teaching of the Gurus'. (Introduction to *Translation of the Adi Granth*, p. cxii.) The teaching of Nanak was, however, very practical. His followers are daily reminded in the *Jap-Ji* that, 'Without the practice of virtue there can be no worship'.

In all that has preceded we have confined ourselves strictly to the intimate relationship subsisting between early Sikhism and the Muhammadan religion. It is, however, necessary to allude to the fact that certain surviving relics of Buddhism had no small share in moulding the thoughts of the Founder of the Sikh religion. A full examination of this part of the subject would be out of

141

place in the present work. It must suffice to say that Buddhism held its position in the Punjab long after it had disappeared from other parts of Northern India; and the abundance of Buddhistic relics, which are continually being unearthed in the district, prove the widespread and long-continued influence of the tenets of the gentle-hearted Buddha. Indications of this influence on early Sikhism are seen in its freedom from caste, in the respect for animal life, the special form of metempsychosis accepted, the importance ascribed to meditation, the profuse charity, the reverence paid to the seat of the Guru (like the Buddhistic worship of the throne), Nanak's respect for the lotus, his missionary tours, and the curious union subsisting between the Guru and his Sangat. In the *Travels of Guru Tegh Bahadur,* translated from the original *Gur-mukhi* by an excellent scholar Sirdar Atar Singh, we find the following remarkable sentence: 'The Guru and his Sangat are like the warp and woof in cloth — there is no difference between them' (p. 37). In the *Adi Granth* there is an entire Sukhmani, or poem, by Guru Arjun, wholly devoted to a recitation of the advantages of 'the society of the pious', the term employed being, however, in this case, *sadh kai sang. (Indian Office* MS., No. 2484, fol. 134.) In addition to these points of resemblance, there is found in early Sikhism a curious veneration for trees, offerings to which were sometimes made, as will be seen by reference to pp. 67, 70 and 83, of the *Travels of Guru Tegh Bahadur,* just cited. In precise conformity with the tradition that Buddha died under a Sal tree, we have seen that Nanak purposely breathed his last under a Sarih tree. Anyone familiar with Buddhism will readily recognize the remarkable coincidences stated above; but the most conclusive of all is the positive inculcation of views identical with the crowning doctrine of Buddhism — the Nirvana itself. The following is what Dr. Trumpp says on the subject:

'If there could be any doubt on the pantheistic character of the tenets of the Sikh Gurus regarding the Supreme, it would be dissolved by their doctrine of the

142

Nirban. Where no personal God is taught or believed in, man cannot aspire to a final personal communion with him, his aim can only be absorption in the Absolute Substance, i.e., individual annihilation. We find, therefore, no allusion to the joys of a future life in the Granth, as heaven or paradise, though supposed to exist, is not considered a desirable object. The immortality of the soul is only taught so far as the doctrine of transmigration requires it; but when the soul has reached its highest object, it is no more mentioned, because it no longer exists as individual soul.

'The Nirban, as is well known, is the grand object which Buddha in his preaching held out to the poor people. From his atheistic point of view, he could look out for nothing else; personal existence, with all the concomitant evils of his life, which are not counterbalanced by corresponding pleasures, necessarily appeared to him as the greatest evil. His whole aim was, therefore, to counteract the troubles and pain of this existence by a stoical indifference to pleasure and pain, and to reduce individual consciousness to its utmost limit, in order to escape at the point of death from the dreaded transmigration, which he also, even on his atheistic ground, had not ventured to reject. Buddhism is, therefore, in reality, like Sikhism, nothing but unrestricted Pessimism, unable to hold out to man any solace, except that of annihilation.

'In progress of time, Buddhism has been expelled from India, but the restored Brahmanism, with its confused cosmological legends, and gorgeous mythology of the *Puranas,* was equally unable to satisfy the thinking minds. It is, therefore, very remarkable, that Buddhism in its highest object, the Nirban, soon emerges again in the popular teachings of the mediaeval reformatory movements. Namdev, Trilochan, Kabir, Ravidas, etc., and after these Nanak, take upon themselves to show the way to the Nirban, as Buddha in his time had promised, and find eager listeners; the difference is only in the means which these Bhagats (saints) propose for obtaining the desired end'. (Introduction to *Translation of the Adi Granth,* p. cvi.)

Such then was the Sikh religion as founded by Guru

Nanak. It is based on Hinduism, modified by Buddhism and stirred into new life by Sufism. There seems to be superabundant evidence that Nanak laboured earnestly to reconcile Hinduism with Muhammadanism, by insisting strongly on the tenets on which both parties could agree and by subordinating the points of difference. It is impossible to deny that Nanak in his lifetime actually did effect a large amount of reconciliation and left behind him a system designed to carry on the good work. The circumstances which led to the entire reversal of the project and produced between Muhammadans and Sikhs the deadliest of feuds does not come within the purview of the present article. It is enough to state that the process was gradual and was as much due to political causes as to a steady departure from the teachings of the Founder of Sikhism.

The Sikh fraternity was under the guidance of individual Gurus from 1504 A.D., when Nanak received the spiritual impulse which gave birth to the new sect, until 1708 A.D., a total of 203 years. After the death of Guru Govind Singh, the *Adi Granth* itself was taken to be the ever-present impersonal guide.

Govind Singh was the tenth and last Guru; he succeeded his father Tegh-Bahadur when only fifteen years of age. He was brought up under Hindu guidance and became a staunch devotee of the goddess Durga. By his pronounced preference for Hinduism he caused a division in the Sikh community. He introduced several important changes into the constitution of Sikh society. The chief among these was the establishment of the *Khalsa,* by which he bound his disciples into an army and conferred upon each of them the name of *Singh,* or lion. He freely admitted all castes to the ranks of his army and laboured more earnestly over their military than over their religious discipline. The nature of the changes which Govind Singh effected in the fraternity is best shown by the fact that the followers of Nanak's own teaching separated themselves from him and formed a community of their own, rejecting the title of *Singh.* In

144

other words, they clung to the religious and rejected the military idea. The spirit of tolerance so marked during the lifetime of Nanak was clearly gone and in yet later times this hostility gave birth to the saying that 'a true Sikh should always be engaged in war with the Muhammadans and slay them, fighting them face to face'. After a turbulent reign, Guru Govind Singh was treacherously slain by the dagger of a Pathan follower. He refused to name a successor, telling his followers that after his death the *Granth Sahib,* or 'the Lord of the Book', was to be their guide in every respect. (*Sikhan de Raj di Vithia,* p. 79.)

The religion of Nanak began in large-hearted tolerance but political causes operated to convert its adherents into a narrow-minded sect. The Hinduism which Nanak had disciplined reasserted its superiority under his successors and ultimately became predominant. While this change was in progress the religious aspect of the movement became gradually converted into military and political propaganda. No contrast indeed could well be greater than that between the inoffensive and gentle-minded Nanak and the warlike and ambitious Gurus of later times. But while we cannot help being painfully impressed by the apparently undying feud which still subsists between the Sikhs and the Muhammadans, it seems perfectly clear that the intention of the Founder was to reconcile the differences between these creeds and that in this excellent work he attained a large measure of success.

(Adapted and abridged from the original.)

145

4/iii.
Yoga and the Sufis
Pundit Kishan Chand

Nearly sixty years ago I was undergoing Yoga training in Northern India, when I developed an intense interest in the history, antiquity and relationships to other systems of philosophy and practice. My teacher first told me that these interests were irrelevant and stood in the way of the attempted re-yoking with the Infinite. As a somewhat Westernised product of nineteenth-century India, however, I persisted, until he said:

'Refusing you leave to study this matter will only produce a greater barrier to self-realization. Therefore go and find out about it, afterwards returning to me when you feel that you can put it into an appropriate place in your mind'.

Thus released from immediate conflict between discipline and worldly matters, I begged the reverend gentleman to tell me, first, whether there was any relationship between Yoga and other systems; and, if there was, why it should be that Yoga teachers and practitioners claimed such primacy and such almost personal possession of the system.

'There is,' he told me, 'such a relationship. All higher knowledge is in fact one knowledge: therefore all who attain to it, by whatever path, share the same knowledge and the same being. But most of the people who teach and who practise Yoga do not know this. Therefore they cleave to a narrow interpretation. Furthermore, the relationship between Yoga and the Sufis is very close. But how can we admit this on the ordinary, the social and mental, level? For centuries, the Hindus and the Moslems have been enemies. To admit that they share something is politically unwise'.

Now I knew, of course, that many Hindus worshipped at Sufi shrines throughout India: but I had always put this down to sheer superstition. After all, Yogis

146

themselves were declared to be absurd apostates by Hindu Brahmins who were the repositories of the Hindu faith. The Imperial Mogul Prince Dara Shikoh, in his book *The Meeting of the Twin Seas,* had, too, stated categorically that the experiences of the Sufis and of the Yogis and Vedantins were identical. That, according to many Moslem scholars, was evidence of the Prince's unbalanced mind. His brother, the Emperor Aurangzeb, agreed to have him put to death, on the advice of zealots, partly on the basis of this book, which has been published by the Asiatic Society of Bengal.

From the tenth or eleventh centuries of this era, as the Indian historian Ameer Ali had noted in a then recently-published book, 'A large number of Sufi saints, both men and women, flourished in India and acquired great fame in their lifetime for sanctity and good work. Their tombs are to the present day the objects of pilgrimage to Moslems, and, remarkable to note, to Hindus as well . . . They called themselves dervishes or *Fakirs* . . . by their followers they were honoured with the title of Shah or king'.

As far as the Vedantist interest was concerned, it seemed that Sufism was recognized by Indians as its equivalent; indeed, the illustrious Nawab Amin Jung Bahadur was to write:

'I use Vedantism and Sufi-ism as synonymous terms, and the Arabic word *Tasawwuf* as a generic term meaning "divine sentiment" to cover both. I have not found any material difference between the two systems, if "systems" they can be called. In my opinion, they are not systems at all; nor indeed are they any kind of "religion" in the sense of a course of practices allied to a set of beliefs . . . nothing more nor less than an attitude of mind . . . preparedness or readiness to act in a certain way in the circumstances of each situation . . . a tendency to tolerate any form of worship which is neither unreasonable nor inhuman. It is this tolerant spirit which makes religious fanatics everywhere its deadly enemies . . . Their tolerance of all faiths is at once their virtue in the eyes of their friends and their vice in the eyes

147

of their enemies . . . All religions are so many ways or paths (*mazahib*) leading to the same Infinite and Absolute, call it Truth, beauty, or what you like'.

Then, if these people had the same goal, did they perhaps have the same origins, which social and national, cultural and sectarian — even racial — considerations had at times been allowed to obscure? I went to the foremost Hindu scholar, Radhakrishnan. He put into my hands the Indian classic which contains a review of major religions, *The Dabistan,* and pointed out a passage:

'The Sufis always were, and are, scattered among all nations of the world, and are called in Persian *vezhahderun*, "internally pure", or *roshan-dil*, "enlightened minds", or *yekana-bin*, "seers of unity"; in the Hindu language they are called *rashisher*, Rakhasas and *Tapisher*, Tapisis, *Gyanisher* and *Gyani,* Jnanis, or Atma-Jnanis'.

If this was the tradition of the mystics of India, they not only connected with the Sufis on the plane of experience: they also went back far beyond the *Yoga Sutra* of Patanjali: for he was some time between 300 and 150 B.C., while the Persian tradition dated from the time when the Aryans of Central Asia had not split into the Eastern and Southern branches which were later to be regarded as Persians and Hindus. Zoroaster himself, even, according to today's scholars predated Patanjali by centuries. As Professor E. W. F. Tomlin noted, Patanjali 'probably engaged in the codification of many traditions'.

If the Yogis of India claim the origins of their science in the teachings of the ancient Aryans, and the Sufis concur in a similar representation of their Path among the same peoples, what other sources of traditions are invoked?

Certainly Sufi history claims that Mohammed was a Sufi, and the first of the truly historical ones. They are able to avoid the necessity of characterising the Prophet as the initiator of Sufism by the same formula which they use in the explanation of the Islamic faith itself.

148

According to this conception, Mohammed was the reintroducer of the same monotheistic religion taught by Abraham, Moses, Jesus and other inspired men of the past. But what else does Sufi history reveal about Sufism?

First of all, such great teachers in the Sufi chain of succession as Suhrawardi claim that it has always existed and that many of the pre-Islamic sages and lawgivers were Sufis as well as establishing social and philosophical systems.

But the recognition of the Sufis as being of the same kidney as members of ancient philosophical schools, if there were substance in the matter, would have to come from sources outside Sufism itself. If the Sufis were anciently active in Persia, there should be traces of their contact with, for instance, the Greeks, their neighbours; and with the Egyptians, if there was a connection with Moses and others in that country, as the Sufis claim; and, indeed, with Jewish thinkers and devotees, if the relevance of the constant use of such Jewish figures as Elias in Sufi tradition were to be admitted.

In 1856 the traveller Ubicini, in his *Letters on Turkey*, noted that the doctrine and institution of the Sufis was 'nothing else than the Sufism which existed in the East long previous to the coming of Muhammad'. He continued to link it with 'the secret schools of the Pythagoreans and the Neoplatonists of Alexandria . . . It is thus that we see, more than a century before Muhammad, the two great sects which divide it: the *meshawans* (Walkers) and the *Ishrakiuns* (Contemplatives) reminding us by the similarity of the names of a certain point and by the conformity of doctrines of the two great philosophical schools of Greece . . .'

And the Hebrews? Ameer Ali notes:

'Although the Persian word "dervish" is significantly Moslem in its origin and meaning, "dervishes" have always existed in Western Asia. The minor prophets of the Hebrews, designated *nabiin*, were only the prototypes of the modern "dervish". John the Baptist, who lost his

149

life for his temerity before Herod's wife, acted exactly as hundreds of dervishes have done in later ages, challenging kings and princes in their palaces". It is perhaps worth noting that John the Baptist is honoured in the Middle East as a great Sufi master: and his tomb, in a mosque in Syria, is a place of pilgrimage for them. The Sufis in many parts of the East, because of their acceptance of Jesus as a Teacher of the Way, are characterised as 'secret Christians', and they regard the Baptist as the Sufi introducer of the great Sufi Jesus.

So when Robert Graves speaks of identifiable Sufi traces in literature antedating our era by three milennia, and the earliest prescribed rules of Yoga by upwards of a thousand years, he may well be speaking of the stream of transmission which is different only in appearance, not in content. Naturally, in the Hindu environment the teaching would have its roots in the Hindu culture, developed at an angle from the Persian-Aryan form. Similarly, in the Hebrew, Christian and Islamic manifestations, the cultural overlay would require a similar diversity of expression.

It is noteworthy that in the modern world, where the emphasis is away from religion and towards psychology and physique, that the two systems Yoga and Sufism should find protagonists in these fields. It is well known, and much abominated by Hindu traditionalists, that the current emphasis on tranquillity and bodily health among Yoga mentors is not consistent with orthodox Hindu preoccupations. To some Western people, on the contrary, contemporary Yoga is the thin end of the wedge of Hinduism. To the orthodox Hindu, it is blasphemy, with its admission of outcastes, with its admission of women, and with its placing the exercises first and not the inner development before permitting exercises.

Similarly, in the case of the Sufi projection for a new community and in today's atmosphere, we find Idries Shah, the authoritative chief of the Sufi tradition, following his father in presenting the facets of Sufism which accord with present-day needs. As one orientalist, Professor Williams, in a scholarly journal puts it:

'Sirdar Ikbal Ali Shah, starting about fifty years ago, was among the first of the Sufi leaders to express Sufi tenets and methods in terms which the West could understand, and he laid the foundation of much of the growing interest which now finds expression both in this country and throughout the English-speaking world in the determination to know more of the Sufi approach to life ... This interest has taken the form, in many countries of the West as well as of the East, of a renewed study of the Sufi classics with the aim of applying to the conditions of modern life the lessons which they teach and the methods by which the teaching is conveyed'.

These words, written five years ago, for me substantiated the unerring intuition of my Yoga teacher; for, on the first occasion upon which I had raised the subject with him, he had handed me an article published in a British journal of religion: 'The General Principles of Sufism' by — Sirdar Ikbal Ali Shah. The powerful link between the realized men and women of each tradition could be seen by the fact that the Sirdar (in spite of addressing himself in psychological terms to Western people) retained his skill in working with a local context by publishing such monographs as the one in *Indo-Asian Culture* in 1962, 'Sufism and the Indian Philosophies'.

So it seems to me that the words of the twelfth-century Sufi illuminate Ghazzali in his *Alchemy of Bliss* are relevant to the differing projections of mysticism, where he says: 'The enlightened man has three modes of expression: the first to those who know nothing: with them he must not upset them; those who have local beliefs: he must express himself in terms of them; and those who can really understand reality: with them he can use whatever terminology or apparent ideas which ensure the necessary communication, without fear of opposition'.

By choosing the psychological path, and illustrating Sufic truths by means of it, Sayed Idries Shah (his father,

151

whom he succeeded, died in 1969) has not only acquired an audience far beyond any which a cultist or ecstatic could; he has also perhaps shown a way in which Yoga research could move in learning how to present Yogic ideas and practices far beyond the present very restricted circles in which they are cramped at the moment. In a nutshell: nobody will today object to psychology and its study — but how many millions still regard Yoga as only Indian, only for slimmers, only a spiritual path, or only studied and practised by a tiny minority of people?

One way of looking at the possibilities of expanding Yoga interest could be to seek for a possible range of ideas and practices beyond, predating even, the relatively few categories presented by Patanjali. Health, hygiene and tranquillity are fine; and probably make an excellent introduction to something which is in other places represented as entirely a means of attaining release from Karma laws; something which attracts only feebly those who do not believe in such a law. But the parallel tradition of Sufism — perhaps because it lacked a Patanjali to restrict or summarise — concerns itself with human evolution, with living in the ordinary world, with ecology, psychology and anthropology. Its protagonists, as poets and scientists as well as social activists throughout the centuries, have left a treasure of precedent and theory which powerfully attracts people all over the world. Hindus, Moslems, Christians, Jews, Zoroastrians, Atheists and Shintoists, Buddhists and scientists: these are only some of the people who are involved in the current projection of Sufi thought and action everywhere.

There are, it is true, many imitative groups, run by people of varying quality and intentions, going under the label of 'Sufi' throughout the world today. But it is easy to discern the true tradition from the cult: all we have to do is to accept the definition of the Sufis themselves. By Sufi tradition, the true Sufi is the one who — in addition to any inward qualities — can show by social and vocational contributions in the community in which he

152

lives that he excels. He can prove that he is 'In the World, but not Of it', to borrow their slogan.

Sufi classical literature warns against teachers who accept all comers; against wearing strange clothes; against applying the same exercises and theories to everyone; against appearing odd and also against claiming to be able to teach. All these are the crutches of the 'teacher' who has nothing else. Perhaps, above all, the real Sufi insists on not allowing his pupils to estrange themselves from the rest of the community to which they belong. This is why true Sufi communities and their members are never to be found where you see all those strange people with fixed places of meeting, fixed practices, parrot-cries and a concentration upon the teacher and not the teaching.

As my first teacher, still to my mind the greatest because he neither revered anyone nor allowed himself to be revered, insisted: 'Every cult is a form of *Yoga*, "yoking": but ninety-nine out of a hundred people, both putative teachers and imagined pupils, are "yoked" to the secondary. This is the Yoga of failure. Aim for the Yoga of the Primary'.

REFERENCES

1. Ali, Ameer, S, *The Spirit of Islam,* London, 1931.
2. Bahadur, Nawab Amin Jung, *The Philosophy of Fakirs,* 1931; Lahore (Pakistan), 1963 edition.
3. Fani, Mohsin, *The Dabistan,* Translated by D. Shea and A. Troyer, Paris, 1843.
4. Ghazzali, Al-, *Alchemy of Bliss/Kimiai-Saadat,* Persian text: Tehran, 1901–2.
5. Graves, Robert, *Introduction to The Sufis by Idries Shah,* London and New York, 1964.
6. Keay, E. E., *Kabir and His Followers,* Calcutta, 1931.
7. Sachan, E. C., *Alberuini's India,* London, 1910.
8. Shah, The Sayed Idries, *The Way of the Sufi,* London, 1968.
9. Shah, The Sirdar Ikbal Ali, 'The General Principles of Sufism,' in *The Hibbert Journal,* London, 20 (1921–22), pp. 524ff.

'Sufism and the Indian Philosophies', in *India-Asian Culture*, 10 (1962), pp. 419ff.

10. Shikoh, Prince Dara, *Meeting of the Twin Seas (Majmu al Bahrain)*. Translated by M. Mahfuz al Haq, Calcutta, 1921.

11. Tomlin, Professor E. W. F., *Great Philosophers of the East*, London, 1952.

12. Ubicini, M. A., *Letters on Turkey*. Translated by Lady Easthope, London, 1856.

13. Williams, Professor L. F. Rushbrook, in *Asian Affairs* (Journal of the Royal Central Asian Society) Vol. 61 (NS Vol. V), part III, October 1974, p. 360. (Editor) *Sufi Studies: East & West*, London, 1973.

5. THERAPY AND THE SUFI

5/i.
Specialized Techniques in Central Asia
Ja'far Hallaji

Abstract: During a visit to Afghanistan in 1961, the author was allowed to observe the hypnotherapeutic techniques of a mystical group which appear to be uninfluenced by Western medicine. The semi-monastic Sufi practitioners differ from most healers or religious workers in that they impose no fees and attempt no proselytizing. The Sufis treat physical as well as psychosomatic disorders by a method which is reminiscent of mesmerism, and they claim cures even for illnesses such as tuberculosis and cancer. A treatment session for 18 patients was observed. The patients were assigned beds in the one-room clinic, and hypnosis was induced individually in each patient, with induction periods varying from 10 to 20 minutes. Chanting, dim lighting, hand passes and eye fixation played a role in the induction. No attempt was made to test for the presence or depth of hypnosis. Fifteen patients claimed immediate cure, one case could not be evaluated at the time, and two patients seemed unaffected. It was reported to the author at a later date that these two initially refractory cases returned for further treatment and were cured.

During a sojourn in Afghanistan in the spring of 1961, I had the opportunity of observing hypnosis among the people of an ancient culture. I feel that the following notes on my experience may contribute to a knowledge of

155

the nature of hypnotherapy in places which have been relatively unaffected by modern developments, and hence shed some light on the historical use of this technique.

The community which I observed is a semi-monastic one, known as Naqshbandi Sufis. The culture is similar to that of the Yogis of India, in that the training of mind and body is stressed, while supernatural elements are rigidly excluded in practical work. Sufism has, however, a respectable literature of transcendental character, and most of the mystical poets of the Persian, Turkish and Urdu classical periods were Sufi practitioners.

Training of the Sufi practitioner is done in secret, given only to selected disciples, and it claims to be the only real 'occult training'. Its purpose is the production of a 'perfect man' complete in mind and body. Disciples have to prove their fitness by undergoing tests and training. Many Sufis are known as *Hakim* (Doctor), meaning that they have passed through a 16-year course in their art.

A description of the activities of the Sufi doctor or practitioner will be the main purpose of this paper.

In the community which I observed, a 'clinic' is held each Thursday night prior to the group devotions and exercises of the entire body. This clinic is composed of 60 devoted practitioners of the Sufi methods. The precise method of the training of practitioners for this clinic was not available. The Sufis are opposed to any investigation of their art because official medical science has not accepted their activities. They were even reluctanct to let me observe their methods in a clinic because they feared that I might be associated with an official inquiry into Sufi methods. However, after these difficulties were overcome, the *Pir-Hakim* (Elder Physician), a man of about 60 years, accompanied by his six senior practitioners, took me to their place of operations.

The clinic was a large, whitewashed building which contained one large room and several smaller ones; the rooms were dimly lighted by oil lamps which hung by

156

chains from the roof. In the large room string-bedsteads were arranged against the walls, each covered by a cotton quilt. During the particular night on which I was observing, there were 18 male patients, ranging in age from approximately 18 to 50. Their ailments included insomnia, headaches, indigestion, lack of appetite, impotence, undefined fears, and backache. The patients consisted of Caucasian and Semitic-type nomads, farmers and other local residents; most of them appeared to be uneducated.

Each applicant was first seen by the chief and his assistants in one of the small rooms and then assigned a bed in the clinic. After the patient had been assigned a bed, he lay on his back, with his eyes fixed upon one of a number of octagonal mouldings. Set in the ceiling, these mouldings were embellished with a nine-pointed diagram. The chief practitioner and his assistants now visited each bed in turn. While the rest of the group maintained a chant of the syllables, 'Ya HOO, Ya HUKK!', the chief passed his hands, held together with palms downward, horizontally over the patient. His hands were held about six inches over the patient's body and passed with a rhythmic movement from the eyes to the toes. The technique thus resembled that of the Mesmerists. An integral part of the proceedings was that the chief practitioner rhythmically blew upon the patient at a rate of about two breaths a second. It is this aspect of the procedure which is responsible for its name, *Chuff* (Breathing). The hypnogenic effect of this technique is probably facilitated by the relaxation of the body, the warmth of the room, the patient's concentration upon the diagram, and the occasional interruption of the light when the palms are passed across the face.

The subjects appeared to enter a hypnotic state in about six minutes. The induction, however, continued for an average of about 12 minutes with younger patients; in the case of patients over about 40, up to 20 minutes was usual. Not all of the patients closed their eyes. Rather, a sharp intake of breath and cessation of

157

minor bodily movement generally signalled the onset of hypnosis for these patients. However, no attempt was made to test for the presence or depth of hypnosis.

After the long period needed to deal thus with each of the 18 patients, the party of practitioners sat down on a bench in the middle of the room while more lights were brought. Tea was now served to the operators, and for half an hour, conversation in low tones with me was permitted. I was assured that the patients were now unconscious, although no verbal suggestions of sleep had been given. The practitioners also informed me that the patients had not known what the nature of the treatment would be before coming to the clinic because all patients who had ever been treated here were cautioned when first interviewed that they should not repeat to anyone, on pain of recurrence of their malady, the form which the therapy took.

At the end of this half-hour period, the practitioners again visited each case in turn. A small gong was beaten once near the patient's head. If he did not stir, the chief, reading the symptoms from a piece of paper, informed him that the curative powers of *Baraka* were entering him, would continue to work in him, were curing him, in every possible way, and would complete the cure before he woke up. This was repeated five times. During this phase of the procedure, the chief made two occult references. The first was that the clinic was 'Haykal'i'Khaab' (The Temple of Sleep), and the other was that the healing took place by virtue of curative power transmitted through the sanctity of the founder of the Order of Sufis, Sheikh Bahauddin Naqshband.

If, however, the patient did stir or move when the gong sounded, he was told that at the end of the proceedings he should rouse himself and return the following Thursday evening for further treatment; he was instructed to lie still meanwhile until the proceedings were finished. Of the total, two patients were evidently not in hypnosis.

All were eventually awakened by being shaken by the shoulder and by being told to arouse themselves. They then kissed the hand of the chief and were sent to another building where they were fed and allowed to stay until morning.

The mandate to teach the technique is still held by the Hashemite family (of which Mohammed was a member), and the present chiefs, who maintain this mandate are the three senior male members of the family: the Princes Ikbal Ali Shah, Idries Shah, and Omar Ali Shah. Their hypnotic knowledge and power thus can be seen as deriving from three sources: that they are Sufi practitioners which gives them the curative power of Bahauddin, that they are tribal chiefs, and that they are Sayeds, descendants of Mohammed.

The following day the patients were again examined for symptoms, and 15 claimed that they were cured. The 16th, the case of impotence, withheld judgement as to his state of health until his return to his village.

According to an informant, the two unsuccessful cases were subsequently hypnotized. It is stated that their maladies — insomnia and migraine — were at that time banished.

The Sufi method of treatment seems to differ from most other religious healing methods in certain respects. Despite the fact that the practitioners are viewed as holy men, I observed no Sufi propaganda being offered to the patients. The practitioners themselves maintained that their method of cure differs from techniques of faith-healing, such as the orthodox Islamic, in the sense that the patients are *not* expected to have faith that they will be cured by the treatment. Further, although one might expect that the practitioners would receive some kind of payment for their services, they accepted no gifts beyond the amount of food which could be held in the palm of one hand.

According to the chief practitioner, cases of cancer, tuberculosis and poisoning had been successfully treated by Sufi methods, though it was sometimes necessary to hypnotize a patient as many as 300 times before effecting a cure. It was also claimed that numerous referrals to the

Sufi method had been cases which defied treatment by physicians trained in the West.

As far as could be ascertained, there was no knowledge of hypnosis as used in the West and no member of the community had any knowledge of any foreign language other than Persian. The books in their library were exclusively classical ones or poetry. The chief practitioner claimed that the Sufi method of treatment originated in the 12th century but had been used for many centuries prior to that by certain Sufi 'masters'. This hypnotic technique of treatment is claimed to have been brought to Afghanistan by a family of descendants of the prophet Mohammed. This claim may be somewhat substantiated by the historical incident in 620 A.D., in which Mohammed placed his son-in-law and companion, Ali (subsequently the Fourth Caliph), into a trance and was able to withdraw without pain a fragment of a lance which was embedded in his thigh.

5/ii.

Nasrudin Looks at Mental Health

Marjory A. Bancroft

Let us put it to the doctors: what is mental illness? When that famous figure of Eastern folklore, Mulla Nasrudin, was challenged by the philosophers, logicians and doctors of law for having dared to call them ignorant and confused, he confronted them in court and asked them each and every one to write an answer to the question, 'What is bread?'

The answers described bread as being anything from a food to a gift of God, to baked dough, to 'Changeable, according to how you mean bread', down to 'Nobody really knows'.

Nasrudin remarked, 'When they decide what bread is,

160

it will be possible for them to decide other things'.

How can one pretend to cure what has never been satisfactorily, let alone unanimously, defined, least of all by those supposedly responsible for its treatment? And if by mental illness we refer to ingrained aberrant and destructive or self-destructive methods of coping with life, leaving aside periodic depressions or other temporary problems, we immediately perceive that success in this field is hardly overwhelming. This fact alone should surely encourage us to stand back and examine not only our methods of dealing with mental illness, at best rarely effective, but our attitudes, individual and collective, which daily and over the generations shape those methods.

Are modern medicine and psychiatry sufficient? It would appear not. Yet do we ever consider treating mental illness outside their confines?

When someone noticed Nasrudin looking for something on the ground and asked him what he had lost, Nasrudin replied it was his key. The neighbour helped him look, and asked exactly where it had been dropped. 'In my house', Nasrudin told him. The neighbour then asked what he was doing looking outside. 'Oh, there is more light here than inside my house', he said.

So with us. That aspect of our culture predominantly concerned with developing rational, analytical thought has generally neglected the possibility that there is another way of dealing with the world. Consequently, our left-hemisphere-oriented society is making great strides technologically in many fields, lighting up Nasrudin's garden with brilliant electric sunshine, while the keys to so many of our dilemmas besides mental illness remain lost in the shadows of a more efficient but necessarily less intellectual manner of dealing with our problems.

Modern psychiatry, of course, would frown on this attitude (though ironically, established scientific thought and psychology — psychiatry and 'pop' psychology in particular — have often found themselves at odds). But is

161

there not a certain amount of intellectual snobbism in the idea that other ways of treating mental illness, not to be found in psychology books, are necessarily exotic drivel founded on unscientific principles? When Nasrudin in his ferry-boat was asked by a learned pedagogue whether the journey would be rough, he replied, 'Don't ask me nothing about it'. The pedagogue inquired whether he had ever studied grammar, and being told 'No', informed Nasrudin that half his life had been wasted. When a sudden storm later threatened to capsize the ferry, Nasrudin asked the teacher whether he had ever learned to swim; he had not, it appeared. 'Then *all* your life has been wasted — we're sinking', said Nasrudin.

In short, it is not necessarily the universities or the medical colleges which are teaching us how to cope with our survival as integrated, constructive and healthy individuals. There is another school; that of experience. One could do worse than read Bacon on this point. Nor is there any reason whatsoever to suppose that it is only the experiences of members of this society or Western culture in general which are of importance or ultimate use to us in this regard. If we could admit that we have failed, and certainly in the case of mental illness I believe we must (The World Health Organization states that ten times as many people were mad in 1975 as in 1900, even allowing for population growth), then surely it is only a healthy humility which could lead us to investigate whether other cultures at other periods in history have perhaps had more success than we ourselves.

Psychiatrists would not appreciate that such primitive societies as the African Zulu tribes, American Indians and others had evolved a more sophisticated approach to certain aspects of mental illness than modern medicine. Yet a former anthropologist turned psychotherapist has adapted, from these cultures, a trance therapy technique for modern victims of anorexia nervosa, a disease notorious for its almost entirely negative response to hospital therapy of any kind; he has since achieved considerable success among a large percentage of his

162

patients, more than can be said of any 'legitimate' psychiatrist practising today. The therapy furthermore appears to possess a previously unsuspected but convincing mathematical basis, as outlined by Professor Zeeman in the condensed exposition of his introduction to catastrophe theory in the April 1976 issue of *Scientific American*.

And if the mass of the populace could reduce the jargon of the Freudians, Jungians and others to their simplest precepts, would they have any interest or belief in these doctrines at all? Or is it their very obscurity which inspires a certain respect-from-afar? When a sage from the Far East visited Nasrudin's village, he began philosophizing abstrusely and at great length until Nasrudin interrupted him, saying that he must tell of his own adventures as a spiritual teacher. After the sage had impatiently sat through tale after tale of Nasrudin's marvellous reception in far-off lands, he finally asked abruptly if no one had ever opposed the Mulla's views. 'Oh yes', he replied; it appeared that in one village he had been beaten and driven away. The sage asked why. 'They understood the language I was speaking in', Nasrudin replied. The sage then asked about all the villages where he had been received with such enthusiasm. 'Oh, they only spoke Kurdish, I was safe as long as I stayed with *them*'.

In the case of the more extreme branches of psychology, from shock treatment to Primal therapy, it is more than the jargon, it is the novelty and the alien approach which 'hook' so many followers (followers who are not, after all, so very different from the avid converts to today's cults, sects and pseudo-Eastern religions; indeed, the memberships of the two reputedly different bodies overlap a good deal). Nasrudin was once stealing apricots in an orchard when the gardener approached; he immediately climbed a tree. When the gardener asked him what he was doing, he replied, 'Singing; I am a nightingale'. The gardener then invited him to sing, and was amused to hear the painfully unmusical sounds the

163

Mulla came out with.

'That isn't like any nightingale I've ever heard', he smiled. 'Then you obviously haven't travelled', replied Nasrudin with hauteur. 'I chose the song of a very rare and exotic nightingale'.

Another problem, apart from a tendency to intellectualize experiences which anyone who has ever suffered from mental illness will confirm are not at all intellectual, is the tendency of psychiatrists to apply blanket treatment. If they are Freudians, then they administer Freudian analysis within its strictest boundaries, whether or not that is what the particular patient in question happens to need. The same is true of all the other specialist branches of psychology. Even the eclectics are generally limited by the concept of modern psychiatry itself.

Perhaps psychiatrists are simply incapable of approaching patients from outside the confines of one strictly-defined, intensely-studied field, or of a mixture of two or more. Or there may be a fear that they would be considered inconsistent if they dealt with individual patients in different ways, resembling the man who had heard so much of Mulla Nasrudin as a sage and therefore journeyed a great distance to visit him and was totally repulsed by the shocking inconsistency of a man who, in the cold of winter, used his breath one minute to *warm* his hands, and the next minute to *cool* a bowl of soup. 'Undoubtedly a fraud', thought the man as he left.

And if this is the case, the psychiatrists may well be right, in that we are probably no more perceptive than Nasrudin's visitor and would, indeed, condemn such inconsistency on their part. But that is scarcely a laudable excuse for failing to deal constructively, open-mindedly and efficiently with such a disabling enemy of humanity as mental illness.

It is surely the restrictions governing the limited knowledge encompassed by psychiatry and medicine as a whole (a difficulty compounded by an often grudging slowness on the part of the doctors and psychiatrists

164

themselves to admit these limitations), especially in comparison with our technological achievements, which prevent us from actually seeing how little we know.

It is like the man whom Nasrudin offered to teach Kurdish, although he knew only a few words of the language himself. Nasrudin started off with the word for hot soup, and was promptly asked how one said 'cold soup'. 'Oh you never say that in Kurdish,' Nasrudin replied. 'The Kurds only ever eat their soup hot'.

Which is, in one sense, similar to the psychiatrists telling patients that there is nothing wrong with them apart from 'normal' periods of acute depression, simply because the patients' problems do not fit in with their own preconceived ideas or definitions of mental illness. It may even be this very fact which contributes to many suicides: 'officially' there is nothing wrong with so many people, yet interior pain and pressure mount to such a degree that the limits of their endurance are surpassed. Nasrudin, in the doctor's waiting room, was repeating loudly over and over, 'I hope I'm very ill', and demoralizing the other patients. When he saw the doctor he almost shouted at him that he only hoped he was very ill. 'Why?' asked the doctor. 'I would hate to think anyone who feels as I do has nothing wrong with them!' exclaimed the Mulla.

Today's victim of mental illness is, in fact, in a rather desperate situation. No one really seems to *know* what to do in practical terms (apart from prescribing drugs, which is consequently done with absolutely alarming regularity and abandon), though everyone is convinced that his own therapy, however limited, is the best available. Like Nasrudin, one may decide to opt for the approach best described as, 'Three heads are better than one': when he was ill, he visited first one physician, who prescribed a purgative, decided on a second opinion and found another doctor who ordered an operation, then found still a third who insisted he needed massage. 'There's the answer', said Mulla Nasrudin. 'One-third of a cut, one-third of a purge and one-third of a massage

165

ought to clear things up in no time'.

I mentioned earlier that despite psychiatry's obvious failure to come to grips with mental illness, no one seemed to consider treating the one outside the confines of the other. Now does this arise solely from our conditioned attitudes towards the idea that anything else would be weird, or esoteric, or superstitious? Or is it simply because there is no other way to deal with mental illness?

Nasrudin once walked into a shop full of various odds and ends. 'Do you have any nails?' he asked the shopkeeper. It happened that he had. 'Any decent leather?' That too. 'Twine?' There was some. 'And dye?' That as well. 'Then why don't you make yourself a pair of boots?' Nasrudin asked.

On another occasion, the Mulla was heard to mutter to himself, 'If I knew what two and two were, I would say, "Four!"'

In short, it is not moaning about what is not being done that *gets* something done. Rather it is examining the tools and material at our disposal, and then conscientiously searching for the knowledge that will allow us to make our own boots, so that we are no longer dependent on pills, weekly visits to the 'shrink', alcohol, an inflated standard of living or constantly excessive exterior stimulation of one kind or another in order to hold us together. The individual has his own contribution to make.

When a group of friends went hunting, Nasrudin was given the slowest horse, and was left well behind the rest. When it began to rain, the Mulla simply got off his horse, removed his clothes and sat on them, partly sheltered by the horse, until the rain had stopped. Then he put on his dry clothes and joined the others, who had tried to dash for shelter and consequently became soaked. 'It must have been the horse you gave me', said a dry Nasrudin in answer to their amazed stares.

So, the next day, his host took the slowest horse and Nasrudin the swiftest one. When it rained again,

166

Nasrudin did as he had done before, while his host, on the slow nag, got even wetter than before. When he returned, he shouted at Nasrudin that it was all his fault for getting him to ride such a slow horse. 'Maybe', suggested Mulla Nasrudin, 'you did not contribute something of your own to the problem of remaining dry'.

As a well-known London specialist once remarked, 'A doctor is only as good a doctor as he is a person'. Certainly medical and psychiatric training today is flawed insofar as this is a factor it stubbornly refuses to take into account. Thus for every medical person of real perception, there may actually be numerous blind automatons.

Nasrudin was once with a sick friend when the doctor arrived, and was stunned when, after only looking at the patient's tongue, the doctor said, 'When you stop eating green apples, you'll be fine again'. 'How did you do it?' he asked the doctor later. 'Simple, when you've had enough experience', he replied. 'When I realized there was nothing more serious than a stomach-ache involved, I looked about for a cause, and noticed a pile of green apple cores under his bed, so it was quite obvious'.

The next time Nasrudin went to visit a sick friend the wife told him abruptly they needed a doctor, not a philosopher, but Nasrudin eagerly pushed his way forward. First thing off, he looked under the bed. 'Nothing to worry about', he said to the wife. 'He'll be fine as soon as he cuts down on this habit he has of eating saddles and bridles'.

And if you think that is too silly and unsophisticated a story to apply to modern medicine, I have an anecdote of my own to relate: a ballet teacher I know was once stricken with a puzzling and painful illness about which she naturally consulted her doctor. 'Malaria', he said. 'But it can't be!' she replied in astonishment. 'From everything I know about malaria the symptoms just don't fit at all'. He shook his head sadly. 'Pity', he said, 'I've never had a case of it. It would have been nice'.

The recent tendency when it comes to searching for the causes of mental illness, particularly with the advent

167

of transactional analysis, Primal therapy, the anti-Spockians, and so forth, is to put the blame on the upbringing of the child, on the parents in fact.

Now is this fair, accurate or helpful? Nasrudin was once trying to get a terribly stubborn calf inside a pen, and ended up by shouting at the mother. Someone asked him why. Nasrudin answered, 'It's all her fault anyway; why couldn't she have taught him better?'

So, in fact, many psychologists and psychiatrists are, like Nasrudin, blaming the mother or father for not teaching the child to do either (a) what the parents themselves never knew how to do, or (b) were only so effectively conditioned that they did it automatically. (In the second case, should we not rather encourage the independence of the child from our conditioning systems, if this independence does not hurt others but instead actually helps him develop to such a point that he progresses beyond behavioural problems or mental illness and can operate as a healthy and effective human being?)

Guilt seems to lie at the root of every known mental illness. In an intriguing story entitled, 'The Burden of Guilt', we are given some clearer insight into how the mechanism operates in almost all normal individuals, and in a far more extreme degree, in disturbed and deranged individuals.

Nasrudin and his wife returned home one day only to find they had had burglars, and that virtually everything in their house was gone. 'You're the one to blame', said his wife. 'You ought to have checked that it was all locked up'.

The neighbours joined in. 'You didn't even have the windows locked', said one. 'Why didn't you anticipate a break-in?' said another. 'You never replaced those faulty locks', put in a third.

'Hold on', Nasrudin said finally. 'It isn't only *my* fault'.

'And who's to blame then?' they all cried.

'Well', said Nasrudin, 'for a start, what about the thieves?'

168

Here we have it in a nutshell: every conceivable interior and exterior voice is constantly shouting at us, 'It's all your fault, you're bad, you're wrong, you should, you shouldn't', and so forth. What has been stolen from us? Perhaps our real faculties of perception, the ones that would enable us to see things as they really are (without the bias of continual and almost incomprehensibly powerful conditioning that, in the short as in the long term, affects our every observation, action and reaction), and therefore be in a position accurately to assess our situation and, if it is an unhealthy one, to remedy it.

And because of these constant voices, be they the internal or external voices of our parents, of television and other media, of our 'Conscience' or that of others, we feel so guilty that we are paralysed when it comes to developing our potential or dealing with our problems.

If, on the other hand, we take Nasrudin's attitude, namely, that instead of sitting there feeling guilty we could point a finger at the real culprits, the thieves, we are then in a position of relative psychological freedom from guilt pressures, freedom which may allow us to make an effort to search for, identify and apprehend the thieves, thereby recovering our 'stolen' faculties. In the absence of the strength or ability to do this, we would be well advised to search out people with some knowledge about catching thieves; unfortunately, psychiatrists do not tend to be such people.

I submit, as a hypothesis, that in the case of mental illness, the normal guilt of the individual, usually quite sufficient to prevent him from realizing his real potential or doing anything more efficient in his life than being a consumer, is distorted and exaggerated to such an extent that the resultant anxiety cripples the individual. To face that guilt head-on would provoke a confrontation with what has variously been described as 'the hole', Primal pain, suicidal panic-depressions, 'the demon of Self-Hate', the Devil (particularly, as Doris Lessing has pointed out, in the case of mystics of the Christian tradition), hell, and so forth. The 'normal' individual finds

169

that the usual distractions of everyday life — food, work, TV, radios and newspapers, sex, alcohol, legal and illicit drugs, fighting with one's spouse or family, fashion, holidays, books, pets, etc. — are all he needs to avoid confronting his inner self for most of his life. If, however, the person attempts to do nothing at all for any period of time, or to deprive himself of his normal, excessive daily intake of external stimulation, he then finds he is not nearly so balanced and calm as he had imagined. Most people, in fact, have projects they would like to (and imagine they should) work on; but instead, on arriving home, they pick up the newspaper, turn on the TV and think about what they'll have for dinner.

As I see it, in the case of the victim of mental illness, such escape is not so simple. A more and more elaborate series of defence-systems is erected to close off the possibility of any internal confrontation. A study of the illness anorexia nervosa is particularly useful and instructive in this regard. Here the incredible guilt over eating and being fat (a great deal of it incidental conditioning on the part of modern society) reaches such a fever-pitch that, to an anorexic, putting on even one or two pounds involves experiencing such a harrowing near-confrontation with the root of the guilt, that the effort to lose weight is redoubled and intensified. The mere prospect of weighing twenty pounds more than his present weight, a conceivable if not pleasant idea in the mind of the normal person, represents a surpassed pain-threshold of such agony that perhaps the only possible solution would be (and sometimes is) suicide.

Anorexia nervosa is an excellent illustration of this precept, because the guilt is so clear and undisguised. In paranoiacs, it seems fairly obvious that to avoid feeling the guilt themselves, they project it onto those around them; with schizophrenics, the division is conceivably a way of escaping the guilt by leaping from one personality or world to another whenever one is threatened; and so on.

Since 1952, drugs have been employed as the single

170

most powerful weapon in the battle against mental illness. Analeptics, anti-depressants and tranquillizers are given out by the handful daily to virtually every patient in mental institutes all over the Western world. Pain-killers, sleeping pills and amphetamines, many of them addictive and harmful in the long run, are also subject to widespread abuse by the population at large. Yet the benefits of drugs in either category are highly questionable. The first three are widely prescribed for schizophrenics, manic depressives and others with severe psychological disturbances; yet Dr Erwin Lausch reports, 'The most significant effect of the new drugs, however, is surely the attitude of the healthy to their mentally sick fellow-beings. Slowly but irresistibly, recognition is gaining ground that the mentally sick should not be treated as lepers, bear no guilt for their sickness and are not hopeless cases'.

It would rather seem as though the effect of the patients' taking the pills is that the *rest* of us start behaving like normal human beings! It calls to mind the story where Nasrudin stole a bull and killed it, taking the animal's skin as well, when the owner discovered this and began crying out and wailing. 'Strange case of cause and effect', thought the Mulla. 'I kill a bull, and the *owner* acts as though he were being flayed!'

Rather than treating the victims of mental illness as lepers then, we might find it constructive to examine their situation from another point of view. If we chose to look at them as symbols rather than 'cases', metaphors in the language of experience or reality, what could they conceivably represent? Mirrors, surely: the circus distorting-mirrors that exaggerate our every flaw. Rather than be repulsed by these images, we could find in them, on closer inspection, a high enough distortion to enable us to see more clearly what we find too small, or too close to us, to see in ourselves: the obstacles to our fulfilment as human beings.

When Nasrudin saw something shiny in the gutter and picked it up, he found it was a metal mirror. Not

171

knowing what a mirror was, he looked more closely and found the reflection of his own face. 'I'm not surprised this was thrown away', he muttered to himself. 'Whatever would anyone see in anything as ugly as this, I wonder?' and deciding it was not worth keeping, threw it back again.

We have been examining mental illness for decades from a single point of view, that encompassed by Western psychology. There are surely many others, and the argument that these would take too much time, effort and initiative to investigate and develop is obviously a weak one. We must think of future generations, and not only of immediately perceptible benefits, in our efforts to broaden the horizons of psychology.

Nasrudin was looking over a wall one day, lost in admiration over a superb lawn, of a hue and texture that surpassed the finest velvet. He asked the gardener, busy watering the lawn, where its secret lay. The gardener explained there was no secret in it at all, it simply involved planting the lawn, weeding it, making sure it was always smooth and cutting it at frequent intervals. Nasrudin thought this was marvellous, was all ready to rush away and make one of his own. 'And about how long does it take to begin looking like this?' he asked. 'Eight hundred years or so', replied the gardener. 'I rather like the view from my house — without grass', said Nasrudin abruptly, and hurried off.

A point I would like to stress here is that perhaps the reason why psychiatrists fail in their attempts to cure mental illness is that they are in no way in real contact with the patients themselves. The sickness is one layer of the individual, and they make the mistake of treating the layer, never coming to terms with the person himself. The patient may be drugged, shocked and put through therapy until he is a co-operative vegetable, but he will have learned nothing of ultimate use to him. The experience will slide off him, and he will remain essentially untouched.

If we dismiss drugs and shock treatment as stop-gap

172

measures, we see that words are the psychiatrist's tools. It has however been established that language is primarily a property of only half the brain, usually the left hemisphere. How may we reach the other half?

We are in need of more effective, practical methods in order to 'get through' to the patient. Nasrudin was once called down from the roof of his house by a fakir asking for charity. Nasrudin asked why he hadn't simply called up to him, and the fakir replied he had been ashamed to. 'You needn't have any false pride', Nasrudin told him, and invited him to come up with him to the roof. When they were both there and he had begun working again, he said to the fakir, 'I haven't got anything to give you'.

In some of the specialised branches of psychiatry, bioenergetics for instance, attempts are being made to include, say, the body over the course of a given therapy, rather than only to treat the mind. But this in the end is hardly more effective, since (a) the inner person remains in most cases entirely unaffected, and (b) such therapies are in the hands of people knowing little if anything more in human terms than the patients themselves. Even if a wonderful new method of coping with mental illness were suddenly to arise, in the hands of an ineffective practitioner, it might well be useless. Nasrudin bought some liver and was taking it home with him, carrying also a recipe for liver pie. An audacious buzzard swooped and made off with the liver. Nasrudin shouted at him, 'You may be glad of the meat, but *I* still have the recipe!'

A buzzard will never make a liver pie; a bad psychiatrist will never truly help a patient, whatever the outer appearances. We must become less concerned with appearances then, and more absorbed by the reality of our precarious situation. The degree of illness in any individual is only relative, as are the means we have of coping with them. Pretending that one or the other is absolute is therefore at best useless, at worst dangerous. Therapy will not make a patient well; whereas becoming attuned to his inner self, his real needs, his own potential and the real nature of his obstacles may bring him to the

173

stage where being well is not a point of relevance, but one of relativity. He may then be in a position to carry out practices which will bring him to a stage beyond being ill or well, where he may take his place in the evolution of humanity as a fulfilled and conscientious individual. On this unscientific note then, I would like to conclude the essay, closing with a story entitled, 'How Nasrudin Created Truth'.

'Laws as such do not make people better', said Nasrudin to the King; 'they must practise certain things, in order to become attuned to inner truth. This form of truth resembles apparent truth only slightly'.

The King decided that he could, and would, make people observe the truth. He could make them practise truthfulness.

His city was entered by a bridge. On this he built a gallows. The following day, when the gates were opened at dawn, the Captain of the Guard was stationed with a squad of troops to examine all who entered.

An announcement was made: 'Everyone will be questioned. If he tells the truth, he will be allowed to enter. If he lies, he will be hanged'.

Nasrudin stepped forward.

'Where are you going?'

'I am on my way', said Nasrudin slowly, 'to be hanged'.

'We don't believe you!'

'Very well, if I have told a lie, hang me!'

'But if we hang you for lying, we will have made what you said come true!'

'That's right: now you know what truth is — YOUR truth!'

5/iii.

Sufism and Psychiatry

Arthur J. Deikman, M.D.

The questions 'What is the purpose of living?' and 'Why do I exist?' haunt modern Western civilization and the absence of an adequate answer to them has given rise to the 'illness' of meaninglessness or anomie. Psychiatrists themselves are afflicted with this same illness, partly because the problem of the meaning of life is solved by a special type of perception rather than by logic; psychiatry is trapped by its commitment to rationalism.

Sufism, on the other hand, is a tradition devoted to the development of the higher intuitive capacity needed to deal with this issue. By taking advantage of the special science of the Sufis, Western civilization may be able to extricate itself from its dilemma and contribute to the development of man's full capacities.

'I think it not improbable that man, like the grub that prepares a chamber for the winged thing it has never seen but is to be — that man may have cosmic destinies that he does not understand'.

Justice Oliver Wendell Holmes (3, p.vi.)

Psychiatry can be defined as the science of reducing mental suffering and enhancing mental health. To date, the field has been primarily concerned with the first part of the definition. For example, in the Index to the *Standard Edition of the Complete Psychological Works of Sigmund Freud* (19), the word 'neurosis' has over 400 references. In contrast, 'health' is not even listed. The imbalance tends to be true of contemporary texts, as well. This situation is understandable because psychiatry originated to deal with disordered function. The question, 'What is the

175

function of a healthy person?' which requires the further question 'What is the purpose of human life?' is not usually asked because it is assumed to be answered by simple observation of the everyday activities of the general population.[1] (18, p.122.)

Underlying all our activities are purposes that give meaning and direction to our efforts. One might go to college to become a lawyer, or save money to buy a car, or vote to elect an official; all of these actions are vitalized by purpose and if the purpose is removed, the activities may cease. That being the case, what is the purpose of human life, itself? What answer do we have to the question, 'Why am I?' A direct answer is not usually attempted in our culture but an indirect answer is there, implicit in scientific publications and in the world view that permeates from scientific authority to the public-at-large. We are told either that the question lies outside the scope of science or that the question is false because the human race has developed by chance in a random universe. Erwin Schrodinger, the physicist, commented on this problem:

'Most painful is the absolute silence of all our scientific investigations towards our questions concerning the meaning and scope of the whole display. The more attentively we watch it, the more aimless and foolish it appears to be. The show that is going on obviously acquires a meaning only with regard to the mind that contemplates it. But what science tells us about this relationship is patently absurd: as if the mind had only been produced by that very display that it is now watching and would pass away with it when the sun finally cools down and the earth has been turned into a desert of ice and snow'. (9, p.149.)

---

[1]In fairness to Freud it should be noted that in his later philosophical writings, he did consider that question and when he did his answer was more in keeping with mystical literature than with modern psychology. 'I may now add that civilization is a process in the service of Eros, whose purpose is to combine single human individuals, and after that families, then races, peoples and nations, into one great unity, the unity of mankind'. (18, p.122.)

We pay a price for the non-answer of science. Psychiatry has recognized the existence of 'anomie' — an 'illness' of meaninglessness, of alienation or estrangement from one's fellow men. Anomie stems from the absence of a deeply felt purpose. Our contemporary scientific culture also has had little to say about meaning, itself, except to suggest and assume that man imposes meaning; he does not discover it. That this assumption may be incorrect and productive of pathology is a possibility that needs to be considered. It may be that the greatest problem confronting psychiatry is that it lacks a theoretical framework adequate to provide meaning for its patients, many of whom are badly handicapped in their struggle to overcome neurotic problems because the conceptual context within which they view themselves provides neither meaning, direction, nor hope. That context derives from the modern, scientific world view of an orderly, mechanical, indifferent universe in which human beings exist as an interesting bio-chemical phenomenon — barren of purpose. Survival is a purpose, but not enough. Working for the survival of others and to alleviate suffering is a purpose but it loses its meaning against a picture of the human race with no place to go, endlessly repeating the same patterns, or worse.

The issue of meaning increases in importance as one's own death becomes less theoretical and more probable. Life goals of acquisition become utterly futile, for no achievements of money, fame, sex, power, and security are able to stop the relentless slide towards extinction. Our bodies age and our minds grow increasingly restless seeking a solution to death. As former goals lose their significance, life can easily appear to be a random cycle of trivial events and the search may end in the most profound despair or a dull resignation. The widespread use of sedatives, alcohol, and narcotics is related to the wish to suppress despair and substitute sensation for meaning.

Such 'existential' despair is so culturally accepted that it is often defined as healthy. Consider the following

177

extract from *The American Handbook of Psychiatry*:

'To those who have obtained some wisdom in the process of reaching old age, death often assumes meaning as the proper outcome of life. It is nature's way of assuring much life and constant renewal. Time and customs change but the elderly tire of changing; it is time for others to take over, and the elderly person is willing to pass quietly from the scene'. (5, p.251.)

So we should end, according to the voice of reason, neither with a bang nor a whimper, but in a coma of increasing psychological fatigue.

The problem is illustrated concretely and poignantly by the dilemma of many psychiatrists, themselves. A recent article in the *American Journal of Psychiatry* concerned a number of professional therapists, aged 35 to 45, mostly of a psychoanalytic background, who formed a group which at first provided peer supervision and later attempted to function as a leaderless therapy group for its members who, as it turned out, were in a crisis:

'The original members of the group we have described were remarkably homogeneous in their purposes in joining. The conscious reason was to obtain help in mastering a phase in their own development, the mid-life crisis. We refer to that stage of life in which the individual is aware that half of his time has been used up and the general pattern or trajectory of his work and personal life is clear. At this time one must give up the normal manic defences of early life — infinite faith in one's abilities and the belief that anything is possible. The future becomes finite, childhood fantasies have been fulfilled or unrealized, and there is no longer a sense of having enough time for anything. One becomes aware that one's energy and physical and mental abilities will be declining. The individual must think of prolonging and conserving rather than expanding. The reality of one's limited life span comes into sharp focus, and the work of mourning the passing of life begins in earnest'. (4, p.1166.)

The 'healthy' attitude recommended here would seem to be a stoical and courageous facing of a reality defined by certain assumptions prevalent in our culture: limited

178

human capacity and limited meaning to life. From this point of view, it can be maintained that the second half of life should be used to adjust oneself to the final termination of individual consciousness. The grimness of such a goal may have resonated in the authors' minds for they go on to brighten up the picture.

'In Erikson's terms, the individual must at this time struggle to achieve intimacy and creativity and avoid isolation and stagnation. If the work of mourning one's lost youth is carried through and the realities of the human situation are fully accepted, the ensuing years can be a period of increased productivity and gratification'. (4, p.1166.)

'Increased productivity' and 'gratification' are invoked to suggest that something good is still possible after 40, but the possibilities still would seem to call more for resignation than for vitality and continued growth. This ultimately circumscribed view of human life is widely held by psychiatrists. Even in the relatively affirmative writings of Erikson the Eight Stages of Man have some of the flavour of a survival manual(1).

In contrast to our scientific culture and its psychology, Eastern introspective (mystical) disciplines have focused on meaning and purpose but have employed a strategy in which the use of intellect and reason is neither central nor basic to the process of investigation. Procedures such as meditation, fasting, chanting and other unusual practices have been employed as part of an integrated strategy whose exact pattern and content depended on the nature and circumstances of the individual and of the culture in which the teaching was taking place.

Unfortunately, the literature of Eastern psychological disciplines has not been of much practical use for contemporary Western readers. Academic study of such texts does not seem to develop wisdom or improve personality functioning, and exotic practices themselves have proven to be elusive and tricky instruments. For example, procedures such as meditation that were once part of a unique and individually prescribed pattern of development are now extracted from their original context and offered for consumption as if they were a kind of vitamin that was good for everyone, ridiculously cheap, and devoid of side effects. Those who use these components of a specialized technology may obtain increased calmness, enjoyment, and improvement of efficiency — but without noticeable gain in wisdom. They answer the question 'Who am I?' by reciting dogma, not by realization, and for all of the 'bliss' that may be displayed, the person's essential knowledge appears unchanged. For those who fare less well with meditation, schizoid withdrawal, grandiosity, vanity, and dependency flourish under the disguise of spiritual practice. Perhaps the worst effect of indiscriminate and unintegrated use of these techniques is that people come to believe that the effects they experience are the measure of Eastern esoteric science. The end result is that they confirm and strengthen their customary conceptual prison from which they desperately need to escape.

The crux of the problem is that modern Westerners need technical means specific to their time and culture. Although such a statement makes perfect sense to most people when the subject concerns the training of physicians or physicists, training in the 'spiritual' is believed to be a different matter. Programmes and techniques 2,000 years old are assumed to be adequate to the task: indeed, it seems that the older and more alien they are, the better they are received.

Fortunately, some traditional materials have recently been made available in a form suitable for contemporary needs; they offer practical benefits of interest to psychiatry as well as the general public. These materials address themselves to the question, 'Who am I?' but they do so in a unique manner:

WHY WE ARE HERE
Walking one evening along a deserted road, Mulla Nasrudin saw a troop of horsemen coming towards him.

His imagination started to work; he saw himself captured and sold as a slave, or impressed into the army.

180

Nasrudin bolted, climbed a wall into a graveyard, and lay down in an open tomb.

Puzzled at his strange behaviour, the men — honest travellers — followed him.

They found him stretched out, tense and quivering.

'What are you doing in that grave? We saw you run away. Can we help you?'

'Just because you can ask a question does not mean there is a straightforward answer to it', said the Mulla, who now realised what had happened. 'It all depends upon your viewpoint. If you must know, however: *I* am here because of *you*, and *you* are here because of *me*'. (11, p.16.)

'Why We are Here' is a teaching story adapted from the classical literature of Sufism. Teaching stories, in a form appropriate to the modern reader, are the means now being made available to prepare Western intellects for learning what they need to know. The stories, such as 'Why We are Here', are built of patterns, depth upon depth, offering resonance at the reader's level, whatever that may be. Teaching stories have more than one function. They provide the means for people to become aware of their patterns of behaviour and thinking so as to accomplish a refinement of their perception and the development of an attitude conducive to learning. Some stories are also designed to communicate with what is conceived to be the innermost part of the human being. Speaking metaphorically, Sufis say that stories make contact with a nascent 'organ' of superior perception, supplying a type of 'nutrition' that assists its development. It is this latter function that is of particular importance to understand; it is the key to the possible role of Sufism in helping to diagnose and cure, eventually, the basic illness that afflicts psychiatrists as well as their patients.

Sufism is usually thought of as a Middle Eastern mystical religion. According to Idries Shah,[2] that

---

[2] Idries Shah has written many books on Sufism and his position as spokesman for contemporary Sufism has been accepted by a large number of authorities (22).

description is misleading. Referring to copious Sufi classics, he states that Sufism is the method of developing the higher, perceptual capacity inherent in human beings and vital to their happiness.

This method is referred to by classical Sufi authorities as a 'science' in the sense that it is a specific body of knowledge, applied according to the principles known by a Teacher, to achieve a specific and predictable result. That result is the capacity to *know*, directly (not through the senses or the usual intellectual functions) the meaning of human life and the inner significance of ordinary events. The change in consciousness that results is regarded as the next step in the evolution of the human race, a step that we must take or perish.

Ordinarily, we do not consider that the zone of normal perception may be so limited as to preclude the experience of a significant dimension of reality, the one with which mystical disciplines were ordinarily concerned. According to the Sufis, meaning is just such a perceptual problem.

An illustration of this issue at the level of biology has been described by C. F. Pantin, former Chairman of Trustees of the British Museum:

> 'A danger in this sort of behaviour analysis — one which I fell into myself — is that it looks so complete that if you are not careful, you may start to imagine that you can explain the whole behaviour of the sea anemone by very simple reflexes — like the effect of a coin in a slot machine. But quite by accident, I discovered that apart from reflexes, there was a whole mass of purposive behaviour connected with the spontaneous activity of the anemone about which we simply know nothing. (Actually, this behaviour was too slow to be noticed; it was outside our sensory spectrum for the time being.)' (2, p.60.)

Similarly, the purpose of human life may be outside the perceptual spectrum of the ordinary person. To widen that spectrum, to provide 'sight', is the goal of Sufism.

The Sufis claim that mankind is psychologically 'ill'

182

because people do not perceive who they really are and what their situation is. Thus, they are 'blind' or 'asleep' because their latent, higher capacity is underdeveloped — partly because they are too caught up in the exercise of their lesser capacities for purposes of vanity, greed and fear. The development of the necessary perception itself is called 'awakening' and the perception, itself, is called 'Knowledge'. It is often said that the science of awakening mankind has been present for many thousands of years, but because of the special nature of the process and of the Knowledge that it brings, the dissemination of the science has fluctuated throughout history and has never taken place on a large scale, partly because of the resistance this idea provokes. (14, p.18.)

RADIOS

I was once in a certain country where the local people had never heard the sounds emitted from a radio receiver. A transistorized set was being brought to me; and while waiting for it to arrive I tried to describe it to them. The general effect was that the description fascinated some and infuriated others. A minority became irrationally hostile about radios.

When I finally demonstrated the set, the people could not tell the difference between the voice from the loudspeaker and someone nearby. Finally, like us, they managed to develop the necessary discrimination of each, such as we have.

And, when I questioned them afterwards, all swore that what they had imagined from descriptions of radios, however painstaking, did not correspond with reality. (12, pp.13–15.)

If, instead of talking of a radio receiver, the term 'intuition' is used, the meaning of the analogy might be more clear. Ordinary intuition, however, is considered by the Sufis to be a lower level imitation of the superior form of intuition with which Sufism is concerned. For the moment, however, some consideration of the place of ordinary intuition in the activity of the scientist may be helpful in illustrating the practical reality of the Sufic position.

183

Although the scientific method is taught as if data plus logic equal discovery, those who have studied how discoveries are actually made come to quite different conclusions. Wigner, a Nobel prize-winning physicist, comments:

> 'The discovery of the laws of nature requires first and foremost intuition, conceiving of pictures and a great many subconscious processes. The use and also the confirmation of these laws is another matter . . . logic comes after intuition'. (2, p.45.)

An extensive, detailed study of the process of scientific discovery was made by Polanyi, formerly Professor of Physical Chemistry at the University of Manchester and then Senior Research Fellow at Merton College, Oxford (7). Polanyi studied scientists' descriptions of how they arrived at their 'breakthroughs' to a new view of reality. He found, like Wigner, that logic, data, and reasoning came last — another channel of knowing was in use. There was no word for that channel in ordinary vocabulary so he used an analogy to convey its nature:

> 'And we know that the scientist produces problems, has hunches, and elated by these anticipations, pursues the quest that should fulfil these anticipations. This quest is guided throughout by feelings of a deepening coherence and these feelings have a fair chance of proving right. We may recognize here the powers of a dynamic intuition. The mechanism of this power can be illuminated by an analogy. Physics speaks of potential energy that is released when a weight slides down a slope. Our search for deeper coherence is guided by a potentiality. We feel the slope towards deeper insight as we feel the direction in which a heavy weight is pulled along a steep incline. It is this dynamic intuition which guides the pursuit of discovery'. (2, p.60.)

Not only do the Sufis contend that man needs more than intellect and emotion to guide him, but that those two 'servants', in the absence of the 'master', have taken over the house and forgotten their proper function:

184

THE SERVANTS AND THE HOUSE

At one time there was a wise and kindly man, who owned a large house. In the course of his life he often had to go away for long periods. When he did this, he left the house in charge of his servants.

One of the characteristics of these people was that they were very forgetful. They forgot, from time to time, why they were in the house; so they carried out their tasks repetitiously. At other times they thought that they should be doing things in a different way from the way in which their duties had been assigned to them. This was because they had lost track of their functions.

Once, when the master was away for a long time, a new generation of servants arose, who thought that they actually owned the house. Since they were limited by their immediate world, however, they thought that they were in a paradoxical situation. For instance, sometimes they wanted to sell the house, and could find no buyers, because they did not know how to go about it. At other times, people came inquiring about buying the house and asking to see the title-deeds, but since they did not know anything about deeds the servants thought that these people were mad and not genuine buyers at all.

Paradox was also evidenced by the fact that supplies for the house, kept 'mysteriously' appearing, and this provision did not fit in with the assumption that the inmates were responsible for the whole house.

Instructions for running the house had been left, for purposes of refreshing the memory, in the master's apartments. But after the first generation, so sacrosanct had these apartments become that nobody was allowed to enter them, and they became considered to be an impenetrable mystery. Some, indeed, held that there was no such apartment at all, although they could see its doors. These doors, however, they explained as something else: a part of the decoration of the walls.

Such was the condition of the staff of a house, which neither took over the house nor stayed faithful to their original commitment (15, pp.211–212.)

The Sufis specify that the development of man's superior capacity has its own rigorous requirements:

185

adequate preparation of suitable students, the correct learning situation, and the activity of a Teacher — one who has reached the goal and by means of that special knowledge is equipped to teach according to the needs of the particular culture, the particular time, historical period, and the particular person. Because of these requirements, there is no set dogma or technique that is utilized in a standard fashion: the form is only a vehicle and is constantly changing.

'All religious presentations are varieties of one truth, more or less distorted. This truth manifests itself in various peoples, who become jealous of it, not realizing that its manifestation accords with their needs. It cannot be passed on in the same form because of the difference in the minds of different communities. It cannot be reinterpreted, because it must grow afresh'. (17, p.264.)

Thus, Sufis differentiate their science from traditional religions, whether Christian, Judaic, Buddhist, Moslem, or Hindu, because such religions have solidified around set rituals, forms, exercises, and dogmas that tend to be handed out to everyone regardless of the context and individual differences. According to Idries Shah, even organizations designated as Sufi Orders may undergo this

'. . .crystallization into priesthood and traditionalism. In the originally Sufic groupings where this fossilization has indeed taken place, their fixation upon a repetitious usage of Sufi materials provides a warning for the would-be Sufi that such an organization has "joined the world."' (17, p.259.)

We have examples of this problem within the field of psychiatry, itself. In Freud's time, for example, the Vienna Circle was open to all who had sufficient interest and capacity to participate, regardless of what formal degrees or titles they possessed. Today, the American Psychoanalytic Institute will not accord full membership to anyone not possessing an M.D., even though the functional relevance of a medical degree for the theory and practice of psychoanalysis can scarcely be discerned. A similar stiffening, sclerosing process seems to invade

186

every human organization. With this in mind, we can understand the Sufic contention that religions were initially based on the development of a higher form of perception but, inevitably, they became ossified, lost their capacity to function in that way, and now persist as archaic structures, hollow shells good only for fulfilling social and emotional needs. Furthermore, most 'mystical experiences' are regarded by the Sufis as being primarily emotional and have little practical importance — except for the deleterious effect of causing people to believe they are being 'spiritual' when they are not. Self-deception is at work in such cases and blocks progress towards the development of higher perceptions.

STRANGE AGITATION

Sahl Abdullah once went into a state of violent agitation, with physical manifestations, during a religious meeting.

Ibn Salim said: 'What is this state?'

Sahl said: 'This was not, as you imagine, power entering me. It was on the contrary, due to my own weakness'.

Others present remarked: 'If that was weakness, what is power ?'

'Power', said Sahl, 'is when something like this enters, and the mind and body manifest nothing at all'. (17, p.182.)

The ordinary man is said to suffer from confusion or 'sleep' because of his tendency to use his *customary* thought patterns and perception to try to understand the meaning of his life and reach fulfilment. Consequently, his experience of reality is constricted, and dangerously so, because he tends to be unaware of it. Sufis assert that the awakening of man's latent perceptual capacity is not only crucial for his happiness but is the principal goal of his current phase of existence — it is man's evolutionary task. Rumi, the great Sufi poet, stated this explicitly:

THIS TASK
You have a duty to perform. Do anything else, do any number of things, occupy your time fully, and yet, if you do not do this task, all your time will have been wasted. (17, p.110.)

HOW FAR YOU HAVE COME!
Originally, you were clay. From being mineral, you became vegetable. From vegetable, you became animal, and from animal, man. During these periods man did not know where he was going, but he was being taken on a long journey nonetheless. And you have to go through a hundred different worlds yet. (17, p.102.)

According to the Sufis, only with the knowledge that perceptual development brings can human beings know the meaning of human life, both in terms of the particular events of a person's life and the destiny of the human race.

CITY OF STORMS
Once upon a time there was a city. It was very much like any other city, except it was almost permanently enveloped in storms.

The people who lived in it loved their city. They had, of course, adjusted to its climate. Living amid storms meant that they did not notice thunder, lightning and rain most of the time.

If anyone pointed out the climate, they thought he was being rude or boring. After all, having storms was what life was like, wasn't it? Life went on like this for many centuries.

This would have been all very well, but for one thing: the people had not made a complete adaptation to a storm-climate. The result was that they were afraid, unsettled and frequently agitated.

Since they had never seen any other kind of place in living memory, cities or countries without some storms belonged to folklore or the babbling of lunatics.

There were two tried recipes which caused them to forget, for a time, their tensions: to make changes and to obsess themselves with what they had. At any given moment in their history, some sections of the population would have their attention fixed on change, and others on possessions of some kind. The unhappy ones would only then be those who were doing neither.

Rain poured down, but nobody did anything about it because it was not a recognized problem. Wetness was a problem, but nobody connected it with rain. Lightning started fires, which were a problem, but these were regarded as individual events without a consistent cause.

You may think it remarkable that so many people knew so little for so long.

But then we tend to forget that, compared to present-day information, most people in history have known almost nothing about anything — and even contemporary knowledge is daily being modified — and even proved wrong. (12, pp.140–141.)

Most psychotherapy focuses on uncovering the fantasies that shape neurotic action and on clarifying and resolving the conflicts of wishes and fears that lead an individual to the repetitive, self-defeating behaviour for which they usually seek therapy. These functions of psychotherapy are necessary and important. However, the resolution of neurotic problems, while it may be a necessary first step for an individual, is neither the measure of health nor of human potentiality. Freud's model of man as an organism seeking relief from tension, forced to negotiate a compromise among instinct, reason, and society, leaves even the most successful negotiator in a position of impoverishment as pathological, in its own way, as any illness listed in the diagnostic manual. This is because the usual psychiatric concept of health is both barren and narrow. Even the most 'humanistic' of current psychologies that offer, in principle, equal attention to such dimensions of human experience as the playful, the creative, and the 'spiritual', have no clear concept of the nature of the problem and little to suggest for its solution. 'Self-realization' is advocated, but just what the self is that is to be realized and what that realization might be are not made explicit.

All of these therapies and theories are in the same boat because they share the fundamental limiting assump-

189

tions about man that are basic to our culture. Unwittingly, they help maintain the lack of perception that is the basic dysfunction of the human race and hinders the development of the higher capacities that are needed. In this sense, psychiatry, whether of the neurochemical or psychoanalytic variety or a combination of both, perpetuates the endemic illness of meaninglessness and arrested human development — it has no remedy for the cultural affliction that cripples normal people. Thus, we arrive at the dilemma of the group of psychiatrists in 'mid-life' crisis described above. They illustrate the point. Their science is caught within the same closed room in which they find themselves; indeed, it helps to bar the door. Psychoanalytic theory, the masterpiece of a genius, is so powerful and encompassing a schema that all phenomena seem to be contained within its walls; its proponents have come to love their city — storms notwithstanding — and they are almost never forced to reappraise their world.

However, existentialism has helped some psychiatrists look to the underpinnings of their profession. Rychlak, writing in the *American Handbook of Psychiatry*, summarizes:

'Building on the theme of alienation first introduced by Hegel, and then popularized in the writings of Kierkegaard, the existentialists argue that man has been alienated from his true (phenomenal) nature by science's penchant for objective measurement, control, and stilted, non-teleological description'. (8, p.162.)

Through existentialism, purpose and meaning have come to have advocates such as the psychoanalyst, Avery Weisman:

'The existential core of psychoanalysis is whatever nucleus of meaning and being there is that can confront both life and death. Unless he accepts this as his indispensable reality, the psychoanalyst is like a man wandering at night in a strange city'. (21, p.242.)

How can the psychoanalyst find that nucleus of meaning, let alone accept it? The group of psychiatrists in

190

mid-life crisis are missing that centre because it is missing from the very discipline they practise and teach. Psychiatry cannot address the issue of meaning because of the limited nature of its concept of man and because of its ignorance of the means needed to develop the capacity to perceive it.

In contrast, Sufism regards its task as the development of the higher perceptual capacity of man, his 'conscious evolution'. According to Sufi authorities, the knowledge of how to do this has always existed. It had a flowering in Islam during the Middle Ages, during which the term 'Sufis' came into use, but it had other names, centuries before. The Sufis regard Moses, Christ, and Mohammed as Teachers of the same basic process — their external forms and the means they employed were different, but the inner activity was the same. The traditional forms that we see around us in current times are said to be the residue of a science whose origins extend back to the beginnings of man's history. The problem is that our thinking has been conditioned to associate 'awakening' to vegetarian diets, chanting, chastity, whirling dances, meditation on 'chakras', koans and mantras, beards, robes and solemn faces — because all of these features of once vital systems have been preserved and venerated as if they were still useful for achieving the same goal. The parts, or a collection of them, are mistaken for the whole. It is as if a car door, lying on the ground, were labelled 'automobile' and hopeful travellers diligently opened and closed its window, waiting expectantly for it to transport them to a distant city.

Meditation, asceticism, special diets and the like, should be regarded as technical devices that sometimes had a specific place in a coherent system prescribed for the individual. When used properly by a Teacher, they formed a time-limited container for a content that was timeless. Now, many old and empty containers labelled 'spiritual' litter the landscape. The importation and wide use of these unintegrated forms attest to the immortality of institutions and customs, rather than the present usefulness of the activities.

The Sufis maintain that, nevertheless, amid all this confusion, the science of 'conscious evolution' continues in a contemporary form, invisible to those expecting the traditional. 'Speak to everyone in accordance with his degree of understanding' was a saying of Mohammed. (10, p.18.) Idries Shah states that he is one of those speaking now to contemporary man, Eastern as well as Western, in a way appropriate to the task of educating people who do not realize how much they have to learn. R. L. Thomson, writing in *The Brook Postgraduate Gazette*, agrees:

> 'The problems of approaching the Sufis' work are such that Idries Shah's basic efforts do seem necessary. Little help is to be found in the academic approach based on linguistics and history.' (20, p.8.)

Most of Idries Shah's writings consist of carefully selected and translated groups of teaching stories, including the ones I have quoted. His translations are exceptionally clear and digestible to a modern reader. The stories provide templates to which we can match our own behaviour. We accept them because they are so deceptively impersonal — the situations are presented as the history of someone else. The story slides past our vigilant defences and is stored in our minds until the moment comes when our own thinking or situation matches the template — then it suddenly arises in awareness and we 'see' as in a mirror, the shape and meaning of what we are actually doing. The analogical form can evade the categorizing of our rational thought and reach other sectors of the mind.

THE DESIGN

A Sufi of the Order of the Naqshbandis was asked:
'Your Order's name means, literally, "The Designers". What do you design, and what use is it?'
He said:
'We do a great deal of designing, and it is most useful. Here is a parable of one such form.

192

'Unjustly imprisoned, a tinsmith was allowed to receive a rug woven by his wife. He prostrated himself upon the rug day after day to say his prayers, and after some time he said to his jailers:

'"I am poor and without hope, and you are wretchedly paid. But I am a tinsmith. Bring me tin and tools and I shall make small artefacts which you can sell in the market, and we will both benefit".

'The guards agreed to this, and presently the tinsmith and they were both making a profit, from which they bought food and comfort for themselves.

'Then one day, when the guards went to the cell, the door was open, and he was gone.

'Many years later, when this man's innocence had been established, the man who had imprisoned him asked him how he had escaped, what magic he had used. He said:

'"It is a matter of design, and design within design. My wife is a weaver. She found the man who had made the locks of the cell door, and got the design from him. This she wove into the carpet, at the spot where my head touched in prayer five times a day. I am a metal-worker, and this design looked to me like the inside of a lock. I designed the plan of the artefacts to obtain the materials to make the key — and I escaped".

'That', said the Naqshbandi Sufi, 'is one of the ways man may make his escape from the tyranny of his captivity'. (16, p.176.)

Teaching stories, such as the above, are tools that depend on the motivation of the user and his or her capacity or level of skill. As understanding increases, the tools can be used for finer and deeper work. The more one experiences and uses them, the more remarkable they seem to be. They lend credence to Idries Shah's claim that Sufism is a science whose boundaries contain modern psychology but go beyond it. He states:

'. . . Sufism is itself a far more advanced psychological system than any which is yet developed in the West. Neither is this psychology Eastern in essence, but human'. (14, p.59.)

According to Shah, the initial step needed to be taken

193

by most human beings is to become aware of automatic pattern-thinking, the conditioned associations and indoctrinated values that limit human perception and receptivity. The teaching story is used for this purpose, illustrating, at one step removed, the egocentric thinking of which we are usually oblivious:

THAT'S WHY THEY BUNGED IT UP

Nasrudin was very thirsty and was happy when he saw by the roadside a water-pipe whose outlet was bunged with a piece of wood.

Putting his open mouth near the stopper, he pulled. There was such a rush of water that he was knocked over.

'Oho!' roared the Mulla. 'That's why they blocked you up, is it? And you have not yet learned any sense!' (13, p.48.)

PERSONAL WISDOM

'I don't want to be a man', said a snake.

'If I were a man, who would hoard nuts for me?' asked the squirrel.

'People', said the rat, 'have such weak teeth that they can hardly do any gnawing'.

'And as for speed . . .' said a donkey, 'they can't run at all, in comparison to me'. (12, p.157.)

Teaching stories such as these have clarified patterns of my own thought, permitting me to notice similar patterns in my patients and to make appropriate interventions. One such story whose content is explicit, is the following:

VANITY

A Sufi sage once asked his disciples to tell him what their vanities had been before they began to study with him.

The first said:

'I imagined that I was the most handsome man in the world'.

The second said:

194

'I believed that, since I was religious, I was one of the elect'.

The third said:

'I believed I could teach'.

And the fourth said:

'My vanity was greater than all these; for I believed that I could learn'.

The sage remarked:

'And the fourth disciple's vanity remains the greatest, for his vanity is to show that he once had the greatest vanity'. (12, p.47.)

Having read this story, I later observed myself using the same strategy as the fourth disciple; specifically, I was berating myself for a personal failing. The context differed from the specific situation of the story but the *pattern was the same*. The story flashed in my mind like a mirror and I understood the role of vanity in my self-reproach. The 'illumination' provoked a wry smile and ended my self-flagellation. Sometime later, I listened to a patient present a similar pattern, recognized it, and, using humour, was able to point out the concealed intent.

The point of view and the learning principles presented in the teaching stories are tough-minded and emphasize the responsibility of each person for his or her own conduct and fulfilment. Such an attitude is not unfamiliar to psychiatry. However, developing a correct attitude is only the first step in Sufic science, a step called 'learning how to learn'. Responsibility, sincerity, humility, patience, generosity — these are not ends in themselves but are tools that must be acquired before a person can proceed further. It is what comes after this first step that sharply distinguishes Sufism from all of the psychotherapeutic and 'growth-oriented' disciplines with which we are familiar. The Sufis regard their system as being far in advance of ours because it extends beyond conceptual and technical limits of our psychology and embodies a method for assisting man to develop the special perception upon which his welfare, and that of the human race, depends. When asked to prove their assertion, Sufis insist on the necessity for undertaking preparatory training and then *experiencing* the domain in question. Such claims and requirements often provoke a haughty dismissal:

THREE EPOCHS

1. *Conversation in the 5th Century*
'It is said that silk is spun by insects, and does not grow on trees'.

'And diamonds are hatched from eggs, I suppose? Pay no attention to such an obvious lie'.

'But there are surely many wonders in remote islands?'

'It is this very craving for the abnormal which produces fantastic invention'.

'Yes, I suppose it is obvious when you think about it — that such things are all very well for the East, but could never take root in our logical and civilized society.'

2. *In the 6th Century*
'A man has come from the East, bringing some small live grubs'.

'Undoubtedly a charlatan of some kind. I suppose he says that they can cure toothache?'

'No, rather more amusing. He says that they can "spin silk". He has "brought them with terrible sufferings, from one Court to another, having obtained them at the risk of his very life".'

'This fellow has merely decided to exploit a superstition which was old in my great-grandfather's time'.

'What shall we do with him, my Lord?'

'Throw his infernal grubs into the fire, and beat him for his pains until he recants. These fellows are wondrously bold. They need showing that we're not all ignorant peasants here, willing to listen to any wanderer from the East'.

3. *In the 20th Century*
'You say that there is something in the East which we have not yet discovered here in the West? Everyone has been saying that for thousands of years. But in this century we'll try anything: our minds are not closed.

Now give me a demonstration. You have fifteen minutes before my next appointment. If you prefer to write it down, here's half a sheet of paper'. (12, p.25.)

If history has any value as a guide, it indicates that we should pay attention to the information now being provided to us by contemporary Sufism and not pass this opportunity without investigating it. Robert E. Ornstein, in his textbook, *The Psychology of Consciousness*, concludes:

'A new synthesis is in process within modern psychology. This synthesis combines the concerns of the esoteric traditions with the research methods and technology of modern science. In complement to this process, and feeding it, a truly contemporary approach to the problems of consciousness is arising from the esoteric traditions themselves'. (6, p.244.)

Psychiatrists need to recognize that their patients' psychological distress stems from three levels: (a) from conflicts of wishes, fears, and fantasies; (b) from an absence of perceived meaning; and (c) from a frustration of the need to progress in an evolutionary sense, as individuals and as a race. The first level is the domain in which psychiatry functions. The second and third levels require a science appropriate to the task. The special knowledge of the Sufis may enable us to put together materials already at hand: our present knowledge of psychodynamics, our system of universal education, our technology, our resources, and our free society, to create the conditions that will permit the development of man's full capacities, as yet unrealized.

REFERENCES

1. Erikson, E. *Childhood and Society*, New York, 1950.
2. Greene, M., Ed. *Toward a Unity of Knowledge, Psychol. Issues* 6: (2). International Universities Press, New York, 1969.
3. Holmes, O. W. Cited in Murphy, G. *Human Potentialities*, New York, 1958.
4. Hunt, W., and Issacharoff, A. History and analysis of a leaderless group of professional therapists. *Am. J. Psychiatry*, 132: 11, 1166, 1975.

5. Lidz, T. On the life cycle. In Artieti, S., Ed. *The American Handbook of Psychiatry*, New York, 1974.

6. Ornstein, R. E. *The Psychology of Consciousness*, San Francisco, 1972.

7. Polanyi, M. *Personal Knowledge*, Chicago, 1958.

8. Rychlak, J. F. The personality. In Artieti, S., Ed. *The American Handbook of Psychiatry*, New York, 1974.

9. Schrodinger, E. *What is Life? Mind and Matter*, London, 1969.

10. Shah, I. *Caravan of Dreams, London, 1968.*

11. Shah, I. *The Exploits of the Incomparable Mulla Nasrudin*, New York, 1972.

12. Shah, I. *The Magic Monastery*, New York, 1972.

13. Shah, I. *The Pleasantries of the Incredible Mulla Nasrudin*, New York, 1971.

14. Shah, I. *The Sufis*, New York, 1971.

15. Shah, I. *Tales of the Dervishes*, New York, 1970.

16. Shah, I. *Thinkers of the East*, Baltimore, 1972.

17. Shah, I. *The Way of the Sufi*, New York, 1970.

18. Strachey, J., Ed. *The Standard Edition of the Complete Psychological Works of Sigmund Freud*, XXI. London, 1961.

19. Strachey, J., Ed. *The Standard Edition of the Complete Psychological Works of Sigmund Freud*, XXIV. London, 1974.

20. Thomson, R. L. Psychology and science from the ancient east. *Brook Postgrad. Gaz.*, 2: 1, 1973.

21. Weisman, A. *The Existential Core of Psychoanalysis*, Boston, 1965.

22. Williams, L. F. Rushbrook, Ed. *Sufi Studies: East and West*, New York, 1974.

5/iv.
Report on Mysticism
A Review by Arthur J. Deikman, M.D.

Mysticism: Spiritual Quest or Psychic Disorder? Group for the Advancement of Psychiatry, New York, 1976.

The report by the Group for the Advancement of Psychiatry entitled *Mysticism: Spiritual Quest or Psychic Disorder?* is intended to supply the psychiatric profession with needed information on the phenomena of mysticism, of which most psychiatrists have only a sketchy knowledge. Certain of the sections, especially those on Christian and Hindu mysticism, show an objectivity and scholarship that are quite commendable. As a whole, however, the report displays extreme parochialism, a lack of discrimination, and naive arrogance in its approach to the subject.

From the point of view of scholarship, the basic error lies in the committee's ignoring the importance of the distinction made by both Western and Eastern mystics between lower level sensory-emotional experiences and those experiences that go beyond concepts, feelings, and sensations. Repeatedly, the mystical literature stresses that sensate experiences are not the goal of mysticism; rather, it is only when these are transcended that one attains the aim of a *direct* (intuitive) knowledge of fundamental reality. For example, Walter Hilton, an English mystic from the 14th century, is quite explicit about this distinction:

> '... visions of revelations by spirits ... do not constitute true contemplation. This applies equally to any other sensible experiences of seemingly spiritual origin, whether of sound, taste, smell or of warmth felt like a glowing fire in the breast ... anything, indeed, that can be experienced by the physical senses'. (7, pp.14,15.)

St. John of the Cross, 16th century, states:

> 'That inward wisdom is so simple, so general and so spiritual that it has not entered into the understanding

199

enwrapped or clad in any form or image subject to sense; it follows that sense and imagination (as it has not entered through them nor has taken their form or colour) cannot account for it or imagine, so as to say anything concerning it, although the soul be clearly aware that it is experiencing and partaking of that rare and delectable wisdom'. (3, p.457.)

A similar distinction between lower (sensate) and higher (transcendent) contemplative states may be found in Yoga texts:

'When all lesser things and ideas are transcended and forgotten, and there remains only a perfect state of imagelessness where Tathagata and Tathata are merged into perfect Oneness . . .' (5, p.332.)

Western mysticism, from which the authors derived most of their examples, constitutes only a minor segment of the literature in the field of mysticism, and its basic contemplative tradition actually derives from Eastern sources, as acknowledged in the report. Yet the goal of Eastern (Buddhist, Hindu, Taoist, Sufic) mysticism — 'enlightenment' — is not visions of angels or Buddhas but the awakening of an inherent capacity to perceive the true nature of the self and the world. Over and over again, these texts warn that the type of mystical experience on which the GAP Report focuses is not the goal of the mystical path. Such visionary experiences are regarded as illusions and, at worst, snares for the poorly prepared or the ill-guided. An example from the Zen literature follows:

'Other religions and sects place great store by the experiences which involve visions of God or hearing heavenly voices, performing miracles, receiving divine messages, or becoming purified through various rites . . . yet from the Zen point of view all are morbid states devoid of true religious significance and hence only *makyo* (disturbing illusions)'. (8, p.40.)

In the Sufi literature, we find many explicit statements that Sufism is a science of knowing and is not a religion in the way that term is ordinarily understood.

'The Sufis often start from a non-religious viewpoint.

200

The answer, they say, is within the mind of mankind. It has to be liberated, so that by self-knowledge the intuition becomes the guide to human fulfilment'. (11, p.25.)

The Sufis regard most mystical experience as being essentially emotional with little practical importance — except for the harmful effect of causing people to believe they are being 'spiritual' when they are not:

'Sahl Abdullah once went into a state of violent agitation with physical manifestations, during a religious meeting.

'Ibn Salim said: "What is this state?"

'Sahl said: "This was not, as you imagine, power entering me. It was, on the contrary, due to my own weakness".

'Others present remarked: "If that was weakness, what is power?"

'"Power", said Sahl, "is when something like this enters and the mind and body manifests nothing at all".'

(12, p.182.)

Despite these clear warnings in the mystical literature, the GAP publication emphasizes lurid, visionary phenomena which lend themselves readily to standard psychiatric interpretations. Because of this, the authors have failed to come to grips with the fundamental claim of mystics: that they acquire direct knowledge of reality. Furthermore, the authors follow Freud's lead in defining the mystic perception of unity as a regression, an escape, a projection upon the world of a primitive, infantile state. The fact is we know practically nothing about the actual experience of the infant, except that whatever it is, it is not that of a small adult. No one who has read carefully the accounts of 'enlightenment' can accept this glib equation of mystical = infantile. An infant mind could hardly have had the experience that conveyed the following:

'The least act, such as eating or scratching an arm, is not at all simple. It is merely a visible moment in a network of causes and effects reaching forward into Unknowingness and back into an infinity of Silence, where individual consciousness cannot even enter. There

201

is truly nothing to know, nothing that can be known.

'The physical world is an infinity of movement, of Time-Existence. But simultaneously it is an infinity of Silence and Voidness. Each object is thus transparent. Everything has its own special inner character, its own karma or "life in time", but at the same time there is no place where there is emptiness, where one object does not flow into another'. (8, p.268.)

To confuse lower level sensory-emotional experiences with the transcendent 'Knowledge' that is the goal of mysticism seriously limits the usefulness of the report and tends to perpetuate in the reader the ignorant parochial position that was standard in most psychiatric writings before the GAP publication and now, unfortunately, is likely to be reinforced.

This naive reductionism is all the more striking in the context of the numerous reports from physicists indicating that the world is actually more like the one that the mystics describe than the one on which psychology and psychoanalysis are based. Contemporary scientists have ample evidence that the world of discrete objects is an illusion, a function of the particular scale of our perception and time sense. For them, it is commonplace that the phenomena of biology and physics point to a continuous world of gradients, not a collection of objects. Percy Bridgman, Nobel Laureate in physics, comments:

'It has always been a bewilderment to me to understand how anyone can experience such a commonplace event as an automobile going up the street and seriously maintain that there is identity of structure of this continually flowing, dissolving and reforming thing and the language that attempts to reproduce it with discrete units, tied together by remembered conventions'. (1, p.21.)

What is missing from the GAP Report is any acknowledgement that the mystic who has completed his or her development may have access to an intuitive, immediate knowledge of reality. The authors assume that the known sensate pathways are the only means to acquire knowledge of what is real. In fact, studies of how

202

scientific discoveries are actually made show in almost every instance that this is not the case at all. Another Nobel Prize-winning physicist, Eugene Wigner, has remarked:

> 'The discovery of the laws of nature requires first and foremost intuition, conceiving of pictures and a great many subconscious processes. The use and also the confirmation of these laws is another matter . . . logic comes after intuition'. (6, p.45.)

'Intuition' can be considered a lower order example of the latent capacity to which mystics refer.

The eclectic ignorance of the authors has led them at one point to lump together Einstein, Jesus, Abraham Lincoln, biofeedback, Vincent Van Gogh, and St John of the Cross. Interestingly enough, if the authors had pursued the case of Einstein alone, they might have come to the epistemological issue that is the core of mysticism — and paid proper attention to it; for Einstein's modern discoveries, as well as the discoveries of natural philosophers thousands of years earlier, were based on an intuitive perception of the way things are. Such perceptions are the source of our greatest advances in science. Michael Polanyi, at one time Professor of Physical Chemistry at the University of Manchester, made an extensive and thorough study of the actual process of scientific discovery and found that the revolutionary ideas of geniuses such as Einstein had 'come to them' by some form of direct intuition, often presented as imagery (10). Polanyi was led by his data to propose a theory of knowledge and human consciousness that is clearly 'mystical'. Furthermore, at least two books have been published recently documenting the strikingly close correspondence between the scientific conceptions of physicists and the insights of mystics. (2, 9.)

Thus, it is truly remarkable to have a group of psychiatrists issue a report in 1976, in which the only comment they make on the mystic perception of unity is that it represents a 'reunion with parents'. Nowhere in the report do we find a discussion of the possibility that the perception of unity occurring in the higher forms of mysticism may be correct and that the ordinary perception of separateness and meaninglessness may be an illusion, as mystics claim. Clearly, mystic perception could be true whether or not a particular mystic might wish, in fantasy, to be reunited with his or her mother.

The GAP report states:

'The psychiatrist will find mystical phenomena of interest because they can demonstrate forms of behaviour intermediate between normality and frank psychosis; a form of ego regression in the service of defence against internal or external stress; and a paradox of the return of repressed regression in unconventional expressions of love'. (p.731.)

How totally provincial our profession has become if this is a summary statement from a group that claims to be devoted to 'advancing' psychiatry!

It is interesting that the only place in which the authors are able to allow themselves to think in positive terms of mysticism is when they discuss the concept of 'creativity'. Apparently, creativity is OK. In this section of the report, the authors venture to speculate:

'At the same time, internal or external perceptions may be heightened, and this sensitivity may open a path to hidden aspects of reality'. (p.795.)

Unfortunately, that one sentence, like a lonely ray of sunshine, is soon swallowed up by a return of the monotonous clouds of reductionism. The very next chapter, entitled 'Case Report', concerns a woman in psychotherapy who reported having had the sort of low level, sensate mystical experience on which the authors focus. The report provides the following conclusion:

'Her interests were reinvested in the fantasy universe, representing God, in which such problems do not exist, and she felt herself united with this God-Universe, a substitute for an unavailable or rejecting parent. The mystical union made up for the rejection she feared from her father, now represented by the therapist in another man . . . so, while a psychiatric diagnosis cannot be dismissed, *her experience was certainly akin to those described by*

204

great religious mystics [!] [my italics] who have found a new life through them'. (p.806.)

In the last paragraph it becomes even more presumptuous and confused:

'The mystical state itself provided the illusion of knowledge. But unlike many mystical states in which the search ends with illusion, it stimulated her to seek further knowledge and led directly to the disappearance of her inhibition to serious reading. [!] This continued search is characteristic of those in whom mystical states contribute towards creative activity'. (p.807.)

The authors of this report are intelligent, educated, sincere men. It is hard to believe that they would display such provincialism, carelessness, and bias if they were discussing schizophrenia. Judging by this and other similar psychiatric discussions, our profession, when it comes to mysticism, does not feel the need to ask serious questions about its own assumptions, nor to take the devil's advocate's position toward its too-easy conclusions. Ironically, the authors are capable of pointing out the problem in others. In discussing 'the naive Western observers of the Indian scene' they say:

'Confronted by such common symbols as that of the representation of the divine activity in sexual form, and bewildered by the profusion of deities in the Hindu pantheon, they could impute to Hinduism a "decadence" following from its essence, and they fail to apply to that religion the discrimination between enlightened and superstitious observance which they would be sure to demand for their own'. (p.747.)

Exactly.

In trying to understand the phenomenon of the GAP Report itself, I am led to two principal considerations. First, in order to understand and have some appreciation of 'mysticism', it is necessary that psychiatrists participate to some extent in the experience. When it comes to its own discipline, the psychiatric profession is unwavering in its requirement that one must 'know' through experience, not just description. Who can really understand 'transference' without experiencing it?

Actual experience is necessary because the position of the outside observer has its limits, particularly in areas not well adapted to language. I can give an example of the necessity for participation from my own research on meditation and mysticism. In surveying the literature, I had noticed that contemplation and renunciation were the two basic processes specified for mystical development by almost all mystical authors, East and West. I proceeded to study the effects of meditation in the laboratory and, naively, assumed that renunciation meant giving up things of the world — in a literal sense. It was only later, when I both studied and participated in Soto Zen training, that I came to understand that renunciation refers to an attitude, not to asceticism, *per se*. That understanding enabled me to formulate the hypothesis of 'biomodal consciousness,' based on motivational considerations (4). The hypothesis, in turn, enabled me to understand a wide variety of unusual states of consciousness.

Perhaps by stating that I have, myself, practised meditation, I will automatically disqualify myself in the eyes of some readers as having any credibility in these matters. I refer those readers to the paper by Charles Tart, wherein he presents a compelling case for the development of 'state-specific sciences' — sciences whose mode of investigation is specifically adapted to the area it is investigating (13). Indeed, participation by scientists in these areas of mysticism would result in an understanding that is less exotic and less religious — and would help rid ourselves of the claptrap associated with mysticism that constitutes a burden to scientist and mystic alike.

Unfortunately, such participation is not likely to occur because of the other basic problem confronting psychiatrists when they approach this field: arrogance — reflecting the arrogance of Western civilization. In this connection, it is interesting that the fundamental requirement for participating in any of the mystical traditions has been, and still is, humility. This is so, not because humility is a virtue, something that earns one credit in a heavenly bank account, but because humility is instrumental — it is the attitude required for learning. Humility is the acceptance of the possibility that someone else or something else has something to teach you which you do not already know. In crucial sections of the GAP Report, there is no sign of humility. It seems to me that in our profession we display the arrogance of the legendary British Colonial who lived for 30 years in India without bothering to learn the language of the inhabitants, because he considered them to be inferior. Perhaps medicine's long battle to free itself from religious control, from demonology and 'divine authority' has left us with an automatic and costly reaction against anything that bears the outward signs of religion. In point of fact, mystics outside the Western tradition tend to share our suspicion and describe their disciplines as a science of development — not a religion, as ordinarily understood.

The authors of the GAP Report have selectively ignored the central issues of mysticism and have made traditional interpretations of the secondary phenomena. If our profession is to advance, we must recognize our defences against ideas that would change our assumptions. Mysticism, studied seriously, challenges basic tenets of Western cultures: (a) the primacy of reason and intellect; (b) the separate, individual nature of man; (c) the linear organization of time. Great mystics, like our own great scientists, envisage the world as being larger than those tenets, as transcending our traditional views. By not recognizing our defensiveness and by permitting our vision to be narrowed so as to exclude the unfamiliar, we betray our integrity as psychiatrists, showing no more capacity for freedom from prejudice than persons totally ignorant of psychodynamics — perhaps less.

Psychiatry's aversion to things ecclesiastical should not blind the profession to the possibility that 'real gold exists, even though false coin abounds'. It is unfortunate that the GAP Report carries us little further towards gaining for ourselves that wider base for human fulfilment that we need. The attitude reflected in the report is myopic and unnecessarily fearful of an avenue of human endeavour, aspiration, and discovery thousands of years old — one productive of outstanding achievements in science and literature that we are only now beginning to recognize. Yet, if we learn nothing more from mystics than the need for humility, they will have contributed greatly to Western culture in general and to the profession of psychiatry in particular.

REFERENCES

1. Bridgman, P. W. *The Nature of Physical Theory*, New York, 1964.
2. Capra, F. *The Tao of Physics*, Berkeley, 1975.
3. *The Complete Works of St. John of the Cross*, Vol. 1, Westminster, 1953.
4. Deikman, A. Bimodal consciousness, *Arch. Gen. Psychiatry*, 25: 481–489, 1971.
5. Goddard, D., Ed. *A Buddhist Bible*, Thetford, Vermont, 1938.
6. Greene, M., Ed. Toward a Unity of Knowledge, *Psychol. Issues*, 22: 45, 1969, International Universities Press, New York, 1969.
7. Hilton, W. *The Scale of Perfection*, London, 1953.
8. Kapleau, P. *The Three Pillars of Zen*, Boston, 1967.
9. LeShan, L. *The Medium, the Mystic and the Physicist*, New York, 1974.
10. Polanyi, M. *Personal Knowledge*, Chicago, 1958.
11. Shah, I. *The Sufis*, New York, 1971.
12. Shah, I. *The Way of the Sufi*, New York, 1970.
13. Tart, C. States of consciousness and state-specific sciences, *Science*, 176: 1203–1218, 1972.

6. THE PRACTICE OF THE SUFI

6/i.

Learning and Teaching

Peter Brent

There are, as we have seen, the classics, by Jalaluddin Rumi, by Saadi and Hafiz and the rest, books galore by generation after generation of teachers, sages, scholars, saints and the illuminated. Above all, there is the Koran. The Message of Islam is itself Islam's — and Sufism's — greatest instrument. Its meaning lies not only in what it says, but what it is. Where Christians centre their meditations upon Jesus, God made flesh, Moslems centre theirs upon the Koran, God made word. And, perhaps because God is infinite, the meanings of the Koran are endless.

Yet that infinity is bewildering; even the dissertations of a Rumi, stemming as they do from a man on the far side of self-realization, are full of an equivocal mystery not to be penetrated by the uninitiated. Thus the books (especially for non-Muslims) may become a barrier rather than a gateway to truth. And the paths and means of learning, of development, of meditation are many, the pitfalls for the untrained are without number. Byways beckon, false rewards, deceptive versions of the longed-for experience.

How, in this complexity, is one to find one's way? How is one even to determine what that way should be? How is one to decipher the codes hidden in the writings of the great? How is one to prepare for the overwhelming experience of ecstasy, and understand it when it occurs?

And how is one, truly knowing neither oneself nor one's goal, to choose among the infinity of possible methods, disciplines, techniques?

Ibn El-Arabi wrote, 'The Teacher is he who hears you, then unveils you to yourself'. And Rumi tells us, 'Soul receives from soul that knowledge, therefore not by book nor from tongue'. What is to be learnt is not knowledge, but a means of gaining knowledge. An inner capacity has to be developed; it is, in other words, not like learning a language, but like learning to talk. The baby is surrounded by people who have long known this skill, and it lies within him, too, in undeveloped form. For month after month, aided by the encouragement of parents, by their love and patient little tricks, he struggles to reach the part of himself where that skill lies. His lips move, he blows bubbles, he gesticulates, he gurgles: one day he says a word. He has made his breakthrough. He, too, is on his way to joining the élite who have learned so to communicate with each other.

Yet no intellectual element entered into the teaching, rather he was coaxed and prompted, he was influenced and rewarded, until on his own account he discovered the ability that took him one more step toward becoming fully human. He had seen, by observing those more advanced than himself, what was possible. In his struggle to be like them, they had helped. But above all, there had been in him and in them an overwhelming desire that he should be as they were, able to speak, a conviction that this was part of his human destiny. Everything that was done, by him to achieve the goal and by them to aid him, was because of this overriding imperative. It was the medium in which their instruction and his learning came together. They were taking part in a drama that had to end well, in the child's victory, because it was part of the wider drama of the human race. Defeat would have been a set-back for humanity as a whole. This element of the relationship was never articulated and probably never became conscious. But because of this element, conscious or not, there was an urgency in the adults' efforts and the

210

baby's struggle that would not have been there otherwise. An essence, the essence of the race, of what it means to be a human being, was being directly transmitted, and the child's learning to speak was a function of that transmission. It is at this level, above all, that the teaching of a Master and the learning of a novice take place. 'Soul receives from soul . . .' — the transmission is direct.

For good or ill, we are not when adults as intellectually uncluttered as babies. Our heads are filled with 'knowledge', a knowledge that in some areas pre-empts our seeing anything at all; or being truly aware of any part of the world that surrounds us. Everything arrives in our understanding already packaged and labelled. How are we to take the wrappings off and test the truth of the labels? The fact is that we are in no condition to do so: we are helplessly hidden from ourselves, even when we attempt to discover what we really are, since the imperfections that we are trying to seek out exist in the very perceptions with which we search for them. It is as though we looked for the colour red through spectacles fitted with a red filter. Until the filter is removed we cannot see what is certainly there, but hidden from us. It is the task of the Teacher, not to remove the filter, but to make us so aware of its presence that we remove it ourselves.

It is for this reason that Professor Shushtery, in *Outlines of Islamic Culture*, warns us, 'The selection and following of a spiritual guide is the most important duty of a Sufi. A bad or imperfect guide may lead him to evil or leave him imperfect and bewildered. He must use all his intellectual ability and human endeavour to find out the true guide and once obtained, he must obey his direction'. Yet the phrase 'true guide' does not entirely sum up the requirement either, for one man's guide may be another's tyrant, or a third man's fool. It is the seeker's *particular* true guide who must be found, the right person to teach the *particular* him or her who is in need. We cannot enter into relationships at this level with just anyone, whatever their qualifications; it has to 'feel right' before we entrust ourselves and our destinies to another.

Even then, how can we set about selecting our guide? Rumi tells us, 'Do not look at his figure and colour; look at his purpose and intention'. In a sense, however, this begs the question, since the novice by the nature of things has not developed the criteria by which to judge. Yet he is on the verge of making so momentous an act of self-surrender that its consequences may stretch forward for many years. The situation is complicated by the fact that his own sincerity may manage to extract relevant truths, and thus the impetus for progress, even from a manifest charlatan. He may, nevertheless, consider certain traits as warnings.

The self-styled teacher (and the assertion is itself enough to make one beware) will sometimes imply, or even insist on, his own knowledge and spiritual development with an emphasis intended to still the newcomer's doubts; such firmness may, indeed, enthuse the latter for a while. Yet even a novice might ask what the real value and true purpose of such protestations might be. The teacher may, on the other hand, go out of his way to flatter the novice, praising him for the high level of his spiritual qualities. Again, even a neophyte might question what value there is for him in such fulsome acceptance. Alternatively, the would-be Teacher may damn him as of small consequence and less potential, yet in lordly fashion accept him into his circle. The novice might remember that the true guide will not waste his time on those he cannot help, nor theirs in harnessing them to a teacher who can do nothing for them. One might say that one test of a teacher's worth lies, not in seeing how many disciples he has, but in how many aspirants he turns away.

There is also the question of authority. All guides will have a background of training, a line of Teachers stretching to them down the generations, perhaps also a family connection with Sufi traditions. On occasion, when faced by some kind of incalcitrance, they may call

212

on this to support their precepts or admonitions. But they will not in themselves stand upon such borrowed authority, nor make it the condition of their teaching. They do what they do because they are what they are. The insecure teacher, on the other hand, will reveal his inadequacies by frequently calling upon his background to validate him. His authority comes not from within himself, but is filched from the past. The quality that fills the true guide, however, both witnessing to and providing the basis for all the authority he needs, may often be sensed by the aspirant. Not possessing it, the over-ambitious teacher may attempt to hide the lack by promising knowledge that only he can dispense; in other words, he will appear in the guise of a magician, offering miraculous powers and curious abilities to those willing to apprentice themselves to him. Alternatively, he may disguise his lack of true authority by continuously oppressive behaviour, substituting tyranny for benevolence. Such a person will harness his disciples to him for ever, will try to keep them his lifelong subjects, will, in short, halt their progress at the level of dependence. The 'true guide', however, acts very differently from this. He will attempt to be the means by which knowledge develops in the pupil. He will not simply pretend to a body of knowledge as such, but will demonstrate a condition of being into which, in time, the novice too can enter. He will never feel threatened by the disciple's progress, precisely because he will realize that only when both guide and guided are in the same spiritual dimension will his work have proved successful.

Even with such general propositions to aid him, the would-be novice is still, on the face of it, inadequately equipped to select his 'true guide'. He will, therefore, be forced to use other methods than the ordinary to make his selection; in other words, he will 'know' when he meets the right teacher in ways other than the logical. In effect, he will experience a sort of 'falling in love', a sensation of mutual sympathy so strong that no other recommendation will be necessary. As we have seen,

213

Rumi's self-surrender to Shamsuddin of Tabriz seemed wholly unsuitable and even absurd, insane, to everyone else.

This level of sympathy is essential, since whatever may be the formal trappings of the master-disciple connection, its essence is wholly flexible and living. Each process of instruction is unique, however much it may resemble others, since each is the outcome of a personal relationship. The teacher never really has only a group of disciples whom he instructs; he has around him selected individuals with each of whom he stands in a unique relation. Even when he appears to speak to all, he bears in mind the different impact of his words on each.

The guide, after all, is the person who has made the journey that the novice wants to make. He not only knows what the novice wants to know, he is what the novice wants to become. As a result, the disciple, once accepted by the teacher, cannot judge the latter's words or actions: he must trust him. In practice, this means his total acceptance of the fact that his teacher knows better than he what he should do, the pace at which he should progress, the exercises he should perform and the disciplines he should undergo. If the disciple does not accept this, there is no point in his sitting at a teacher's feet. He will reject the only truly valuable thing the teacher has to offer. Theories, arguments, dissertations can all be found in books; the impact of one person on another is a quite different matter. It is this acceptance of what amounts to the teacher's omniscience, certainly in the matter of the pupil's development, that is the basis for the surrender that the novice must make: it is precisely for this reason that he is not a student but a disciple.

Because, therefore, he cannot anticipate what methods the teacher will use to alter him, but knows nevertheless that those methods will be total, involving every aspect of himself, the novice must have the courage to pick the teacher by a sort of inspired guess. He must, in other words, rely on his own intuition in making his choice. And precisely in that lies his first and greatest lesson:

214

that it is within himself that he must seek for truth. It is his inner voice, his inner certainty, that he must, as it were, rediscover and cultivate. It is in these that the secret of his full humanity always lay, and these that reason and instinct have combined to distort. If his first task on setting out on this path is to discover, not what one learns, but how, then his best beginning is to become aware of his own reactions, listen to his inner voice, and in their light make the crucial choice of who is to guide him.

The teacher's early function must be to alter the patterns of the novice's thinking and thus of his behaviour. If the novice's mind operates in a set way, dominated by prejudices and automatic responses of which he may not even be conscious, it interposes itself as a barrier between himself and the fact of the teacher, the activity of the teaching. In order for mind, intelligence, to become a channel for the teaching, it must be made aware, so that it can seize on the multiplicity of truth and snap up the complexities of meaning. The different components of what the mind takes in will then begin to work on each other, altering perception and breaking down the rigid processes of a learned logic.

Learning as we do largely through books, we have been forced to think in sequences we designate as rational. This leads us to define existence and everything that makes it up in a dictionary way. It is the drawback of such a definition that its very precision robs a word of resonance. There is a complex series of echoes emitted by every word, just as filaments of meaning stretch from fact to fact, making nonsense of our Cartesian clarity. The language of logic, like that of dictionaries and the constructions of mathematics, leads us to a truth which is of one kind, truth as particular, singular, arrived at by the elimination of alternatives. The fact that we simplify the world in this way does not, however, mean that the world is equally simple. Neither does the fact that this is how we have learned to understand the world mean that it is the only way the world can be understood. Nor, indeed, does it mean that the world so understood is the only world open to our understanding. We create what we become aware of, at least to some extent, by the sense we use to apprehend it. If you show a dog a book of philosophy, the dog will use its nose in order to decide what it is. It will have a series of categories — *food/not food, dog/not dog* and so on — that will serve as its criteria for judging the scents that are its primary data. It will as a result very soon lose interest in the book. That will not be because of a defect in its sense of smell, it will be because ability, instinct and experience force it to use the wrong sense for the task. In the same way, the manner in which we perceive the world may not be inadequate, given the senses we are employing; it may simply be irrelevant because we are employing the wrong senses.

This is the condition that it is the teacher's first task to change. Once he has accepted the novice, he must assess him, determining how much and in what manner he can learn. The teacher must then, by any means that seem to him suitable, create in the aspirant states of mind that will of themselves cause the latter to progress. Precept is here of little value; the learning is always from within and it is the conditions for it that are set up by the guide. For this reason his behaviour may appear at times bizarre, unpredictable or meaningless; he may act in ways that are flippant, domineering, cold, manic or tyrannical, he may scream as though gripped by fury, sit in disapproving silence or set the disciple a flurry of apparently inconsequential tasks. Any outsider might well conclude from his behaviour that he is mad; even the novice himself may realize only long afterwards what the teacher's true intentions were.

Nevertheless, if he follows his teacher's instructions, picks up his hints, reacts to the stimuli he provides, strange though these may be and tending in directions he cannot guess at, the aspirant will surely begin to break through the mental barriers, the rigidities, blocks and distortions, that previously hampered him and prevented his progress. Meanwhile the teacher will carefully

216

monitor his advance, always making sure that the disciple does not pass beyond his capacity.

Know your own capacity, don't mention that garden of union.

Isn't it enough that you have become aware of its thorns?

Thus Rumi, setting words in the mouth of Shamsuddin of Tabriz. And of the disciple's capacity in this chartless area the teacher can be the only judge. Understanding the uniqueness of each disciple and certain of the goal, he needs no orthodoxy upon which to rely. Indeed, the unorthodoxy of the teacher expresses that of Sufism itself. Since it is a direction and not a dogma, it submits to no clear definition; why then should those who teach it, or their methods? It achieves itself in being, through action; and so do they. Exercises done in unison, as in most 'mystical' groups, can only be false to the true Sufi.

Of necessity the first stages in a novice's progress will often seem to him threatening, even destructive. Rumi makes Shamsuddin ask, 'Unless you are first disintegrated, how can I reintegrate you?' The breakdown of long-established modes of thinking, of being, is bound to be experienced by the immature as some sort of personal demolition. It will frequently be painful, and it is because of such moments of anguish that the novice's trust in the teacher must be absolutely established. Only on that basis will he be able to go through the desperate struggle in which he is engaged. For it is often at the start a darkness and a turmoil, an overturning of what had seemed established, an obliteration of all north and south. Only as the novice continues will he understand with his newly-developed perceptions the beginnings of a different logic, a differently ordered cosmos. Once he has glimpsed it, all his efforts will make retrospective sense; he sees that he has after all been moving steadily along the path. It is lack of resolution, or unfitness for the Path, which make people criticize or abandon the teaching at this point, and makes outsiders object.

Partly because the relation of teacher to taught is such

a dynamic one, partly because there is in what must be learned a highly important ethical layer, the teaching does not take place in a vacuum. Neither teacher nor novice will, in the normal course of events, withdraw into ascetic seclusion. It is while still active in the world's ordinary tasks that they pursue their most deeply-felt desire. One reason for this is that the moral alteration the disciple must undergo is not to be achieved while contemplating, in hair shirt and with busy scourge, the sins he has committed in the past. The Sufi way, here too, demands a refreshing directness; it is by altering his behaviour, by seeking to commit the good action, that the disciple changes the tone of his ethical being. There is therefore none of that distortion, almost preciosity, that at times seem to falsify the activities of monastery, *ashram* or hermitage; by not withdrawing from the world, the novice ensures that his development will be tough in texture and firmly rooted.

In the Market Place

The kind of withdrawal that must take place is not physical, but psychological. By being forced to re-examine his values, his conceptions and perceptions of the world, the whole systems of ideas that hitherto he has accepted as self-evident, the novice is levered out of his previous emotional and intellectual environment. It may have been one in which he felt secure, but that very security encouraged in him precisely the kind of automatic thinking and behaviour that made any new self-knowledge impossible. By learning to question, at deeper and deeper levels, the reasons for the actions he performs: and thus to understand what truly motivates him, who he really is, the disciple is slowly detached from the pointless, the uncreative or unworthy activities in which he may previously have spent much of his time. The process is slow, step by step; action by action, insight by insight, the aspirant must make his way forward.

218

There is no point in his heading, as though by some short cut, for the ultimate goal, for this presumes that he knows what it is, and that he knows where he is. He may know, like any reader of a book, what it is *called*, but to discover what it *is* he must experience it. To do so he must arrive at it by the route his teacher prescribes, a route that will see him throwing away the intellectual and emotional clutter of a lifetime, not through any effort of will, but because it becomes stage by stage, inevitable that he does so.

This cleansing process, as it might be called, is itself no more than a beginning, though it may take many years. As it continues, the teacher may prescribe certain techniques, rather as Rumi taught his Mowlavis the whirling dance, in order to induce meditative states in his disciple. *Sam'a*, the expression of religious emotion through song, music and movement, is a well-known element in Sufi practice — passion for the divine both induced and expressed, in the Sufi way, through action. As action, it both bursts through inhibition and avoids all chance of intellectualization. Of itself, however, it is neither mark nor method of those chosen to make their way towards perfection; it is a means to an end, selected for given individuals in a given situation by their preceptor. It may be practised to 'wear out' harmful emotion. At some point, the disciple may develop an ecstatic veneration for and eventually a feeling of identity with the teacher. He may then seem to lose any sense of the difference between the teacher and God: 'My Shams and my God', wrote Rumi, as we have seen. Yet the teacher, however revered, is never thought of as in himself a god. The essence that identified him with the deity is that of the divine, permeating all creatures and things. The developed individual is in direct contact with it; the disciple, identified with him, sees him as a channel through which to make a similar contact. Thus it is in that essence, by virtue of that essence, that teacher and disciple may have the sensation that they have become, in some indefinable way, united.

219

Happy the moment when we are seated in the palace, thou and I,
With two forms and with two figures but with one soul, thou and I.

Despite such feelings as those that Rumi had for Shamsuddin, the teacher is by his nature transient, operating upon the disciple for the necessary length of time, then moving on. What he represents is permanent in the disciple and remains with him, often personified in the remembered shape of the teacher. But the teacher himself is neither permanent nor immortal. He is not an idol to be worshipped, but truly exists, to state it once again, only in action. Indeed, were he venerated as and for himself, he might be said to have failed in his task, for there is a limit to the dynamism possible in such a relationship. At some moment there would have to be an end to the disciple's development, since it would be implicit in his standing with such a teacher that he could not, perhaps even must not, aspire to the latter's level. Yet Sufism teaches that the process, not the person who inducts one in it, is primary, and that its end is self-perfection. Perfection, after all, is absolute; in this religious context, it implies, too, that one may be directly filled with a sense of the Absolute. At that level, hierarchy vanishes, and erstwhile teacher and erstwhile taught become indistinguishable. 'The teacher as God' is thus a kind of shorthand sifting out the essence of this final stage in the disciple's progress *as disciple*.

The process of Sufi learning has of course been formally charted, in a general sense, despite its extreme fluidity in the particular; its stages have been named and its goals, as far as is possible, defined. For example, the merging of the disciple with this teacher, the annihilation of the self in the person of the master, the guide, is called *fana-fi-sheikh*. (*Sheikh, pir* or *murshid* are names given to the teacher; the disciple is the *murid*.) When the novice begins to attain true knowledge, in the sense of his mind's illumination, he enters the stage called *marifah*, knowledge. But when he not merely knows but realizes

220

the truth, when he is filled with an awareness of the Absolute beyond anything that can be apprehended by the unaided intellect, he is taken to have entered the stage called *haqiqah*, Truth. This culminates in *fana-fi-lah*, the annihilation of the self in the Absolute, the experience of unity that is finally what gives such blazing significance to the Sufi path.

Yet, as has been mentioned, there is a stage even beyond this. There is a story, told by Rumi and now famous, of a merchant who on the eve of his departure for India on business asked his parrot what gift she would like him to bring back for her from her native land. 'All I ask', said the parrot, 'is that when you see other parrots there, you tell them that a parrot who longs for freedom lies in your cage'. The merchant did as she had requested. One of the Indian birds, on hearing what he had to say, trembled in a terrifying fashion and fell down dead. The merchant assumed that this must have been a relation of his own bird. It was with some reluctance, therefore, that when he returned home he told his parrot what had happened. She immediately trembled in a terrifying fashion and fell down dead. Lamenting his loss, the merchant took the parrot from the cage, only to see her leap from his hand and fly into the nearest tree. From the safety of a high branch the parrot explained, 'By her action the other parrot told me that I would have to die myself before I would be released and so gain my freedom'. It is directly, so this story seems to say, that relevant truths are passed from those who know to those who seek, and their effect is to persuade one that freedom lies on the far side of annihilation.

This final state too has a name: it is called *baqa*, which means 'abiding' or 'continuance'. It is in that condition that a person appears to those round about to have achieved perfection. Complete self-knowledge and constant access to the certainties only glimpsed in ecstasy have released him from all ordinary doubts and trammels. He is fully conscious, conscious of himself and of his unbreakable connection with the cosmic unity that,

221

as it were, flows through him. He is both self and non-self, having made himself aware of his total state, of the way that he manifests in a unique manner, his own manner, the cosmic generality.

Professor Arasteh writes, 'Whosoever achieves this state becomes a "perfect man", who relies on consciousness and is ruled by reason. Aided by intuition the perfect man functions as a totality with spontaneity and expressiveness. Instead of studying life from afar, he is life itself. In this state, indescribable and characterized by silence, the individual is now everything and nothing: everything in the sense that he is united with all, nothing in the sense that there is nothing whose detachment or loss may become a source of grief to him. He embraces all of life; he is beyond good and bad. Consciousness, reason and intuition — with such qualities a person moves among ordinary men like a creature out of myth. He sees everything as it is, and has as a result no need of rules. He feels a direct involvement with every human being, every creature, and has as a result no need of laws. He is complete, and in a way that has no necessity to sustain itself by solitary contemplation. He has taken a vast journey, inward into himself, outward into the universe, and it has brought him back, utterly changed, to work and spread the invisible emanations of his truth in the same world that he left. Once he languished in its carefully baited traps; now he can turn to the endless task of liberating others'.

6/ii.
Sufi Studies Today
William Foster

Students of movements in the Near and Middle East have, during the past three decades, turned up a wholly unexpected wealth of information on Sufism and the Sufis. This has originated with personal investigations by

222

travellers and residents in the area, with a re-examination of traditional Sufic materials, and with an apparent desire by Sufis themselves to make available hitherto restricted information about their beliefs, practices and working structures.

Two major results will emerge from this new information: almost all dictionary and encyclopaedia entries will have to be changed; and the emotionally-religious aura which has been allowed to surround the Sufis will be lifted.

The background of Sufism for the average Western student until the recent discoveries and revelations may be said to have been copies, in the first place, from Moslem divines' writings. Anxious to identify the undoubted prestige of Sufi thinkers with their own view of the Islamic heritage, they have emphasized the points of resemblance (often superficial) between Sufi and Islamic theological thought, and conveniently ignored or played down the areas of Sufic thought and action which do not seem to accord with the social and psychological norms of their part of traditionalistic society. Many quasi-Sufic organizations, dating from the Middle Ages until today, may be said to have been 'taken over' by theologians in the Middle East. As a result such organizations serve mainly to condition applicants to the acceptance of Islam. In the second place, the Sufis' own efforts to represent themselves as wholly compatible in their thinking with Moslem tradition has confused the issue and given the Eastern and Western students alike the opportunity to identify Sufism with Islam.

In Victorian times, an additional complication arose, and it is one which is amply represented in the literature of the time, and one whose ghost is still with us. This was the rise of the theory that the Sufic ideas and activities which could not be explained by reference to Moslem scripture or tradition and some of which were even seen to be opposed to these, must be regarded as fragments of shamanism, or as a reaction of the Persians against the Semitic thought-patterns of the Arabs. As in almost every facile assumption of this kind, it was found possible to produce, by selective extracts, 'evidence' of these influences which are found upon examination to be nothing more than 'proof by selected instances'. The same goes for the energetic attempts to relate Sufism to various forms of Indian philosophy. This reached its apogee of absurdity when Orientalists were to be found using Sufi-influenced Hindu theories to prove the Indian 'origin' of Sufism.

Even in more modern times, Sufism has not had an easy passage in its examination by committed scholars and others who seek to relate it to, or judge it by, some personal preoccupation of their own. Hence followers of Christian, Zoroastrian, Hindu, Theosophical and other cults have, from time to time, all tried to find affinities, resemblances, even origins for Sufism in their own sanctions. Sometimes they have attempted the reverse: trying to show the roots of their own beliefs to be in Sufism. Most of such efforts have failed: but they have still left their mark on the general stock of literature on the subject: to the extent that any objective student of Sufism in Eastern or Western literature may be forgiven for finding himself excessively confused by what he reads. Before he can begin to understand the materials, he has to have a thorough background of the bias of the writers whose works are pieces of polemic just as much as sources of information.

Watered-down forms of Sufism, centred around an Eastern exponent or two visiting or residing in the West, have added their quota of confusion and cultishness, which has often been coloured by the sectarian and universalist tendencies which are so often to be seen as alternating factors in almost all matters which appertain to the human mind.

And yet, in spite of it all, the sheer accumulation of information about the Sufis and their work has made it possible to steer a course through these subjectivities.

When such a course has been steered, Sufism and the individualities of the Sufi exponents emerge as something

224

very different from what they are represented to be. Further, and perhaps more significant, Sufism stands revealed as a series of systems which have only the slightest resemblance to the 'mystical', 'religious', 'idealistic', 'cultish' organizations with which we tend automatically to bracket it.

It is, in short, something on its own. It is a different kind of entity from the inevitable cults with which we are familiar. Because of this, and because of its intrinsic interest, it may well have something to contribute which could be salutary to our thinking patterns. Certainly it is to be welcomed because of its very 'difference'.

But what is it? It is compatible with Islam, though it is claimed by some to have preceded Islam. Moslems and Christians alike have called it a form of Christianity. But Christ is not its central figure. Sufis themselves claim that it is something of which religion is a misguided variety, and a diluted one at that.

Sufism is a study. It is centred around collections of people, includes ideas and practices, aims at some kind of a 'perfectioning' of man.

Here is a literary form of this 'deliberate evolution' theory, from the thirteenth-century *Couplets of Inner Meaning*, by Jalaluddin Rumi, one of the greatest Sufis:

'He came, at first, into the inert world, and from minerality developed into the realm of vegetation. Years he lived thus. Then he passed into an animal state, bereft of memory of his having been vegetable. Except for his attraction to Spring and flowers. This was like the innate desire of the infant for the mother's breast. Or the affinity of disciples for an illustrious Guide. Their attraction originates with that shadow. When the shadow is no more, they know the cause of attachment to the Teacher. . .

'From realm to realm man went, reaching his present reasoning, knowledgeable, robust state — forgetting earlier forms of intelligence.

'So, too, shall he pass beyond the current form of perception. . . There are a thousand other forms of Mind. . . Because of necessity, man acquires organs. So,

225

necessitous one, increase your need. . .'*

In order to develop organs of perception, Sufis have to undergo training. But this is as far as the resemblance with other systems goes, because Sufi teaching, poetry, literature, seemingly having discovered the effects of 'conditioning' long before I. P. Pavlov, claims to be dedicated to preventing the establishment of conditioned reflexes (habit-patterns) in man.

Our mental set may be responsible for making it difficult for us to conceive how this could be done. But the Sufis are insistent upon it, apart from those who have developed their organizations into indoctrination systems, and which by reference to Sufi classics cannot genuinely be called Sufic at all.

Sufis have been bracketed together with Mystics of various persuasions, as a matter of convenience, by almost all observers. This is undoubtedly because they speak of transcendental experiences, ecstasy, discipleship and religious formulation.

But examination of Sufi groups and literature shows that Sufic organization, teaching and personalities alike carry on a far wider series of activities than those which we would normally recognize as of a 'mystical' type.

There seems to be some method of procedure, known to the Sufi teacher, which commands what kind of training and study an individual and/or a group should follow. And, in addition, that procedure will often be found to have no easily seen relationship with mystical or religious thinking.

An analysis of the themes used by Sufi classical authors and exegetists of the past thousand years shows that each preceptor will instruct his pupils in a manner which seems to be chosen with some kind of regard for the natures of the disciples: not from the standpoint that

---

*The London University Zoologist W. Tschernezky showed the inadequacy of the 'environmental' theory of evolution, and cited examples of 'deliberate' evolution, supporting Sufi claims of 700 years before, by his article in the *New Scientist*, 22 August, 1968 (*Dolphins and the Mind of Man*).

226

the individuals are to go through a standard ceremony or course of study. It is precisely this 'strangeness' of approach which baffles the systematic mind. All the questions which we are asking become invalidated when we say, for instance:

'What is your system?' — if the system is peculiar to the community in question; or,

'Where did you get this knowledge?' — if the source is said by the teacher to be unimportant, or directly acquired from another source in another modality of thought.

When the foremost authority on Sufism, Idries Shah, published a book (*The Sufis*, Doubleday, N.Y., 1964) and revealed the Sufi origins and usage of the Mulla Nasrudin stories, specialists in Sufism, admittedly outsiders, replied that this was not so. And yet, three years later a Westerner (Raoul Simac, *Hibbert Journal*, (London) Spring, 1967) recorded a sojourn with a Pakistan Naqshbandi (founded 14th century) group which used nothing else but this figure in their studies. The appearance of this piece in a distinguished religious journal clinched Shah's point: but supposing Simac had not been there, or had not published?

This information problem besets most students of Sufism. I have been able to find hardly a publishing student of Sufism who is an initiated Sufi, or who has not been inducted into some very derivative or narrowed group which would not have been regarded by the classical masters as Sufi-inspired at all.

Some of the most profound Sufi teaching, though translated into Western languages, is so concealed in its inner significance that nobody understands more than a distorted part of it. This is surely true of Omar Khayyam, translated by Edward Fitzgerald. Professor Robert Graves and Agha Omar Ali-Shah have completed (*Rubaiyyat*, London, 1967, Cassell & Co.) a completely new translation of the Quatrains, with a Sufic interpretation.

Sufi thought and activity is comparatively hard to

227

assess, and is only slowly becoming understood, because of the fact that the figures known to researchers, the literature which is avowedly Sufic, the organizations carrying the label, are claimed by Sufis themselves as representing only a small part of the total Sufi activity. Sufis are not secret: their work tends to be private, or iceberg-like because they believe that 'for every ounce which is visible there must be a ton which is active, but not perceived by the ordinary man'.

We, especially in the West, are not accustomed to dealing with things which cannot be trotted out in front of us for instant examination. And yet it could easily be claimed that this attitude is itself based upon a presumption: 'Nothing which cannot be measured by my tools, preferably here and now, can possibly be of any account'.

Typical of the Sufis' claims about their work is this poem, translated in 1962 by a member of the American University of Beirut from Al-Ghazzali (A.D. 1058–1111):

'Many are the roads, but truth is a single path. And those who tread this way are few. They pass unrecognized, their goal unknown, while slowly and steadily they press along. Men do not know for what they were created, and most of them fail to see the path of truth'.

But there are manifestations of Sufism available for study which are becoming better known once the key is available. An example is Professor Rom Landau's work on the arabesque-designs. These existed for a thousand years at least before anyone bothered to look at them from the point of view that they might, as claimed, be special forms of diagram-teaching. In 1955 the American Academy of Asian Studies brought out a monograph on the arabesque. The establishment in the fourteenth century of a Sufi Order called the Designers (*Naqshbandia*) specialising in teaching-design stimulated no academic nor aesthetic interest outside its ranks until the American Academy took up the point six hundred years later! And this in spite of the fact that the Naqshbandi Orders of Sufis are among the most important in documented Sufi and Eastern history.

228

Sometimes there is too much imitation and too little understanding of Sufi materials. Because of its dramatic effect, and perhaps because the Russian mystagogue Gurdjieff made some play of contact with it, 'dervish dancing' of the Sufis found its way into the West as recently as the nineteen-sixties. But the supposed calisthenic and other effects of these exercises having been carefully prescribed for use only by special people and for limited purposes — not for attunement with the Infinite or creating excitement or calm — was forgotten.

In 1957 a translation of a 17th century Sufi's book was published in London, warning against the cultish or random use of 'whirling or turning'. This was before its introduction into Britain and America as something of a cultish fashion:

'The Khilwati have turned their ordained music and their obligatory motions, which their ancient founders prescribed for a sound purpose and which ought to be freely permitted to those worthy, into bait for the trap of imposture and a snare for disreputable fools'.*

While Sufi practices, probably torn from context, have been introduced in the West by mystical 'masters' rather following the pattern of the Hindu gurus who have abounded in the United States since the nineteenth century, it is only in certain instances that Sufism in the West has fallen into the trap of becoming a cult.

To be sure, the followers of this or that Sufi-inspired cult leader or that 'mystical master' trumpet their message as loud as possible. But there are increasing indications that Westerners studying or practising Sufism under more typical and genuine Sufis do not display the proselytizing or conversion-syndromes. This is evidenced by the way in which they write or speak of Sufism, and also by their use of Sufic materials in their everyday work.

Recent examples of Western personalities approving of

The Balance of Truth, by Katib Chelebi, translated by G. L. Lewis, London (Allen & Unwin), 1957, page 43f.

Sufism or influenced by it in some way which have been published include the novelist Doris Lessing; the actor ('Flint') James Coburn and his wife; the poet Ted Hughes; the late Secretary-General of the United Nations Dag Hammerskjöld; Robert Graves; the film producer and artist Richard Williams; the historian and orientalist John Hamilton; and the psychologist Erich Fromm.

Another important result of Western analysis of traditional documents has been the discovery that many of the bewildering cults, beliefs, pieces of literature and other unusual pieces generally supposed to be parts of Christianity, or of occultist society provenance, can be traced to Sufi origins. Hence Professor Asín Palacios has traced work by Teresa of Avila, John of the Cross and Dante to Sufi published originals; the sociologist Daraul has traced Rosicrucianism, much alchemy, and 'witchcraft' to Sufi groups; the Templars and Order of the Garter have been found to have irresistible analogies with Sufism; and much of the 'Hindu' thinking so prized by many Westerners has been shown to be a late development of imported Sufi ideas into India and 'Hinduised' by medieval Indian gurus.

The very novelty and abundance of the newly-discovered Sufi activity in the heritage of the Judeo-Christian, Hindu and Moslem traditions, coming into prominence within a comparatively short space of time has had a predictable, though nonetheless unnecessary, reaction. Many people are unable to adjust themselves sufficiently quickly to the news that Dante and the Blessed Ramón Lull copied Sufi literature, that Najmuddin Kubra anticipated St Francis in an alarming variety of details, that Sufi influence underlay national, social, literary and philosophical movements in the East and West which had until recently appeared to be of totally varying origins. The more paranoid observers either cannot stomach this new flood of information, or regard it as a manifestation of some sort of Sufi hidden hand trying to assert a psychological ascendancy.

230

Such reactions are as unnecessary as that of the synthesizers who are trying to relate Sufism to their established ways of thinking. The latter include authors of books on Sufism and occultism, on Sufism and Christianity, on Sufism and poetry, and so on.

The main defect in current scholarship when it comes to its power of evaluation of Sufism is that traditional intellectualism requires that the material studied shall be explicable. 'Mandarinism' (which operates on a basis comparable to 'Which category familiar to us does this material fall into?') has already been discarded by science. No scientific researcher in existence will say: 'What kind of electricity am I studying?' without first making sure that he is working with electricity . . .

Sufism, when its materials are assembled without prejudice, shows that it has features which seem to place it within the purview of philosophy, but also some features which belong, apparently, to mysticism. At the same time, it is partly manifested in the forms of literature, and literary men tend to study it from this point of view, ignoring almost all others. When Sufic organizations are found which recall to the mind of the medievalist the monastic formulations of the Middle Ages, the treatment of the materials unearthed will tend to be comparative with monkish orders known in the West.

Among the difficulties encountered in studying Sufism is the fact that, as soon as one tries to analyse a Sufi organization's rituals, ideas, manner of proceeding, hierarchy, literature and the rest, one finds that, although complete in itself as a teaching-system, such an organization differs considerably from another — equally important — Sufi body in another place, belonging to another culture, or operating at another time.

This difficulty, if we read what Sufis have to say about it, becomes logically resolved. According to Sufis, their methods of teaching must vary in accordance with the 'individuality' of the teacher, the time, the place and the students. While such an idea may recommend itself to logic (if one grants that Sufism has the knowledge to

231

provide peculiarly apposite formulations) it is not one which forms a part of our Western intellectual tradition. Consequently whilst an electronic computer might be expected to take such a conception in its stride, through lack of culturally-conditioned preconceptions, most of us, as largely Western-trained thinkers (academics or otherwise) are, frankly, incapable of making the psychological adjustment of facing this contention. It has, in short, no parallel in our thought-systems.

The Sufi answer is that this is precisely the thought-system which we have to learn in order to be able to approach Sufism.

Until 'Sufic' thinking-training machines are developed, the traditional method of learning this process remains unsuperseded: the study, with a Sufi teacher, of his thoughts, ways of acting, projects and products.

Recent research and publications on Sufis and Sufism seem to be a particularly useful way of approaching the study of what seems to be an almost totally unfamiliar set of ideas. The alternative is to study with a Sufi exponent, and the literature (apart from that emanating from popularized and diluted 'cultish' recruitment bodies passing as Sufis) tells us that it is hard to find Sufi teachers in the main line of the tradition.

Even if one did find such an exemplar, the indications are that the majority of students would approach him in an uncritical frame of mind, being in psychological dependency need, or else from the mechanical-assumption point of view, trying to relate his instruction to our own preconceptions, and fragmenting it in the process.

6/iii.
Sufi Studies: East and West
A Review by Leonard Lewin, Ph.D.

The word *Sufi* is a comparatively new one for most Westerners. Except for certain scholars, who specialized in research on Eastern mystical sects, few people were likely, until quite recently, to have encountered Sufism in any recognizable form; though writers like Nicholson[1] and Arberry[2] have attempted for some time to present a Western-oriented interpretation. The present book*, a symposium which has been produced in honour of Idries Shah's services to Sufi studies by twenty-four internationally known contributors, also marks the seven hundredth anniversary of the death of the renowned Sufi, Jalaluddin Rumi. But if this book should be read solely as an accolade to Shah, much of immense practical value and importance in this volume would be lost.

The functional key is given in the Foreword by Sir Edwin Chapman-Andrews's version of a Nasrudin story;[3] and it seems sufficiently important to warrant its being quoted here in full.

> 'From the pulpit one day, Nasreddin asked his congregation: "Do you know what I am going to preach about?"
>
> "No", they replied.
>
> "In that case", he said, "it would take too long to explain". And he went home.
>
> Next day he again ascended the pulpit and asked the same question.
>
> "Yes", the people replied, determined to put him on the spot.
>
> "In that case", said Nasreddin, "there is no need for me to say more". And he went home.

Sufi Studies: East and West, L. F. Rushbrook Williams (Ed.), Dutton, New York, 1973.

233

Yet again the following day he put the same question: "Do you know what I am going to preach about?"

But now the congregation were ready to corner him. "Some of us do and some of us don't", they answered.

"In that case", said Nasreddin, "let those who know tell those who don't".'

In this story we see the higher faculties of the mind, represented by Nasrudin,[4] trying to educate the congregation of ideas, thoughts, and attitudes that constitute the basis of our ordinary thinking and modes of everyday operation. But Nasrudin's manoeuvres are too subtle to let him get cornered in argument. His purpose is to teach wisdom to humanity, and he does this indirectly, first by inducing a situation wherein his teaching is requested, and then, by leading his audience on, he provokes a situation wherein they begin to learn how to learn. The approach is, of necessity, of this indirect character because '. . .it would take too long to expalin' — an indication that the material does not lend itself to the customary mode of linear exposition. Eventually the congregation is led into a situation of teaching itself, those knowing, or thinking that they know more, trying to teach the others. In this process they learn something about teaching, and their own understanding, or lack of it, and so, gradually, the knowledge is built up by a sort of 'across-the-board' activity in which all participate in diverse ways. It takes all sorts for this method to function correctly, including, no doubt, a few who are prone to misinterpret.[5] From all these teaching-learning interactions the Sufi knowledge develops. The process having been activated, the yeast has started to work, as it were, and now the dough is beginning to rise in preparation for the eventual baking of the loaf.[6]

The many and varied contributions in the present book can be viewed in this light — twenty-four authors doing their best to teach us what they know. If some appear to be more adept or knowledgeable than others, if some appear as if they might be life-long students of Sufism whilst others seem relatively new to the subject,

234

this is the nature of the mix. Should the reader already be somewhat familiar with the Sufi Teaching Story, and accustomed to trying to seek deeper levels of meaning therein, he may feel a little impatient with a contributor whose piece seems only to depict the more superficial or moralistic content of these tales: but this is his contribution, and there will be those for whom this level is entirely apposite. One might even experience the awakening of a desire to provide an improved interpretation.[7] The essence of the total learning situation is beginning to bubble up before our eyes, and we should try to see the nature of the whole, in its entirety.

The many points of view are indeed diverse. One contributor sees Sufism as a branch of Islam, whilst a second discourses on the psychology of human learning and creativity. A third explains at great length the importance of Shah's lineage, and the great accomplishments and dedication to be expected from an individual with such a tradition behind him. A fourth indicates the importance of Sufism to Western cultural development, whilst a fifth is not even sure if Shah is a Sufi; and much, much more.

Who, then, are these various authors, and what qualifications do they have to lend veracity to their different versions? Ten pages of an appendix are devoted to this question; and it is apparent that, in a sense, we can see that the 'big guns' have been brought out. Every one of these contributors is an outstanding individual, versed in one or more areas of scholarship, diplomacy, teaching, governmental service, consultation, cultural relations, poetry, literature, or historical research; most are well-known writers, some with many internationally recognized books to their credit. They are from many parts of the world, with the majority from Eastern countries, though often with Western university degrees. A much larger assemblage is given acknowledgement for their help at the beginning of the book, and again about three-quarters of them have Eastern names. One gathers, if only indirectly, that important personages of Eastern

235

Sufi groupings are represented here; the significance must be that their support for Shah is implicit in this use of their names and, for what it is worth to those who need this reassurance, the message is that Shah's Sufic contributions are indeed authentic, and his position in the Sufic exposition of the present time is thereby acknowledged.

This support is indeed not irrelevant, because Sufism, for so long most at home in an Eastern setting, is now being expounded also for Western ears, and the Westerner has little to guide him on the question of authenticity. Might not Shah be an Eastern 'drop-out', someone who couldn't quite make it in his own homeland, setting himself up as some sort of guru of a new sect to be launched on Western soil for the seduction of the twentieth-century gullible? The overwhelming support for Shah from scholars and others in both the East and the West tells a sharply different story; and Shah himself has come out most strongly against the whole question of importation of gurus to the West, and the rather ridiculous cults that are growing up around them. This is not the Sufi method, we gather, which has a much more practical and urgent task to achieve world-wide, but particularly in the West, where certain ideas have for too long been under-represented in our culture. If all this is so, one might ask, why the eulogies in praise of Shah? In his own writings he certainly makes it very clear that he eschews this sort of thing, yet here writer after writer, each in his own way, introduces words of praise and tribute for Shah's scholarship, successes, achievements, books, methods, and so on. If genuine scholarship and achievement have little need of this, may it not be that, on this occasion, the tribute paid is not only to Shah personally but, particularly, to the ideas and to the tradition he represents? A pointer, in fact, to the circumstance that, whether we know it or not, we are on the threshold of one of those historically rare public outpourings of the Sufi knowledge, with Shah's functional position as fountain-head hereby formally

236

acknowledged and recorded.

What are the contributors of this book trying to tell us about Sufism? It is not easy at first to gain a coherent picture; the attention may initially be attracted only to relative superficialities. Should, let us say, a strange and elephantine creature begin to emerge from the darkness of the jungle, our attention may be caught at first by such irrelevancies as the mud or other debris associated with its estwhile environment, still clinging to its skin. This is not to be taken as a sensible measure of its real nature, and it may take time and effort for an understanding of its true character to come through.

In a piece entitled 'Contradictions'[8] the seeming opposition within Sufi material is described in the following terms:

'An interchange between a Sufi and an enquirer:

"Which statement should one choose if two Sufi sayings contradict each other?"

"They only contradict one another if viewed separately. If you clap your hands and observe only the movement of the hands, they appear to oppose one another. You have not seen what is happening.

"The purpose of the 'opposition' of the palms was, of course, to produce the handclap".'

It is apparent that this book is, in many respects, a sort of multiple handclap. Shah in a BBC radio interview said, 'Sufism is, in fact, not a mystical system, not a religion, but a body of knowledge'.[9] On both this, and other aspects, too, the various contributors seem not to be in agreement. One says that Sufism is the basis of Islam; another that it is a heterodox Islamic cult; another that it is akin to Christian mysticism; another, that it is an educational and psychological body of knowledge; another that visible Sufi sects are, as it were, the rejects, run by those who failed to make the grade; and much else. It is this very diversity of opinion that is of importance for our present considerations. Like the blind ones and the elephant[10] each is perceiving only a part, is misinterpreting it, and also mistaking it for the whole. If

237

we listen to *all* the partial descriptions we may begin to see the whole taking shape. It is not a question of whether this account or that is right or wrong, so much as that here is the best this or that writer can do to explain how he sees the matter. The accounts at this stage are necessarily partial, but taken together they begin to reveal the nature of the process.

On the nature of Sufism itself we gather that, *in principle*, it cannot be understood by any attempts at systematic analysis, because it underlies, or precedes, all systems of thought; it will not, therefore, yield to conventional methods of investigation. Sufism is a coherent whole, a *Gestalt*, and requires directed effort, work, and a great sincerity to understand. Its manifestations are subtle, and cannot be perceived by a crude approach. It is a body of knowledge grounded in experience, and has deeper meanings that are unlikely to be apparent on first contact. For the same reason its methods of operation cannot be comprehended from without. Only Sufis, i.e., those participating in an authentic course of Sufi studies, and experienced at sufficient depth, can validly claim to recognize what is Sufism, or who are genuine Sufis. All other attempts are but expressions of opinions or personal prejudices, and of no lasting value or significance, though they may tell us something about the person expressing these opinions. This, say the Sufis, goes particularly for many of the academic researchers of the subject, who have concentrated on the visible externals of what, in many cases, are mere vestiges of once authentic schools, the record of past method.[11] As an example, Shah has indicated that the word *Sufi* has a psycho-onomatopoeic origin[12]; yet one after another of the contributors to the book, and many others also, have spent time and effort trying to analyse its etymology and to derive it from such forms as *suf* (wool), from the Greek *sophia* (wisdom) and so on.

Sufism is universal and timeless in its appeal, though the local form taken varies, being adapted to work within the local culture and mental set. Hence, quite different

238

external formulations have often not been recognized by some scholars as stemming from the same ultimate source. A corollary to this is the (mistaken) attempt to use an outdated formulation designed for peoples of another culture and another period and to try to apply it to a present-day situation. In contrast, Shah's formulations are specifically adapted to Western twentieth-century ideas and methods, and this accounts for much of his success in generating support and understanding for his goals.

Sufism is, above all, a practical system. Many great men, especially in the East, are known to have been Sufis. Their ranks include scientists, philosophers, religious teachers, artists, poets, heads of government, military commanders. Sufism encourages worldly excellence, in part as a mark of achievement, and its exponents have always been exemplars in this, encouraging self-learning and high-mindedness in their disciples. Many famous Sufis have been scholars with an international or trans-cultural outlook. Their discoveries in science, not necessarily made by methods which today we call 'scientific' (and which are, therefore, suspect in some quarters), have in many cases, predated modern discoveries by many centuries. We could mention here the anticipation of Pavlov's findings on conditioning, long known to Sufi psychology, and Rumi's anticipation of Darwin's evolutionary theory, if not in zoological detail, then certainly in terms which pay particular attention also to man's psychological development, which runs parallel to his biological and behavioural evolution. (For a note on the anticipation by 900 years of Freud's methods of interpreting symbols, and of the Sufi ancients' knowledge of Jung's Archetypal theory, see Shah's comments in *The Way of the Sufi*, p.35.)

The force of psychological evolution, according to the Sufis, is love. Not love as commonly understood, which is a feeling projected onto secondary phenomena, but a primary force, akin to a profound yearning for oneness or unity. When this advanced development state of Unity is attained, the distinction between 'I' and 'thou' is dissolved, and the condition is called 'ecstasy' (standing outside oneself). This is to be viewed as the attainment of a very profound and significant developmental condition, and not just a vague, wonderful, blissful feeling, a deteriorated meaning often given to this word. The would-be Sufi's aim is the achievement of this state through the renunciation of the conditioned, culturally-determined self. Man's psychological evolution is seen as a journey from an original state of unity, through a separation, to a yearning for oneness, and a return to unity through the 'death' of the conditioned self and a spiritual rebirth. In one way or another, all the world's religions proclaim this message. In the book some examples of traditional Eastern methods are given, and though they do not seem to bear too closely on current Western conditions there may be much here which will be seen to convey a modern equivalent.

Once this initial evolutionary threshold is passed, the Sufi's further development continues. Sufi communities are claimed to be advanced practitioners of telepathy, something that they say underlies the vital support and sustenance of the entire human race. If this claim sounds a little quaint to some ears, it might, nevertheless, be just as well if we began to take it seriously and quite literally. It is certainly a far cry from the card-guessing experiments of many of today's scientific investigations; and it is in an area where, *par excellence*, the material is suited to internal rather than external investigative methods — and this is, after all, the Sufi's home ground.

Sufism involves a higher working of the mind, the attainment of which involves discipline and guidance, and can be attained only in accordance with the disciple's merit and earning of it. The finer qualities are 'caught', rather than taught in any academic sense. Sufism is a practical wisdom based on a whole spectrum of experiences, and the essence of these is encoded in the so-called Teaching Stories. These are not published merely for entertainment purposes, or for inculcating morals, but are highly ingenious technical devices for the purpose of Sufi teaching. The teaching books themselves are designed as a whole for evoking special effects and responses; and perhaps *The Book of the Book* (London: Octagon Press, 1969) is the most visible example, the story itself predicting the entire range of possible responses from different types of readers.

The stories are designed to help the mind's orientation. Their use is effective, and people *are* able to relate to them, because they do indeed enshrine an inner Truth: they embody reality, not a fiction. Thus Sufism can operate as an evocative force via a correct use of these stories. As an example, the wit of the Sufic figure Mulla Nasrudin both helps to preserve the stories, through their retelling, and assists their inner truth to penetrate the thick, outer, culturally-conditioned mental layers. But the Sufi secrets are revealed only by a correct working with the material, and the would-be seeker must relate to it with an attitude of humility, service, love, and with good deeds, aspiration to goodness and a contemplation of the divine. Ultimately, when the state of ecstasy appears, it is by divine Grace. (The religious words that appear here and elsewhere are used as technical terms, and do not convey the more conventional meanings. A consideration of the relationship between some of them is given in Ghazzali's 'Practical Processes in Sufism'.)[13] But the demise of the conditioned self is *inevitable*; either when the body dies, or at some earlier time if the individual is able to achieve the understanding that will enable him to sacrifice it on the altar of Higher Knowledge. In the latter event the state of Union is attained, and the individual's essence is ensured a condition of permanence. It is this that the would-be Sufi strives for while he still lives. Since we cannot know, in fact, whether we will be alive from one moment to the next, a note of special urgency is struck, and several of the book's contributors attest to this.

The world's current need for the Sufi knowledge is stressed again and again by different writers, and this for

241

both Eastern and Western cultures. In the past, European culture has derived much benefit from its contact with the East, especially via Spain in the Middle Ages. Now East and West are in urgent need of understanding each other's culture and ideas, and of awakening to the reality of the world situation, of which they are a part. Sufism, which has been at home particularly in the Middle East during much of the past thousand years, has not always been understood there. It is not an intrinsically Eastern doctrine, for its potential application is world-wide. But it is particularly in Western culture that certain ideas have been inadequately represented, and the West is now ripe for, and, in fact, is in most urgent need of, these ideas.

Sufism is a highly sophisticated integrator, well adapted to the needs of an advanced society. It is, above all, a practical system, and the timeliness of its appearance now in the West is matched by its current format of presentation, which conforms with modern Western thinking.

What, then, is defective with modern Western culture, that it should be in need of such assistance? Basically it is overly materialistic and spiritually weakened. Despite great material and scientific progress, hypocrisy and intolerance are rife, and the deadly failings of greed and vanity are built into the very structure of society. Education in the West is, with some exceptions, too fact-oriented, and is failing to produce men and women of adequate quality. In fact, Western psychology, starting with Freud, has misunderstood the nature of man, the concentration having been on man's similarities to the animals, not on his creativity, which is what distinguishes him from them. (However, Jung's concepts are perhaps a little closer to the thrust of Sufi ideas: bringing the collective unconscious into public consciousness might be one way of trying to describe the present stage of psychic evolution.) But with present materialist trends unchecked, civilization itself is threatened, and Sufism as a counterbalance to the damage stemming from greed and worldly vanity is needed. And the West, particularly, is now ripe for these ideas.

The practical side of Sufism has tended to go unnoticed by many academic scholars, who have so often concentrated their attention on Sufi mystical cults, whose visible manifestations are more closely described as a deterioration of, or misrepresentation of, Sufism. The practical aspect of Sufism is perhaps worth emphasizing, since the Sufis themselves say that knowledge for its own sake is useless,[14] and that attempts at the ordinary, academic transmission of Sufi knowledge subject it to continuous deformation and degradation. Hence the recurrent renewals in history of the Sufi teachings.

The dangers of facile assumptions and hidden bias are stressed again and again by different contributors in the book. Many of the Mulla Nasrudin stories show the Mulla in a situation dominated by false assumptions and defective logic. Sometimes these pieces appear extraordinarily amusing — a sure sign that the reader himself is subject to the operation of the self-same flaws, though he might be quite unaware of when they are actually operating in his own life. 'Cheese for Choice'[15] is an excellent example of a story which shows how a 'rational' decision may be nothing of the sort, but a consequence of the working of selective factors operating outside the normal range of consciousness. Another highly amusing example of defective logic based on false assumptions is 'The Magic Bag',[16] where the interpretation of a certain situation, obvious to an outside observer, has become inverted. People in general seek from each other attention and support for their opinions, not truth, which, unless presented extremely gently and with compassion and understanding, may offend and cause pain. The operation of stories like this one can sometimes bypass the defences in a constructive way, and enable the individual to begin to perceive the dishonest workings of his own mind: a small first step, but a necessary one, toward the substantial task of dismantling the distorted mental structures of the conditioned-self.

The individual responsible for the underlying support of the current world-wide emergence of Sufi ideas and methods of human development is Idries Shah. The appearance at the present time of a man of this calibre from the East is itself something that calls for comment. Born of a line of distinguished predecessors going back in unbroken succession to the Prophet Mohammed, the family moved closer to Western inspection through the recent career of Shah's father, the late Sirdar Ikbal Ali Shah. He was a man of international connections and achievements, who earned great respect for his scholarship, diplomacy, and cultural contributions to the life of many nations. A pedigree of this character is of great importance in the East, where it ensures acceptability in Islam; but in the West, particularly in individualistic, success-oriented America, this sort of thing often tends to be disregarded as of no real relevance. However, it does have several very practical consequences. In the first place it ensures for Shah access to people and places in the East, both religious and secular, which would not be accessible to many a Western scholar, no matter how distinguished. One tangible aspect of this is to be seen in Shah's early account of his travels in the Middle East.[17] Another consequence of the greatest importance is that the tradition of education and upbringing ensured by this lineage determines a degree of dedication and capacity for achievement of the very highest order, and Shah's life so far has been in fact a shining example of such high-minded dedication and practical accomplishments. His task, among other things, is to function as a bridge between Eastern and Western modes of thought. Whatever the superficial differences, their ideas are compatible at a fundamental level, and Shah, with his acceptability in the East assured, is well prepared for this position of mediation. To establish a corresponding bridgehead in the West he has researched historical and social material, taught in

244

universities, written over fifteen books concerned with social studies and Sufi teaching materials, set up a business based on electronics, and another on the manufacture of carpets. He has founded and is now Director of Studies of The Institute for Cultural Research, a learned society in Great Britain. He engages in the work of charitable institutions, and is a member of the Club of Rome. From a study of his writings it can be seen that he clearly understands with great depth and compassion, the nature of the human condition and human weaknesses, and knows how to present the essence of the situation, encoded in narrative form, in Teaching Stories whose operation evokes powerful inner capacities of response. His teaching books have been widely accepted as authoritative Sufi material, and particularly so in the East, where his methods have been likened to those of Al-Ghazzali. By putting Sufism into a modern context he is helping to fashion the modern mind through education and the development of a deep understanding of the human condition. Although Shah comes from the East his presentation here is geared to Western needs. Even so, his in-depth approach has not always been fully appreciated, and this in both East and West.

Shah is very much the generalist, shrewd and understanding. He makes full use of modern scientific ideas and achievements and of scientific discoveries, particularly in the social and behavioural fields, which form part of his presentations. He is not in any sense a 'guru', and he has made it abundantly clear that Sufi teachings are not promulgated in such a fashion. With respect to the promotion of certain Sufi practices today such as Dervish dances, so-called Sufi workshops, etc., whose sponsors lay claim to the use of the title Sufi, it is well to emphasize that Shah has no truck with such methods, claiming that they are but vestiges of outmoded and imported practices, not intended for, and not suitable for, current Western mentation. Neither is he concerned with monasticism or other forms of withdrawal from society; on the contrary, a constructive involvement in the local milieu is now the essence of Sufi developments.[18]

So we see two of Shah's roles; that of communicator and that of practitioner. What other features are there in evidence? Since he is taken, by several of the contributors, to be a Muslim, the question of the relation of Shah and Sufism to religion, and to Islam in particular, is inevitably raised. The East has been the cradle of most of the world's major religions, and it is claimed that Sufism has influenced them all at a fundamental level. There are many similarities, at least at the superficial level, between Martin Buber's *Tales of the Hasidim* and some of the Sufi Teaching Stories. One contributor also likens the latter to Christian parables, and sees an affinity of Sufism with Christian mysticism. There are, of course, many morals to be seen in the stories, and one contributor goes into this in some detail. Another sees Shah as using Sufism to restore vitality to both Islam and other religions. Yet as mentioned earlier Shah says, 'Sufism is, in fact . . . not a religion but a body of knowledge', and we gather that the appearance of religious terminology in Sufism represents a technical, not a religious usage.[19] Even so, the long association of Sufism with Islam is something which has been of great importance in the Middle East. If Sufism is now being projected in the West substantially devoid of this attachment, it says a lot for the versatility of Sufic methodology and techniques of transmission.

To the pious man, of whatever faith, the Sufis seem to be saying that the established religions are to be seen as interim vehicles for an attempt to present something of cosmic importance to mankind. In the twentieth century the authority of religious institutions has, in many places, begun to wane. Where this is so, civilization is in a real danger of collapse, and the very essence of human existence needs to be rekindled in the hearts of men. This is what the Sufis are attempting to do, within a religious framework when that is indicated, but in a non-religious one when this is appropriate. They are governed by neither format.

246

To the materialist, or to the scientist and to others, the message is the same, but may appear in different garb: something essential is being left out of the educational process and of our understanding of the universe. Its omission causes man's vanity and greed to gain ascendance. Hence there is a crisis of morals and of values. There is nothing in Sufism that in any way contradicts established findings achieved by the scientific method. But since, it is claimed, Sufism lies *behind all systemization*, science cannot approach Sufism in a constructive way by its conventional means. If it so tries it will find on the material plane, at most, concurrences, or what it takes to be blind-chance coincidences. Rather it is in the field of individual psychology that the two come closer together, and it is here that the subtleties of Sufism can blend with the domain of science. In his writings, Ornstein[20] discusses the physiological basis, in the functioning of the two hemispheres of the brain, for the two modalities of thought, the logical and intuitive, of the human mind. And it appears that it is at the intuitive level that the link with Sufism is closest. (This circumstance may provide a clue to the meaning of an assertion by one contributor that the Sufis are 'anti-rational'.) In any case, the parallelism between action at the rational level and action in the 'hidden dimension' of the Sufis' mode of operation, or between the two modes of thinking, linear and lateral, as expounded by Ornstein and by de Bono,[21] may be one of the many meanings contained in the story 'The Founding of a Tradition'[22] used by one of the contributors, Rushbrook Williams, to illustrate, among other concepts, the dichotomy of religious orthodoxy and heterodoxy. Commenting on the use of the Teaching Story he says, 'Perhaps one should simply try one out and see what it teaches.'[23] So we will try just that. This story runs as follows:

> 'Once upon a time there was a town composed of two parallel streets. A dervish passed through one street into the other, and as he reached the second one, the people there noticed that his eyes were streaming with tears.

"Someone had died in the other street!" one cried, and soon all the children in the neighbourhood had taken up the cry.

What had really happened was that the dervish had been peeling onions.

Within a short space of time the cry had reached the first street; and the adults of both streets were so distressed and fearful (for each community was related to the other) that they dared not make complete inquiries as to the cause of the furore.

A wise man tried to reason with the people of both streets, asking why they did not question each other. Too confused to know what he really meant, some said:

"For all we know there is a deadly plague in the other street".

This rumour, too, spread like wildfire, until each street's populace thought that the other was doomed.

When some measure of order was restored, it was only enough for the two communities to decide to emigrate to save themselves. Thus it was that, from different sides of the town, both streets entirely evacuated their people.

Now, centuries later, the town is still deserted; and not so far away are two villages. Each village has its own tradition of how it began as a settlement from a doomed town, through a fortunate flight, in remote times, from a nameless evil'.

The tradition being discussed in this description may well be the Sufi tradition itself, which, according to a number of accounts,[24] originated in relation to an unspecified disaster. Does the story throw some light on this? The two parallel streets in the town could refer to the two parallel modes of thinking associated with the two halves of the brain in man, at some earlier stage of his development. The dervish, representing a higher wisdom, was traversing from one region to the other, 'peeling onions'. This could refer to the exposure of successive mental layers as a prerequisite for higher understanding. A side-effect of this process was to cause the appearance of tears, mistaken as a sign of grief at a death; and a situation that was not a 'death' was mis-

248

interpreted as one. In the midst of this confusion a wise man — representing a higher capacity of the mind — appears and attempts to use reason, but to no avail. He does his best but triggers a further fear that the 'infection' will spread, with a consequent disintegration of the community; the inhabitants, becoming panic-stricken, abandon the more highly-structured habitation of the town to replace it by the simpler living in two separated villages. This description could refer to man's present fragmented mental condition. By drawing attention to the misinterpretation of an effect encountered on the journey to higher knowledge, i.e., of tears as grief at decease, this story may provide an indication of how to prepare oneself to cope correctly with a comparable situation that may come, the dissolution of the conditioned-self. (This probably is what is referred to as the 'White Death', the first of three specific experiences, technically termed 'deaths', through which the Sufi initiate must pass.)[25]

If this interpretation is not entirely fanciful, its generation, in the context of the preparation of the present commentary, may provide an instance of enlightenment emerging as a consequence of working with the material in the subject book. Should this appear too complicated and indirect a method of working to the average Western mind, accustomed only to a logical and sequential delineation of ideas, we can only remind it of the explanation contained in Nasrudin's comments in his opening sermon, '. . . it would take too long to explain.' We are dealing here with an extra, if hidden dimension; linear exposition cannot adequately cover the ground, and a different process is necessary if the multiple inter-relationships between what would otherwise be the fragments of a piecemeal approach are to be developed and understood.

As the following piece illustrates,[26] the higher faculties of the mind, through which the Sufi inner voice is heard, are latent within:

INNER SENSES

A certain Sufi was asked:

'Why is it that people have no inner senses?'

He said:

'O man of high promise! If they had *no* inner sense, they would not even appear to be people at all. When people lack inner sense, they behave in a completely destructive or totally passive manner. Being *aware* of inner sense is another matter'.

The Sufi process requires a certain minimum, a willingness to serve, in order to get started.[27] Part of the role of the teacher and the taught in this is depicted in the ensuing story:[28]

PLEASE DO THIS

A certain Sufi was asked:

'How can you teach people to move in certain directions when they do not know your language?'

He said:

'There is a story which illustrates this. A Sufi was in a foreign country where the people knew only one phrase of his "language". The phrase was: "Please do this".

'He had no time to teach them more of his language. So, whenever he needed anything done, he had to demonstrate it, saying, "Please do this".

'And in that way everything *was* done'.

It is in this way that the intuitive and deeper levels of the mind are awakened and brought into healthy operation. Unfortunately, modern Western educational methods, with but a few exceptions, do almost nothing to promote the development of the intuitive mode of thinking. If the Sufis can redress the balance we should be very grateful. And a sense of profound gratitude to Shah for his dedicated efforts in this direction is a part of the message to be culled from this extraordinary book. Not that he in any way needs this gratitude for himself; what is needed is that *we* should come to be able to feel it. For with this will come a deeper and fuller appreciation and understanding of what life is all about, and it is to this end that the current world-wide Sufic activity is directed.

FOOTNOTES

1. R. A. Nicholson, *The Idea of Personality in Sufism*. Cambridge, 1923.
2. A. J. Arberry, *Tales from the Masnavi*. London, 1961.
3. Idries Shah, 'The Sermon of Nasrudin', *The Exploits of the Incomparable Mulla Nasrudin*. New York, 1972, p.44.
4. The reasons for the use of the different spellings is explained in Appendix 1 of the book.
5. Idries Shah, 'Three Villages', *The Dermis Probe*. New York, 1972, p.126.
6. For an account of the symbology of the baking of the loaf, see 'The Parable of the Three Domains' in Idries Shah, *Tales of the Dervishes*. New York, 1970, p.125.
7. See, for example, 'The Time, the Place and the People', *ibid.*, p.121.
8. Idries Shah, 'Contradictions', *The Magic Monastery*. New York, 1972, p.100.
9. L. Lewin, Ed., *The Diffusion of Sufi Ideas in the West*. Boulder, 1972, p.17.
10. 'The Blind Ones and the Matter of the Elephant', *Tales of the Dervishes*, p.25.
11. Idries Shah, 'The High Knowledge', *Thinkers of the East*. Baltimore, 1972, p.153.
12. Idries Shah, *The Way of the Sufi*. New York, 1970, pp.13–16.
13. *Thinkers of the East*, p.180.
14. 'The Man who Wanted Knowledge', *The Dermis Probe*, pp.116–117.
15. *The Magic Monastery*, p.138.
16. *The Exploits of the Incomparable Mulla Nasrudin*, pp.58–59.
17. Idries Shah, *Destination Mecca*. London, 1957.
18. 'Yasavi', *The Way of the Sufi*, p.149.
19. See note 9.
20. Robert E. Ornstein, *The Psychology of Consciousness*. San Francisco, 1972.

21. Edward de Bono, *Lateral Thinking*. New York, 1970.
22. *Tales of the Dervishes*, p.70.
23. *Sufi Studies*, p.156.
24. Idries Shah, 'The Islanders', *The Sufis*. New York, 1971, pp.1–10.
25. *Sufi Studies*, p.421.
26. *The Magic Monastery*, p.166.
27. *Ibid.*, 'Service', p.161.
28. *Ibid.*, p.98.

6/iv.

Abshar Monastery

Julian Shaw

I rode my little *yabou* (pony) up the defile of the Hindu Kush where the Koh-i-Daman curved beyond Paghman. For centuries the bleak fortresses of the highland Saiyid Khans have guarded this entrance to Kafiristan, land of the Infidel, last of the patchwork of communities to be Islamized just after the Second Anglo-Afghan War.

My guide, Abdulmalik Khan, and I, in karacul caps and furlined *postins*, were hunting the elusive Dervish. After many a false start, for orthodox Islam of the Sunni rite suspects these ecstatics deeply and mere imitators abound, we had obtained an introduction to the Mir-Shaikh, presiding over what was described as a select band of ancient contemplatives settled on a hilltop. In the event, they were rather a surprise.

The waterfall of Nimtout, offset by a stern crenellated rampart where the Sulaiman spur had been cunningly used to cover a Ghaznavid fort, concealed the entrance to a cave. Once through this, we found ourselves walking our ponies on a mosaic paving of key pattern, perhaps a relic of Greek occupation some two and a half millenniums ago. We were in a part-natural, partly excavated interior patio, the lower half of a vast and mainly

252

subterraneous monastery complex. That it dated from the Buddhist era seemed certain from the 12 ft. standing statues, rock-carved, with painted haloes, which smiled down on their latest guests.

In the centre of the courtyard stood the Sardar Mir-Shaikh (head teacher) Asaf Beg, towering, turbaned, hook-nosed, with the grey eyes which may have been due to Mongol blood. He was enormously friendly and did in some elusive way remind me of an Eastern Orthodox archimandrite whom I once knew well. All around the court, which was roofed by the sky, were arches. We walked towards the largest of these, giving on to the Durbar Hall. Inside the sandalwood doors was a huge domed room, with immense carpets of Afghan and Turkestani type. The Sardar led us to the raised platform backed by an alcove, where cushions were placed, between two ranks of men, some sixty in all, telling beads.

They wore long shirts buttoned in the Cossack style. Some had shaven heads and the fair skin of the average Afghan hillman. All sat cross-legged in their baggy *shalwars*; one wore an Arab *mishla* cloak. We had walked straight into a ceremonial *muhadira*, a congregation of Derwishin.

There were about 200 permanent residents, occupied in crafts and certain pursuits not specified, the shaikh explained. They did not regard themselves as primarily religious but as the guardians and exponents of an ancient secret knowledge from which all human higher aspirations were ultimately derived in some unfamiliar way. They diffused this, it appeared, at intervals throughout the world, watched its progress and maintained their end of the activity, again not specified, as the impulse for which they were responsible worked its way through the generation.

They regarded as degenerate the Dervishes who gave public dancing or other displays, or who taught through the Moslem scriptures, because 'the essence of the reality is in the inner teaching, not the overcoat'.

253

Long white cloths were brought in and we sat on either side of the narrow strips like people from medieval Samarkand before Genghiz. Water for washing the hands was presented in curiously chased ewers which may have seen duty here in Harun el Raschid's day. Then we all fell to eating succulent lamb *pilao* from the finest china *zarfs*, platters so thin that they seemed like wafers. This was no ascetic community in the usual sense of the word. The People of the Inner Court have, it appeared, settlements in Persia and Iraq as well as in the Central Asian highlands. They do no preaching, but circulate their message in a special way unfamiliar to this age and not specified. When pressed, the Mir admitted to their organizing centres of study which often became usurped in course of time, becoming 'mere philosophical grinding-mills'. Upon them, regrettably but without doubt, there was a curse.

Abdulmalik Khan translated the main outlines of the cult, after the mass 'remembering', the Dervish *zikkr*, of the name of the absent head of the community, the Sarkar. This took the form of the phrase *Idd-rees Shaah!* — which was faithfully and literally translated for me as King Enoch. Mankind, it was stated, lacked a permanent thinking capacity. Mind, one might say, was an alternation. Humanity had to perfect itself by welding together, under rare and secret auspices, the scattered elements that it inherited, as well as imbibing certain secrets which took shape only rarely and under difficult conditions. Some of the methods were conventional study, hearing special music at carefully calculated times, manipulating an ancient mandala or design of high sanctity, carrying out physical exercises.

Since there must also be utter loyalty to a special kind of teacher who appeared but rarely and bore certain physical marks, the likelihood of this creed becoming a vogue outside its present home seemed remote.

I cannot report that the Mir showed any interest in recruiting either of his visitors; though Abdulmalik revered him because of his kinship with the Sarkar

254

(literally meaning 'Head of Work' and once applied to the East India Company in India as a term of respect); did not a certain settlement of sectarians in Badakhshan and the Pamirs call him their Imam? To them he was the incarnation of Ali, and therefore the true Caliph of all those who were waiting for the Hidden Imam to proclaim himself and lead Islam back to glory.

As we left, now encumbered with the regal gifts of gold *ashrafis* knotted in large silk squares, we passed a band of some 20 Pathan plug-uglies carrying rifles who shouted 'Long Live the Khan!' as we passed. 'The Sarkar is near, they come to prepare the Namouss, the Community, for his reception', Abdulmalik said after an exchange of greetings.

Soon enough we were completely away from the Middle Ages. Even the unexpected electric lighting at Abshar monastery, I realised, had not overwhelmed its flavour.

6/v.

The Pointing Finger Teaching System
Ahmed Abdullah

Ahmed Abdullah has specialized for many years in the study of legends and mysterious tales as used in esotericist training. His best-known published works are *Mysteries of Asia, Fifty Enthralling Stories of the Mysterious East*, and *Fighting Through*. He has also published a study of hypnosis among the Arabs.

The Pointing Finger.
(A) *The Legend*.
The Pointing Finger legend is generally attributed in the Middle East to Dhun'Nun Misri, the 9th-century mystic. In summary, it is this:

255

For centuries an ancient Egyptian statue which was reputed to indicate the position of a hidden treasure baffled all attempts at finding it. It was a figure of a man with hand and finger outstretched.

All seekers except one tried to find the hoard in the direction in which the finger pointed. The one dug at the spot where the shadow of the finger rested at midday. He found the treasure.

(B) *Interpretation and Use of the Legend in Teaching.*

The Malamati (Seekers of Opprobrium) mystics state that the statue stands for the teacher, the shadow and its position for understanding, the successful seeker for the student. The apparent message of the teacher (the 'pointing hand') is not what he is teaching. His training is by means of the pointing finger initially, but it is through its development in the student (the shadow) that the understanding of the message comes. The teacher therefore coaches the student to acquire a capacity ('looking at the shadow, not the statue') which will give him an answer, provoking in him the capacity. But before this can be done, the outline of the enterprise must be indicated in some way. Such an outline is the Legend of the Pointing Finger.

6/vi.
The Known and Unknown in Studies
John Grant

Dr John Grant, in addition to spending over a quarter of a century in private studies of Babylonian belief and tradition, has published two semi-autobiographical books in English: *Lion of the Frontier* and *Through the Garden of Allah*. His knowledge of Sanskrit, Hindi and Urdu have enabled him to live in India and Pakistan, collecting unpublished records of beliefs and practices.

The perennial rumour that a secret path to inner knowledge lingers in the East, if it has any truth in it at all, seems to be connected with psychological attitudes common to the East which in our culture can find no place. This is not to say that such ways of thinking should not become possible for us; indeed, were not possible for our forebears. The chief among these in my experience is the role of the individual as an instrument rather than as a name. Some of the most important individuals in Eastern history are practically unknown as personalities. What has been considered important is their message. In many cases we do not know where they were born, where they were buried, what they were like. We only know what they tried to do. The same phenomenon is strong in certain spiritual schools today. Among the Sufis, it may be the least significant-looking person who is the teacher: even the youngest. Books and other teaching materials which circulate, sometimes couched in the greatest poetry of Arabic, Persian and other languages, are anonymous. Works of art are rarely signed. There is not a single authentic portrait known of any of the spiritual teachers of most of Asia before the nineteenth century European influence and interest in personality. Then there is the interchangeability of teacher and pupil; something unknown to our thinking. In some dervish schools, senior members are taught certain things and then sent to complete or improve personal and group characteristics by acting in a lowly capacity in another school. Such an attitude seems almost grotesque to us, who believe, unconsciously, that a man must be distinguished in all ways if he is accepted as of a certain standard in one. That such techniques and attitudes may reflect an ancient knowledge forgotten by us is perhaps borne out by the claim that ideas of a Western kind have been known for thousands of years in Asia. Not long ago I was talking about modern public-

257

opinion testing methods used in the West, and also referring to the trials of new drugs which were made by giving some to patients and having 'control groups' who were not given anything, and also groups who were given inert substances — placebos — to see whether there was a psychological effect. The Sheikh of the Qalandars of Delhi said that this system of testing the 'ripeness' of a population for a spiritual teaching had been in use for centuries. 'We often,' he said, 'have sent out teachers with whole ranges of ideas which were useless, just to see which people would be attracted to them. This not only helped us to choose promising students, but also kept busy the people who would be useless, since they would be occupied believing the "truths" of the concocted cult'.

I have been privileged to see this technique in operation. In its modern form it has given rise to some of the 'Eastern' teachings taken to Europe and America by well-meaning but self-deceived foreigners who have been unwitting subjects tested by this method.

6/vii.
Emulation and Cycles of Study
Ali Sultan

Ali Sultan has travelled and studied extensively in Turkistan, Khorasan and India, publishing some experiences in his English book *And They Died*.

The Tradition

The Bukharan spiritual teachers of the Nakshibendi, Hajegan and Chistiya Schools have for long emphasized the importance of emulation in teaching. To emulate the outward behaviour of a teacher, however, as is customary in virtually all Eastern systems, is regarded by them as the lowest form of practice. The true form of emulation can come, it is believed, only through being involved in

258

activities of almost any kind, initiated by a teacher.

Interpretation and Use of Technique

There is a sharp contrast between Bukharan and European behaviour in the interpretation of emulation and example by the different schools. In the tradition being studied, slavish imitation of a master is regarded as the mark of an unpromising student, and just as bad as criticism. The teacher makes an actual exercise of associating with him, from time to time, all of his pupils in some of the affairs of everyday life. In this way, they learn by observation and by co-operation with 'something greater' — this something greater being believed to be an objective force operating within the teacher himself. In this way, it is stated, the teacher and the students constitute together a pattern. The teacher is in contact with a cosmic intention. That intention informs him; he, in turn, relates the pupils with it by allowing them to take a part in his activity. It is said to be for this reason that teachers sometimes encourage one student, sometimes avoid him: he is when he does this thought to be attaching the student to the operation of the 'Greater Plan', and detaching him from it when it is in a period of suspension. This emphasizes another important Central Asian dogma: that the operation of the 'Great Plan' is cyclic and discontinuous. 'To continue activity when the Great Plan is quiescent (for its own reasons)', says Ahmed Yasavi, 'is harmful to the pupil. He must be told this, otherwise he thinks that the teacher has abandoned him'.

6/viii.

Learning by Contact

Rustam Khan-Urff

Rustam Khan-Urff was born in Bokhara and

educated at Mire-Arab College, where he became Custodian of Manuscripts, as well as being Turkic expert of the Arg (Palace) Library. He settled in Albania in 1936, having lived and studied in India, Kashmir and Yemen. He has published one book in English, *The Diary of a Slave*.

The Bektashi of Albania, as well as the Mahaguru of Ladakh, preserve a belief in learning by contact. This is based upon the theory that a 'current' of knowledge must run through all parts of an organization set up by a teacher or holy man. He starts with the immediate circle of disciples, each of whom will become to a greater or lesser degree imbued with his sanctity. They, in turn, will communicate it to their trainees or to the people with whom they come into contact. There could be an argument for claiming that this knowledge behaves like such a force as electricity, even if only because it is enunciated that, for optimum transmission effectiveness of the knowledge, it has to be exerted upon carefully chosen people, and the people themselves must be collected around a certain 'Point of Concentration' — a place, a series of prayers, etc. In this sense the teacher and the people whom he has influenced may be likened to an organism which has come into being for a purpose, and which derives its nourishment from a total action which radiates from a centre and suffuses the whole. It may be this doctrine which underlies the belief that the mere act of induction or initiation conveys a power or capacity for development which can continue in the person regardless of whether he is constantly carrying out the rituals of the cult or not. There are distinct traces in the above-mentioned and other cults of a belief in the presence of a 'divine current' in men and women associated by means of special routines. The terminology used, however, is not scientific in our modern sense, and it is possible that this has obscured the doctrine as far as we are concerned.

260

6/ix.
Meditation Method
Mir S. Khan

Mir S. Khan is of nomadic extraction, and has written and broadcast on a wide variety of subjects. He has made sociological studies of the Berbers and the Afghan Kochis, and his despatches have been published in *The Times* of London, used by the British Broadcasting Corporation, and appeared widely in the general press in many countries. He is a member of several Sufi Orders.

After following indications of the theoretical dynamic behind traditionalistic meditation activity, it was when I was studying with Gulbaz Khan of Kalat (Baluchistan) that I came across what might be termed a developed theory of pupil-teacher meditation. This is attributed to the remotest antiquity; though why it should be claimed that it was practised by 'Noah, Joseph, Jesus, Elias and Salman the Persian' especially, I cannot say. In summary, the theory holds that there is a certain element in the human being which strives towards perfection. This element (Nafs-i-Haqiqa = The True Being) will attach itself to anything — men, objects, ideas — in the hope of finding some conductor which will bring it to 'maturity' (Pukhtai). When it comes into contact with a correct source of conduction — a teacher, it feeds for a time on his knowledge. This is the phase of attachment to a teacher. If the teacher accepts the pupil, he will first of all teach interchange concentration exercises. In these the mutual bond is strengthened. The next step is for the teacher to induce the students to interchange with one another, which they do by meeting regularly and all taking an interest in some common theme. They may think that they are learning something from that theme. In fact, they are becoming attuned to one another. Next comes the phase in which the pupils are able to spend some time, at will, interchanging with the teacher and

261

with one another. When this stage has been reached, they have attained a form of directing capacity over their spiritual life. The next form of meditation is when different subjects of meditation are given to each student. Now each has three types of practice. After that comes the succession of meditation. The whole community following signals from the teacher or his deputy (Khalifa) first collect themselves, then meditate upon themselves, then upon the teacher, then upon an object or idea, then upon the private objects or ideas. In this way, it is believed by the mystics of the Chishti, Qadiri and other schools, the human capacity for connection with superior cognition is practised and brought to fruition.

6/x.

A Sufi Organization in Britain

Arkon Daraul

Sufi organizations exist in England, Europe and America as well as in the East. They are referred to as The People of the Path; and this passage gives an account of beliefs and practices, as well as an initiation into Sufism, held in a country house in Sussex, England.

People in Britain enter Sufism for a variety of reasons and in a number of different ways. They seem to be mainly of the middle class.

Their beliefs are that 'a certain nobility of mind and purpose resides within every human being . . . this it is the task of the Sufi teacher to discover and develop in the individual'. The Sufis believe that 'if a person were to take their principles alone or piecemeal and apply them, this would result in an unbalanced personality. Sufism, they maintain, must be followed as a training system in its entirety'.

There is a supernatural element in Sufism. 'Members

262

believe (and literature abounds with supposed examples of it) that the members of the higher degrees of initiation are capable of influencing the minds of men and even events in a totally inexplicable manner'.

'Is Sufism a religion; a way of life; something like Yoga — just a ramp? It is none of these things, and yet it is a secret cult whose members believe that it gives them something which they have unconsciously sought for years. In this respect, at least, it resembles a religion'.

Sufis carry out healing processes, and concentration sessions designed to help further various objectives of the Order. 'The disciplines of the Order are six in number; and it depends upon his teacher as to which one is to be used by which Sufi. First comes traditional ritual worship; then recitation of the Koran; after that the repetition of certain formulas; now "Striving" or effort for a goal; then physical exercises, breath-control and the like; and finally contemplation on individual themes, then on complicated ones'.

But there seems to be no standard training: 'There are many paths within the Order which the initiate may take; all will depend upon what his natural bent is: what are his inner capabilities, which will be "developed" by the training which he is to receive'.

In order to enter Sufism, the candidate must somehow make contact with a Sufi, probably on some ordinary basis, not, that is to say, because he specially wants to be a Sufi. He is then prepared and tested (the latter 'for patience, tact, moral probity and sheer endurance') — though there is no standard procedure for this, either. 'One goes by intuition'.

In the initiation ceremony, the Circle (*Halka* — the operative unit) is convened in a traditional manner. Members have 'functions' corresponding to a household, or a ruler's court, or a family. Hence the Groom, the Cupbearer, the Soldier, Emir, the Brother, Nephew, and so on.

The candidate is brought from the antechamber by his sponsor, immediately after having been taught an iden-

263

tification gesture. He removes his shoes and is taken to the Master. His arrival is formally announced, and he is told that he is welcome. His novitiate and sponsor are mentioned.

Now he is asked to speak for himself. He advances, bows and kisses the hand of the Murshid (Director or Master), and, when asked, recites the Rules for Initiates. Having, after repeating each Rule, sworn that he will obey them, the newcomer is invested with a terra-cotta coloured robe, staff and bowl. These latter symbolize uniformity in outward appearance (the robe); work and authority (the staff); and inner and bodily nutriment (the bowl). He may now take his place in the Circle.

Sufi dogma includes:

'Mankind has certain capabilities, certain ideas, certain capacities for experience. These things are all related. The goal is the Ideal Man, who shall use every aspect of his experience to be "In the world and yet not Of the World". These teachings have been passed down to the elect since the beginning of time'.

The Secrecy of Sufism:

'How secret is Sufism? This is something which is very difficult to answer. In the first place, the Orders require initiation, passwords and signs. Secondly, some of their esoteric literature is hard to understand, and has its own technical terminology. Yet on the other hand, it is a canon of belief that a Sufi does not progress merely by passing through degrees and initiations; the "blessing" (*baraka*, sometimes called Power) must come upon him. If this is so, and the baraka is passed on from another Sufi, the conclusion is that there should be no need for secrecy; because no outsider could experience what the Sufis are undergoing in their raptures.

'The answer to this, given by Sufis themselves, is that atmosphere plays a part in the cultivation of enlightenment. Strangers are a barrier and also a superfluity. Sufism is not for an audience. Again, the word "Secret" is used in a special sense. It refers to one or more of the

264

inner experiences of the mind, and not to the mere possession of formal knowledge. In this way Sufism differs from those schools of initiation which used to hold actual secrets, such as those of philosophy or how to work metals, or even how one could supposedly control spirits'.

The Effect of Sufism upon Society:

'On the whole, the effect of Sufism upon society has been creative and wholesome. Sufis do not suffer from fanaticism, are not connected with magic (though they are thought to have special, extra-normal powers) and hold to the principle of honour and effort to an astonishing extent . . . the phrase "the word of the Sufi" is proverbial . . . Attempts have been made to popularize Sufism in the West in a similar manner to that which is used with odd cults of personality. But, with the exception of the schools which have been set up on an experimental basis, this "society Sufism" has never caught on . . .

'But the Path of the Sufi is likely to exercise a fascination over men's minds for many a year yet; and its influence in the West is undoubtedly increasing'.

6/xi.
A Dervish Assembly in the West
Selim Brook-White

During the past twenty years the effects of the practice of Sufism have been palpable in the West.

What is this form of Sufism, and why does it attract the people of the West? In the first place, the Western or technological mind places much importance upon work and the linking of the body and the mind.

Sufism of the Naqshbandi branch stresses the fact

that, if it has any meaning at all, mystical experience must improve the individual. It must make him a better man. The 'Perfected Man' (*Insan-i-Kamil*) is the man who is in the world but not of it. He does not have to grow matted hair and live in a cave. His perceptions, his value to the community have been improved. And he has found an answer to the nagging unfulfilment which is the curse of humanity.

In the West generally, the Naqshbandi principles have been adopted under the general term of the *Tariqa* (The Path). The Sufis are organised in *Halqas* (Circles) under a teacher, and the *Halqas* are combined in the complete organization, the *Tariqa*. The striking thing about the Western members of the *Tariqa* is that among them you will not find the long-haired semi-intellectual, the neurotic who joins every new 'craze', the weakling who seeks guidance. They are straightforward, active, interesting people.

Sufism means to the Westerner in the earlier stages that he is practising something which has brought obvious benefits to others. He can see in the company of Sufis to which he is attached something which he would like to participate in. This is the first principle: that a man wants to become a Sufi because he likes those whom he knows, and that he believes that they are the best advertisement for the goods which they are purveying.

Secondly, again in the early stages, he finds that there are undeniable benefits in the exercises (*Wazifa*) which he is expected to carry out. He can actually feel the benefit of the mental and physical exercises, working upon himself. Sufism is not offering him some undefined and vaguely hinted at eventual satisfaction.

Thirdly, when he has actually tasted the effects of Sufism upon himself, he enters into an understanding of the basis of Sufism. How did it develop? Upon what is it based? How can he enter the wider field which lies within the mysticism on whose periphery he now stands? He may be introduced to the works of Al-Ghazzali and to the *Mashaf* and *Sunnat*, in order to make it clear to him

266

that here is the root of the teaching.

Thus Sufism in its practical expression in the West cuts right across the mental dilemma in which modern man finds himself. It shuns the sensation-seekers, for they congregate around the charlatans and the miracle-mongers who run societies for commercial purposes. There are isolated and static so-called Sufi cults in the West, it is true, modelled upon the occult societies which are known to provide a good living for the Guru if he can only keep his disciples in a state of mystification. Some of these pantheistic societies try to show that Sufism is nothing but a teaching designed to unite all religions and they study all the holy books of all time. But the *Tariqa* Sufis ignore these material aims, and concentrate upon leading people to Sufism through personal experience of happiness and fulfilment.

But how, you may ask, can a sceptical Westerner stomach the practice of something which he cannot understand with his intellect? In the first place, it is nowadays more easily explained than ever before that the intellect arrives at nothing final enough. This is admitted by all Western thinkers. Secondly — and this is vital — you merely say to your candidate that, providing that he practises the preliminary exercises which he is given, he will have clear proof that he is on the 'right Path'. And this is the amazing thing about Sufism. There is something which is known as *Barakat*; the power which, when contacted, will give the man more than the insight which he needs to know that he is at last on the way to fulfilment.

Sufism is neither a Western nor an Oriental cult. It is an eternal one. It has produced some of the world's greatest literature, some of the East's greatest thinkers and sages, as well as giving a stiffening to the moral and material progress of man.

I recently had the honour to attend a meeting of thirty-one *Halqa* delegates from Europe, addressed by the *Tariqa* Grand Sheikh Idries Shah Saheb, who is, of course, a lineal descendant of the Prophet (Peace and

267

Blessings of Allah upon him!) and an Afghan nobleman as well as being the grandson of H. H. of Sardhana. It was here that every single speaker gave the *Kalima* and stressed that the *Tariqa* was leading people to the truth through the methods of truth, and not through propaganda or intellectual sophistries.

There is no doubt that this work of the *Tariqa* will grow and will produce individuals who will carry on the work which provides humanity with the link which is needed in a materialistic world to the ultimate Truth as we already know it.

6/xii.
Use of the Five Gems
Edouard Chatelherault

Edouard Chatelherault is the author of *You and Your Stars*, in which astrology, talismans and ancient methods of seeking information from the skies are made intelligible to ordinary readers. Of Persian, Spanish and English extraction, he has lived and worked in many countries of the Far East.

Taking the points which we are studying in the order in which they have struck me, I find most revealing in the Eastern tradition the freedom which has been lost in the West: the freedom to look at anything as a possible source of experience. Most strongly marked was my own quest when, at first, seeking transcendental knowledge among spiritual people I was recommended to study what appeared to be a book of spells and mantrams — *The Five Gems*. This book is very much in demand in its Persian guise, known throughout India, Pakistan and Central Asia as the *Jawahir-i-Khamsa*. The only clue to any deeper meaning than magical processes lies in the authorship. It is by the mystical saint Gwath Shattar. The run-of-the-mill orientalist or bibliophile would —

268

and often has in Asia itself — dismissed this authorship as an attribution intended to give the book a greater currency. But it is to be found used as a textbook by mystics who could not, by any stretch of imagination, be regarded as occultists. To experience its teaching use occasions almost as much of a shock as if one were to discover that 'Old Moore's Almanac' was a disguised religious or psychological document. The *Gems* frequently quotes the Sage Timtim, and also contains magical processes which appear in the work of the North African 'sorcerer' El-Buni. The reasons why this document is to be found in a magical disguise is given by the Shattari teachers as follows: (1) People are attracted to the magical, and will tend to protect and distribute 'magical' texts; (2) It is traditional among 'men of perception' to conceal their meanings in forms which will not only baffle the inept, but will effectively test them: if they want magic alone, they will be prevented from troubling the Shattaris; (3) The Shattaris are under an ancient obligation to court no high repute in the world. One of their major teachers being considered a magician furthers this end; (4) When the real meaning of the *Gems* is revealed to the disciple, he understands, in a flash of cognition, that all exterior presentations of dogma are only formulae, and that truth can be put in any form. The 'Star Lore' and 'Magical Recitations' in *The Five Gems* is an elaborate coding-system. Until an individual has dropped magical aspirations, he will not face up to this fact, and will not be able to learn.

7. CURRENT STUDY MATERIALS

7/i.
First Principles

There are three main types of human organization:

1. Those designed for mutual exchange of attention and giving the individual a sense of significance; including a social aspect, which is more or less strongly marked and may often be unperceived, being mistaken for something else;

2. Those designed for training, encouraging people to believe things and act in certain ways as a consequence, implanting and maintaining opinions and assumptions;

3. Those designed as a format within which certain experiences can take place, a certain awareness can manifest, certain capacities can be developed.

There are, of course, all kinds of amalgams of these features in various societies and human entities, but a study of any human organization will show it to be biased towards one of these main characteristics.

Yet it is because the surface appearance of the organization is social, political, educational, vocational, and so on, that the ground-plan, the structure is seldom noted at all. If someone says that such-and-such a body is for learning, people seldom imagine that it is really social, and so on. There are certain exceptions, when people notice that students at evening classes are very often there to fill in time or to make friends rather than to learn; or when there are putatively sporting, say, or religious associations where the social side has gone so far as to be regarded as integrally important, or even

271

vital, to its functions: 'If we love one another, we will be more effective'; or 'we do a lot of trout fishing, but the accent here is strongly upon social life'.

You should note, however, that it is often possible to combine two or more of the factors without particularly harming the enterprise: for instance, if you are trying to raise money for charity, you may be able to do it better in a social atmosphere or among commercial associates. The points being made are that, first, it is valuable to *know* the relative quantity of the various ingredients, social, attention-attracting or developmental, so that the organization can be understood; secondly, that certain enterprises will suffer if the ingredients get out of proportion. Perhaps we could take as a very rough parallel the tribe in which there are mostly chiefs and very few Indians.

Education is said to require specific facts as well as a maturing of the mind: but the fact is that the desire for drama and the demand for attention-arousing supposed facts manages to militate against both. Here is one example out of many that could be chosen, and which is familiar in one form or another to most of us:

Sir Max Mallowan* wrote about the 'Hanging Gardens of Babylon' that 'in these matters legend dies hard; it is sometimes better not to proclaim the truth. I remember more than two decades ago overhearing a worthy local guide expatiating on the "Gardens" to a group of tourists. "Let me explain to you what this really was", I said. "It was a prison reserved for the king of Judah, as we know from tablets discovered by the Germans and deciphered by Weidner". "Thank you very much", he said. "What you tell me is most interesting". Alas, when I overheard him some years later in the same role of mentor to the innocent they were described as before. "Hanging Gardens" they remained'.

Some people, at least, know that a group may turn in

---

*Mallowan, M., 'Sampling pre-history', *Books & Bookmen*, July 1976, p.59.

272

almost any direction. It may be founded for study purposes but turn into a power-system, to gratify the desire of some to lead and others to follow. When this happens, the participants may be quite happy with it, but its dynamic effect will be gone as far as its original intention was concerned. People are not learning, but think that they are, or are too contented to care whether they are or not. Among the Sufis, this matter of group integrity is carefully guarded and monitored.

The learning group and the total organization to which it belongs, according to the Sufis, is so important that it is worth regarding as sacrosanct in itself as far as its integrity and maintenance are concerned. Among the people of our tradition the assembly of people comes first; then the teacher; then the arranging or re-arranging of the group in order to enable it to become and remain the learning instrument. Until this is properly grasped, it is hard to learn in such a group; but its existence is always the guarantee of the learning potential being maintained. Once such a group is invaded by personality or power or other considerations from 'the World', it cannot be called one of our groups at all. This is not to say that a group may not be formed with the hope of becoming a learning one. But the dangers are great, since unless the determination to learn and to qualify as an authentic teaching group is stronger than subjective desires to shine in company, to share secrets, to feel important, and so on, the group will go sour, often without anyone realizing that it has. Or, even if it is realized that it has, few people generally suspect *why*.

It is therefore not too much to say that the group and the school are fundamental. When you have these, you have almost everything. It is a test of a study group and for its members if social strains develop, if people leave because there is insufficient emotional stimulus, if a demand for action, information, activities, objectives and so on build up.

Truly effective, real developmental organizations are rare or not well known simply because of the great

273

wastage and metamorphoses through which they go because of these very human — subjective — demands. What makes them difficult to maintain is the self-deception whereby people believe their dissatisfactions or demands from the group to be rooted in laudable and quite other causes. And yet it is easy to see them manifesting themselves. People say: 'I want action, or to know this or that, or to go here or there, or to engage in this or that activity'. If they do, instead of wanting to harmonize themselves with what is necessary and essentially true, which is the initial purpose of the group, they are trying to leave or modify it. Desertion or manipulation is in fact the root stimulus. Desertion may be in order to get stimulus, of course, but in any case, it is muddying the water and holding back the alignment which makes the group a truly functioning whole.

It is not, either, necessarily anyone's fault that they have not studied this factor.

7/ii.
The Known as the Channel to the Unknown

There is an Arabic phrase, *Al-Majaz Qantarat al-Haqiqa*. This is approximately rendered as 'The Manifest is the Bridge to the Real'.

People who have come across this statement *after* they have heard of Neoplatonism have unhesitatingly identified, in most cases, this doctrine with Neoplatonic philosophy. Such a belief, however, does not describe the historical situation. It only means that the describer is describing his own reactions. Paraphrased, it means: 'This sounds like something about which I have already heard — or is similar to something which has another label: therefore it is the same thing, or a derivation of it'. The truth is that two separate things may have the same origins, and need not be derived one from another.

274

The fact that this still has to be stated indicates most clearly the poverty of human thought when faced by something it does not know. This poverty is displayed by the almost indecent haste with which a label is sought and applied. It is for this reason that it has been said: 'Do not entrust thought to people who imagine themselves to be thinkers'.

To proceed with the thesis: It might be said that this doctrine holds that crude, 'terrestrial' things have refined, 'celestial' equivalents: the obvious is the projection of the original. Every action exists on the level of thought as well as on that of action. All coarser manifestations exist on the level of the fine, the subtle.

Hence, when Sufi poets say that 'Human love is a crude form of divine love', they refer to this concept. When Rumi says that every thought has a corresponding action, he refers to this concept. When Hafiz talks of drunkenness, he is referring to a state in the material world which parallels a psychic state. Many commentators, unable to get behind the most obvious, have tried to torture meanings out of the ideas of 'drunkenness', or 'love' and of 'movement', either approving or disapproving according to their own bias, or assigning a sentimental meaning to what are in fact technical descriptions. Others, just as awry, have imagined that this is a crude technical description, and that the mere effort to intensify feelings of love, or to throw oneself into an intoxicated state, or to carry out physical exercises, will produce the desired results. This, again, indicates a primitive stage of understanding little better than magical thinking. Such people have often set up experimental situations in which they have actually tried to make their aspirations come through by going through the motions of 'love, action or induced ecstasy'. The results are always undesirable. Such results include implanting and spreading obsessions, and even mental damage. Relatively harmless results are the formation of fanatical or indoctrinated groups which can become widely known and even respected. But, since they operate only on a mimetic and repetitious basis, they fall into the category of social diversion, disguised as spiritual movements because of the words which they use to describe themselves, and thought to be important because of the absence of basic general knowledge on the subject.

Some spiritual people privately welcome them, because they effectively divert or dissipate attention which would otherwise be an inconvenience: they absorb the energies and hence the irritation capacity of superficial people, who are at the same time able to imagine that they are engaged in something profound.

To resume: conduct on this level, of imitation and based upon greed for progress or fulfilment without preparation, results in no progress. But conduct is extremely important: conduct of the appropriate kind does not *determine* one's progress, as the 'magically-minded' think; but it can, and does, *align* it with the Higher, Finer. Alignment, therefore, makes communication possible.

But what conduct, where, when and how? Changes in the terrestrial pattern require changes in apparent organization. This is the main reason for successive changes in the presentation of Higher Teaching in different communities and epochs.

Terrestrial organizations, by assuming certain characteristics of the Ultimate, help to make communication, which has been interrupted, possible.

Such alignment may not, and frequently does not, accord with expectation about it. Misconceptions have to be shed before alignment itself can be effective. A mirror does not usually resemble the object which it is registering. It needs, however, to have characteristics on which the object *acts*, to manifest itself in a local form.

Genuine organizations with this objective are so structured as to focus, as it were, upon the Ultimate. Remember that the construction of the mirror, as well as its appearance, may appear to have no relationship with the object to be registered upon it.

276

Human organization may be employed as a communications instrument. Human beings endowed with certain insight are always 'followed' and copied externally by others. This 'following' and copying, without direction, will produce only sociological results.

Those who have a need for social or psychological stability will demand this first, and will always employ the observed externals and the associations of a real teaching on this lower level. It is therefore of great importance that people who feel that they want to align to something higher should first stabilise themselves in the social context, so that they will not unconsciously be seeking to transform something higher into something lower. Their social capacities, needs and integration have to be established first.

To pass over this primary requirement will produce great social visibility and may be greatly welcomed. But it constitutes the first hurdle.

People are accustomed to associating certain kinds of social behaviour — appearance — certain traditional practices, and certain otherwise unexplained feelings, even certain places and objects, with inevitable, automatic, basic, undoubted, spiritual significance. Such people are always left behind in any real effort.

Therefore: 'The Manifest is the Bridge to the Real, but not all manifestations are bridges to the Real'.

Groupings of people, type and degree of studies, the right balance between action and inaction, these and other factors must be achieved, under right direction, otherwise effort is spiritually wasted, although it may be emotionally welcomed by the participants.

Such wasteful activity is well summed up by an old phrase, employed also in other connections, 'If the young *knew*, and the old *could*'.

It is possible to achieve the alignment of thought and action which corresponds with the Ultimate Truth by the application in the right manner of order, discipline and service.

But people who are powerfully attracted by the concepts of order, discipline and service for their own sake cannot be regarded as serious. These factors are instruments, not conditioning factors. Similarly, people who are obsessed by inaction, or avoiding organization to a necessary degree, disqualify themselves.

The capacity for order, discipline and service is the basis for discharging the terms of the injunction: 'Be *in* the world — do not be *of* the world'.

7/iii.
Journey Beyond History

1. Let us assume that there is a community of people who, instead of dealing in handed-down literature or tradition, have an actual extra-dimensional view of the origin, possibilities and place of humanity in a large picture.
2. While the idea of such individuals has been conceived from time to time, while it has even been known from time to time, this is not a theory — even though it may be a fact — which commends itself to many people.

This is the first problem of such people: how to make known their existence and capacities to those whom they can help, without producing 'proofs' which only ruin these people by stimulating the wrong emotions?
3. This problem has been tackled by this community in the past in various ways. These ways have always been devised in accordance with the peculiarities of the situation concerned.
4. There have been two main methods used in the past.

(a) The method of projecting the message initially in a 'secondary' form, a form which will appeal to the sense of pride, greed or mystery; or the approved norms of a community, a cultural milieu. These have often been termed 'religious ways'.

278

(b) The method of instituting a 'secret organization' of some kind, with degrees of initiation, in which the member has been successively attracted to an idea and then, equally successively, weaned from one version onto another.

In both these methods (each with a more and a less 'esoteric' or initiatory part) there has been a protection. This resides in the fact that the organization in its external face purports to be innocuous, or to be doing some verifiable good or kindness to humankind.

The grave drawback of this method is that it means that certain attachments (conditionings) are engendered, which have at some point to be rescinded. Not everyone will survive such treatment.

5. Although today, in the countries and among the communities connected with us, the above factors have become essential, there is still a tremendous drawback. This is simply that there is a law of diminishing returns in this teaching, as in all human ideas, whereby people will tend to accept from a teaching what they fancy they want. This is generally release from worry, increase of perplexity, hero-worship, certitude, emotional indulgence. They treat the teaching in the same manner that they treat any other 'food': they settle for short-term gains.

7/iv.
The Regeneration and Degeneration Cycles in Mystical Study

Local and ultimate reality

Reality, says the Sufi — in common with the modern scientist — is not limited to that which comes within the limits of the human faculties. There is a local reality: the world as perceived by our familiar senses. There is a reality beyond this, extra-sensorily perceived. Contemporary science, as Einstein hinted, points towards mysticism (the perception of a greater, commanding reality) just as much as it verifies the small-scale facts of terrestrial existence. He says: 'Science is the attempt to make the chaotic diversity of our sense-experience correspond to a logically uniform system of thought'*; but also: 'The cosmic religious experience is the strongest and the noblest driving force behind scientific research'.**

Contemporary science reports astonishing facts

Scientific discoveries, especially in physics, may have disproved various folklore beliefs, but they have replaced them with information every bit as strange — and support them with the authority of mathematics and observation which is regarded as even more veridical than anything accepted, in the past, from religious doctrine.

Worlds disappearing into black holes; universes in which things grow young and start old, where time runs backwards: back-to-front worlds — such things are today believed as strongly by 'detached' scientists, as was any dogma of the past by obsessionals

Modern emergence from three unviable panacea beliefs:
science, technology, reason

A hundred years ago, Victorians believed that science would solve all problems: whereas it has succeeded only in substituting greater doubts for the certainties which it at first promised. Fifty years ago, as you may read in almost any textbook of those days, technology was going to overcome all humanity's problems: today one of its roles seems to be to show with increasing ferocity that many of them are insoluble. Two centuries ago, the Age of Reason proclaimed that man's sovereign intellect would solve everything. Today, the more that people

---

*Out of *My Later Years*, 1950, p.14.
**His Obituary: 19 April, 1955.

280

think, the less seems to be the value of the intellect itself. Certainly it is not conspicuously solving very much; though constantly throwing up more problems.

Breakdown of idealist systems encourages cranks

These facts have opened the door to every kind of crank and to many a cult which claims that, because the foregoing is true, any absurdity may be true. This is very far from being the case. Because astronomers have often been wrong or stupid, say, this makes no difference to the absurdity of astrology. We need astrology and similar preoccupations like we need basket-weaving in therapeutic contexts: to keep people busy and happy when we can offer them nothing much else.

The religio-intellectual approach has been a means of asserting 'truths' which provide comfort if not real truths. Their effectiveness depends, of course, on the stage of the society in which they are promulgated. Remember the words of Archbishop Ussher:

'The world was created on 22nd October, 4004 B.C., at 6 o'clock in the evening'.*

This was published in 1660. A much-respected reference book of 1881 notes, however, that the dates assigned to the Creation vary between 3616 and 6984 B.C.**

The West at this time — less than a century from the time at which I am talking — needed new disciplines, and it got them. The main weakness of these approaches is that they do tend to extrapolate, like Archbishop Ussher, beyond their capacity. We can use them, but we have to know their limitations. These restrictions, unfortunately, are visible only to those who can see beyond and don't need them. Yet these people can use them to help conduct the awareness of their hearers towards reality; rather as you might describe the roundness of the

---

*Chronologia Sacra, Oxford, 1660
**Haydn's Dictionary of Dates, London, 1881, p.217 (seventeenth edition).

281

moon to someone who needed to know about roundness by referring to a coin, a plate, and so on.

If, by the way, it is doubted whether we have our Archbishop Usshers today, recall the words of the great scientist, in full cry of irresponsible extrapolation from insufficient data:

'Anyone who expects a source of power from the transformation of these atoms is talking moonshine'.* So said one of the most eminent of all physicists, Ernest Rutherford. And he only died in 1937 . . .

Scientifically-minded people, and scholars, seek repeatable demonstration of mystical and spiritual fact *in their own terms*. Because they are looking for things which they can recognize instead of preparing themselves to recognize things which they are not able to, they cannot accept the evidence which they cannot see and will not train themselves to see. There is a story to illustrate this:

In the Land of Fools one of their citizens had fainted and the others decided to bury him. When he started to move, they tied him down onto a plank, so as not to have their intention interfered with. While they were carrying him to the graveyard, he was delighted to see a respected judge by the roadside. He called out to him that he wasn't dead at all. The judge stopped the cortège and asked the mourners, all honourable and solid citizens, whether the man was dead or not. They all swore that they had seen him dead, and so he must be. Then they produced the death certificate. So the Judge said: 'Say what you like, but according to the rules of documentation and witnessing, you are dead, and these people can prove it'. And so they took him away and buried him.

Value of new disciplines of psychology, anthropology and sociology

But the modern disillusionment has made it possible to go back into human history and records, to see whether any of the materials shrugged off by the scien-

---

*Quoted in *Physics Today*, October 1970, p.33.

tific, technological, rational or industrial revolutions might not, after all, be of some value.

Tools for re-examination of the human heritage in knowledge

Furthermore, the infant soft sciences of psychology, sociology and anthropology are valuable tools in this endeavour.

Contemporary society has only recently perceived itself as one civilization among many

It is only in the past few years, of course, that the West's more accurate perception of itself as a civilization among a hundred others has made it open to an effort towards the retrieval of ancient knowledge. It is in an even shorter period that it has been possible again to use the all-but discarded word 'wisdom'. . .

'Discovery' of knowledge held by earlier cultures

Desmond Morris, referring to *Tales of the Dervishes**, once remarked that the meaning and significance of the stories came to one only after going through experiences paralleled in them. Something of the same tends to happen with the community at large: as with the individual, so with the group.

Analogy of Mark Twain

Western disciplines, as they encounter phenomena of human thought and action which they are able accurately to categorize for the first time, tend to rediscover with surprise that others have been along that way before. The ancient literature of the East suddenly seems to be full of insights which were not seen before. It seems all very much like the experience reported by Mark Twain. When he was fourteen, he was annoyed at how ignorant his father was. When he was twenty-one, he was astonished how much the old man had learned in seven years.*

*By Idries Shah. London, 1967 and reprints.
*'The Bee', in *What is Man and other Essays.*

283

Eastern specialization in experiential religion

One area where the East has an acknowledged start is in experiential religion, and particularly in the field known in the West as mysticism.

Western human-behaviour anecdotes can be milked for knowledge

If one takes modern tools of the West — such as psychology, sociology and anthropology — and applies them to the behaviour of Western peoples, wonderful facts emerge. If, further, one takes the traditional insights and teachings of the East and applies them, as well, to human problems which seem so baffling to the West, things become clearer. If, moreover, one takes some of the literature of the West — such as human-behaviour anecdotes: presto! A whole tapestry of meanings, referring to the reasons for and methods of human thought and action, emerges. The odd thing is that people haven't done more of this in the West.

Let us look at some of the common heritage, largely by means of stories of the kind which are found in both cultures. I have chosen eight Sufi and an equal number of Western stories to illustrate this theme.

Value of Easterner's analysis of the West

Before we do that, however, it is worth noting the conclusions which an Eastern observer, steeped in his own tradition, but using Western methods, would draw from an examination of Western religio-mystical behaviour.

Need to distinguish between social and religious behaviour

The first observation surely must be that the methods, organization and even terminology of 'Western' religious life very strongly resemble social, not spiritual, activity. If you take away unsupported beliefs (indoctrination and folklore), subtract emotional stimuli (whether sacred or profane), remove tribalism (group-behaviour), you will be able to say that you have stripped away those elements which can be challenged as externals and as merely the product of outward inevitability in human organization.

This situation, of religion-turned-tribe, is almost equally common in the East. But there is no shortage of people there who can see this clearly, and also of those who insist on the importance of original religion as a transforming force.

Seizing something may obscure the trap which accompanies it

THE VULTURE AND THE KITE

A vulture told a kite: 'I can see farther than anyone else'. Looking down, far away he espied a single grain of wheat upon the ground, and swooped upon it. He failed, however, to notice a snare, and was caught in it. He could see the grain, but he could not see the trap. The kite asked: 'What is the use of seeing the grain; when you could not see the enemy's trap?'

This tale, from Saadi's classical thirteenth-century *Bostan*, The Orchard, underlines the ancient Sufis' concern for just the same kind of facile trap of 'instant illumination' which numerous Western seekers find themselves in.

Loose thinkers demand authoritative, regulative bodies for metaphysics. But such are not successful in any field

People in the West are constantly asking why there are so many false 'spiritual schools' in Europe and America, and why the Eastern exponents of the authoritative and genuine traditions do not establish and maintain legitimate organizations which will show up and defeat these frauds and self-deluded entities.

Now, there are innumerable fakes and idiots practising all kinds of medicine, say, and commerce, art, science, recreation, education, in the West, who make a good living in spite of the existence of regulatory institutions: so the existence and activity of such a body does not have the effect fantasized for it. So much for the official control' idea.

The externalists, in any case, could not assess the legitimate school

But what about the need for a 'source of authoritative teaching active in the West?' The people who clamour for the setting up of this school, interestingly enough, are for us the very same ones who do not, probably cannot, recognize it where it does exist: for there is indeed such a school, and it is in healthy and effective life. So, what our questioners are really asking for is in reality something which *they themselves* would regard as a school of this kind. As we already have one, and it carries on its functions vigorously and effectively, to set up another which would satisfy mere externalists who are looking for certain irrelevant signs as those of 'legitimacy' could only be done if we were to concoct a spurious school to amuse such people. For it is indeed amusement which they subconsciously seek.

If they instead sought the school, they would easily find it, as in fact a large number of people do!

'I fear that you will never reach Mecca, O Nomad —
For you are on the road to Turkestan'.

(Saadi)

Paranoia as an endemic attitude

Sufis constantly come across a paranoid reaction to what they say and do, among both the general populace and specialists in inner thought. And, short of that, there is always the question of the learner himself endlessly questioning (through a misapplication of the principle of judgment) the meaning and motives of authentic mystical systems.

Saadi (*Bostan*) has another telling tale, well worth keeping in mind. It enables one to register that a person's ability to judge situations, if he is not thoroughly competent in the field in question, may seriously malfunction:

Parable of misjudgment of motives

Faridun, the Persian King of about 700 B.C., had a minister who was reported to have lent out gold and

286

silver. He had also stipulated, Faridun learnt, that the loans were to be repaid on the death of the king.

The king was infuriated and charged the man with plotting against him. The minister answered:

'I wanted all the people to wish you long life. By imposing the condition, I ensured that they would pray for your extended health'.

The subjective self must first be prepared — then objective assessment is possible

This kind of misunderstanding, whether between people or within the individual's own mind, leads, so Sufis teach, to an inability to develop the deep understanding which enables people to set aside the subjective self and to reach universal truth.

While people continue to think that they can work out truth while still a prey to confusions and suppositions, they will not find it. That they have chosen not to prepare themselves and instead to try the impossible has not gone unnoticed even in the youthful Western culture. Shakespeare's Banquo said:*

'If you can look into the seeds of time,
And say which seed will grow and which will not,
Speak then to me . . .'

Re-education of self-appointed critics who lack information and ability through vanity

The problem, in fact, is not for the legitimate teaching to project itself in a familiar manner. This is always active. It is for those who imagine that they could recognize a school, if it looked or sounded like what they demand, to re-educate themselves, to perceive the real thing and appreciate it. It is, in short, they who need reorientation. It is no part of a mystical school's work to reprogramme those who are conditioned to look for the wrong thing, or the right thing in the wrong way. After all, the would-be student must do something for himself.

---

*Macbeth,I,iii.

287

This something is to become truly aware of what really *is* there. What holds him back? Vanity and the belief that he can judge the school by his present criteria. These characteristics disable him from being a candidate for the school. Naturally he cannot find it. Why should he? If he did, it would be useless to him.

The Role of automatic associations in confusing analysis

People who have removed the clutter of certain associations from their minds can really look at the publications and activities of spiritual schools and see what is actually there. Until they have done this, they will continue to appear, to the genuine teacher, like the tramp faced by the suitcase, in this anecdote:

Tale illustrating need for right assumptions

A tramp stopped by a market stall and asked the stallholder, 'What are those things for?'

'They are suitcases. You put your clothes in them'.

'What, and walk about in the nude?'

The imposing of his own conditions of study by the would-be student is a state of mind of which he is unaware until he assesses himself; but this incipient state prevents him from understanding what real teaching is; as in a certain famous story:

Tale indicating imprecise thinking

One powerful tycoon had made an arrangement to receive 'special individual spiritual projection' (*tawajjuh*) from a Sufi teacher.

Something cropped up, and he was delayed; but he knew his manners. He sent the sage a telegram which read: 'I SHALL BE LATE BUT DON'T WORRY JUST START WITHOUT ME . . .'

The Latin tag *Quis custodiet ipsos custodes?* (Who will guard the guards themselves?) could be paraphrased in mystical studies by 'Who will prepare the teachers — or students — themselves?' The Western concept that anyone can embark on any kind of enquiry or study,

288

irrespective of ability or preparation, has the solitary but not negligible defect that it simply does not work. This is particularly true in the case of the human mind trying to work with the human mind. The Sufi conception of *Nafs-i-Ammara* — the lower, 'Commanding Self' which 'veils' the ability to discern Reality — insists that anyone who tries to move ahead with spiritual activity without transforming this Self will destroy his gains.

This is illustrated in a Nasrudin tale, also attributed to the joker Joha and others in the Middle East.

One day Nasrudin sold his house to someone, but asked that he should be allowed to reserve for himself a square yard of the inside wall. Since the price was attractive, the buyer agreed. But soon Nasrudin was there, hammering a peg into the wall, on which he hung a pair of old shoes. He came and went, taking down the shoes and putting them up; and he was a slight annoyance — but the bargain that the house had been offset this in the mind of its new owner. But, as the days passed, Nasrudin started to hang more and more odoriferous objects on the wall, until the new owner could not even live there. He knew that Nasrudin was within his rights, and that the law would not help him: so he was forced to sell the house back to Nasrudin for next to nothing.

Thus it is with people who carry on spiritual exercises without a completely clear basis. The permission which they leave for the operation of such things as self-will, greed and the tendency to imagine and to desire emotional stimuli will drive them out, and they will even 'lose their investment'.

Indispensable preparation for a would-be student

By starting through studying one's own assumptions about what spiritual schools might really be like, long before attempting to reach illumination or higher consciousness, people in the East and West find their way to them. Those who do not do this, are not students. I got thunderous applause and a whirlwind of letters when, in

289

California, I said to a questioner who asked whose books one should read 'Read them all!' I was complimented on my even-handedness. But I meant 'Learn what you can — then look for teaching'.

Confusion of essentials with personal desires

There are, of course, people who say that religion would be ruined if you took away incense, chanting, robes and candles, litanies and mantrams, and so on. You may recall the man who said: 'Switzerland? Take away the snow, mountains and lakes — and what have you to make such a fuss about?'

'Spiritual Tourism'

But Switzerland, in this sense, is a land of tourism. The people who want the emotional and superficial appurtenances just mentioned are identifying themselves not as truly religious, but only as spiritual tourists — people for whom social satisfactions mean religion. Their lives are a sub-programme of the entertainment industry, according to the proponents of another, really perceptive kind of spirituality.

Analogy of undeveloped science with undeveloped spirituality

So this is where many 'devout' people are now: in the spiritual equivalent of an undeveloped area: just as foolish regarding higher knowledge of the mind as any primitive man is about matters of, say, technology. They ask the wrong questions because they lack basic information. They lack it because they do not look for it: not because it is not there. Their behaviour, like that of the under-privileged seeking a technological education, is correspondingly low in its potential for success. Such people *are* primitive in this area, no matter how many Ph.D.s or deep-freezers they have.

So much for where they are. But where do they think they are, imagine themselves to be? This could be illustrated by a parable involving a farmyard:

290

Assumption that something actually
is that which it seems to resemble

A child's white balloon drifted into a chicken-run one day and settled beside the resident cock. He looked up and saw, coincidentally, a duck flying overhead.

First he gazed at the balloon. Then he strode up to the hens in their nesting-boxes. 'Ladies', he said, 'have you any conception of what the opposition can really do?'

Where they think that they are, very often, includes the belief that they have a piece of knowledge already, while they generally have it in the least relevant form for their own good, if it is there at all. This is referred to in a further tale of how scraps of undigested information or experience can even be dangerous:

Possession of information or practices is not the same
as knowing their function

A man was looking for a job.

His prospective employer said to him:

'You say that you have held a position of trust with Prince Such-and-Such. Can you prove it?'

'Yes, indeed', claimed the applicant, 'here are the very golden cups which he entrusted to me, so reliable was I at the time'.

People are so deluded about what religion and inner knowledge are that in many cases these are just a means of supporting their vanity. Esoteric traditions, indeed, claim that the reduction of vanity is an essential of preliminary training, not a key to paradise or only a social necessity.

Self-deprecation as a 'shock' technique is comparable
with Western pretensions to dignity

I was once present when a gushing lady, with a world-wide reputation as a devout and enlightened individual, visited a certain Sufi.

She was full of tales of her spiritual experiences, accounts of which poured from her lips like a torrent.

'You see visions of the unknown?' asked the Sufi.

'Oh, yes — all the time'.

'And you have healed the sick?'

'Frequently'.

'And have studied with all the great teachers of the time, living and dead?'

'Absolutely'.

'You are initiated, illuminated, transformed and full of bliss?'

'Exactly'.

'Then', said our teacher, 'perhaps you would condescend to take my place here, for I wish to occupy yours . . .'

Imagined eligibility for teaching may be an almost clinical condition

The problem, then, is as to what people want versus what they need. A spiritual teacher once passed through Britain and was importuned by a youth for money, saying, 'I feel I must get to Katmandu'.

The sage handed the young man £10. 'But this will not pay my fare . . .' he began.

'My child, it is not for your fare, it is the fee to get your head examined . . .'

An inevitable phase of deterioration in spiritual sciences in all cultures

In both the East and West, traditional religionists frequently confuse power and enlightenment. They seek power, or seek to use it, or seek those who seem to have it. The following tale which illustrates more than one aspect of this confusion — and the vanity which is never far behind — could have taken place in almost any civilization in its inevitable phase when spirituality has become muddled:

Unchallenged vanity in putatively great religionists a mark of degeneracy

A group of devout people planned an open-air conference. They could be the self-styled Sufis who nowa-

292

days fill the East and West; a group of Christian clerics, or almost any of the Hindu gurus whom one finds everywhere in India.

These gentlemen suddenly realized that they had forgotten to invite one important and aged sage.

A deputation was at once hurriedly despatched to request the ancient's presence.

'I am afraid that you should have remembered before,' intoned the venerable one, 'for I have already prayed for rain . . .'

Emotion imagined to be devotion, ritual for its own sake, conformism as the rule: three signs of disease

Social and emotional activity, ritualistic behaviour and stylized, superfluous conformism are very frequently confused with something higher, in all societies where the generality of the people have lost track of the difference between these things and the spiritual traditions proper. This is alluded to in the story of the silent fakir.

Example of mindless ritualism as a warning

An Indian and his wife every day respectfully saluted a squatting contemplative who presided over their verandah.

One day the wife said:

'This fakir, this guru of yours is getting very old and troublesome. Can't we get rid of him? After all, you are well settled in life and hardly need his prayers now, after thirty years of putting up with him . . .'

'MY Guru?' spluttered the husband. 'I always thought that he was YOUR Guru!'

Instead of trying to observe what the essentials of a teacher or teaching might really be, people tend to absorb themselves in such burning questions as whether they charge money for teaching.

Attempts at analysis of teachers only display the basis of thought of the observer

As one Sufi once observed, 'This tells you more about

293

the enquirers than about the school: ˙ shows that the supposedly eager aspirants are worrying about and want to hold onto their money: the last thing that spiritual people are supposed to care about . . .'

So this peculiarity can be turned against its victim

One Far Eastern mystical master has solved the problem of reassuring his disciples on the money question, as he recently confided to me. He gives teachings completely free to the stingy disciples who surround him; throwing them into such a strange state of psychosis that only one psychiatrist in the world can get them out of it. The wonderful doctor concerned is the mystic's disciple. *His* fees are very high indeed . . .

Example of originally flexible thought
transformed into sheer prejudice

In the East it is fully understood that dervishes are a mixed lot, rather as were friars in medieval Europe. One current joke underlines how crabbed religiosity can be seen in the failures of this persuasion; who are consequently not on a higher, but actually on a lower, level than the ordinary populace:

A sour-faced dervish was plodding along a road one bright Spring day.

A farmer called out:

'What a glorious day for us!'

'It is', said the dervish, 'but do you not realize that the sinners are getting it, too?'

In an upside-down world, the genuine man must masquerade

This situation obliges the genuine Sufi, when he has to live among the people who imagine things to be as they are not, to play a part and to navigate himself as best he can in an area where people think that religion is the exact opposite, quite often, to what it is.

The incomparable Mulla Nasrudin, the Sufi teaching figure, is found pointing an allegory which shows how difficult it is for the ordinary person, because he is so

294

neglectful of the obvious, to understand the Sufi:

It was starting to rain when Nasrudin called out 'Coward!' at a burly farmer, wearing a heavy cloak, who was beginning to run for shelter across the town square.

The rustic immediately threw himself upon the Mulla and bore him to the ground.

'Now will you yield and apologize?' he roared.

'No'.

They lay like that for several minutes, until Nasrudin said:

'Very well, I yield and apologize'.

'That's better. But why didn't you do it before?'

'What, and let the rain fall on me instead of on you?'

Literature is capable of instilling pre-study awareness

The Sufi's role may be to indicate that truth can be found almost anywhere but where people ordinarily look for it. He can often be found illustrating, through literature, sample equivalent situations with familiar figures in them. These are studied and applied to their own lives by students long before they can aspire to discipleship or real learning. The relative positions of the Sufi and the student may be allegorized as, for instance, interchanges between a doctor and a patient like this one:

Tale stressing the value of coherent thought and its absence

A man who had vivid dreams — so the story goes — decided to make use of them. He found that he could induce himself to dream of the ballet, of which he was very fond.

One night, however, he found that when he tried he could not dream of the opera, and he went to a psychiatrist to discuss the problem.

'Surely', said the physician, 'all you have to do, with your remarkable powers of visualization, is to imagine yourself at the opera house, just as you did with the ballet?'

'Opera house?' said the aesthete. 'Whatever makes

295

you think that I could *afford* their prices?'

The lesson here includes, of course, the reminder that the man in the tale had not stabilized his ideas, but, like self-styled spiritual disciples everywhere, was making up his own rules as he went along.

The tremendous number of misconceptions about what people call the inner path is often illustrated by the application of what are technically termed — and often literally are — 'shocks'. This is one where the Sufi master is dealing with the problem of over-transference ('idolatry') by a group of disciples:

Jolting people who are needlessly idolators

'I fasted throughout the daylight hours for five years', said a certain Naqshbandi sage, 'and then I studied holy books for another seven. After that I did exercises and studied movements and postures, breathing and telling the rosary. For years I examined my conduct and thoughts . . .'

'Master', breathed one of the assembled disciples, 'was that what made you a Great Teacher?'

'No', said the ancient one, 'I had to wait for my father to die before I could be that . . .'

It will be quite obvious that the convention whereby a 'man or woman of the spirit' must be grave and didactic, which is so well rooted in the West, makes it extremely difficult for this kind of teaching to be operated outside of the East. This is, of course, only because dignity has come to be equated with importance: although a moment's thought will show that the one has no essential connection with the other.

'Theft' of genuine ideas and processes back-fires!
Tale of the zealous Malamatis

Imitators, as soon as they come across such arresting ideas as this one, always appear and try to embody such concepts in their own activities. The results are always useless. What happens is that they overdo or underdo things, since they lack the essential ingredient of

296

measure. This is emphasized in the traditional Malamati tale:

Dervishes of the Malamati ('People of Opprobrium') persuasion deliberately annoy people, and behave in what can be considered an atrocious manner, so that only the sincere and perceptive among would-be disciples can bear their company.

The story is told of a community of Malamatis whose director, the Murshid, went on a journey of several months leaving strict instructions that the residents of the settlement were to act according to the rules of the school.

When he returned, he asked:

'Have you adhered to the Malamati Rules?'

'Adhered to the Rules?' echoed the deputy. 'Why, we have applied them so strictly that even the genuine and perceptive visitors have ceased to call'.

This tale, too, is used as an allegory of the random use of exercises and tales. When these are not 'prescribed', but merely repeated endlessly, the higher experiences do not come, the 'visitors cease to call'.

Confusion of mystical and medical questions

Sufi teaching cannot begin until certain facts — which can easily be written down and absorbed from the printed page — have taken effect in the would-be learner. One of the major ones in a society like the present one is the need to distinguish between self-realization and therapy. The distinction, especially in the West, has become so narrow in people's minds that mystics are constantly asked what are in fact medical questions.

Irrelevant demands for solace and reassurance

Solace and reassurance is thought to be a part of a higher aim. Many people employ mantrams and religious formulae merely for this purpose. The situation is very different, if at all, from the one in this interchange:

Patient: 'Doctor, I am too fat, and I worry about it!'

Doctor: 'Take these tranquillizers . . .'

297

Patient: 'Will they make me lose weight?'
Doctor: 'No, but you'll stop caring about it . . .'
One way in which it is possible to affirm the difference between what people think to be spiritual advancement and how it is truly perceived by its real devotees is to use stories like this one:

Clarity of vision and experience as such is nothing . . .

A man went to a dervish master and said that he was getting far more vivid experiences from a certain cult than he did when he was the dervish's disciple. 'In fact', he said, 'when I was with you, my visions actually faded . . .'

'That reminds me', said the dervish, 'of the man who went to a doctor complaining of a buzzing in his ears. The doctor gave him drops to put in them. When he returned after a week, the doctor said: "Any improvement?" "Oh, yes", said the patient, "the buzzing is much clearer now".'

Summary

By the use of quotations and anecdotes, we have been stressing and illustrating certain essential characteristics of metaphysical study and development. We have also affirmed that things orginally intended to be instruments — and once employed as such — become mere totems or symbols, bereft of dynamic function. We are living in a time when this tendency is strongly marked: though not a time, luckily, when it is as powerful as it might be.

The contentions which I have just put before you, extracted from living tradition and emphasized in order of importance, include these:

There should not be a confusion between the relative reality as perceived by the limited senses and an absolute Reality which is referred to by mystics and others. Scientific work itself, in recent years, has suggested very strongly that a further reality is dramatically different from what we take to be the only real thing, the 'evidence of our own senses'.

298

We are perhaps fortunate in that we come later than those ignorant optimists, mere panacea-mongers as it turns out, who believed that the use of reason, or technology, or devotion, even, would solve all problems.

At the same time this argument cannot be used to support the contention that we should abandon all sense and efficiency, as some have sought to do, and espouse spurious cults and useless beliefs. Equally, the emerging and infant enterprises of psychology, sociology and anthropology enable us to examine current as well as ancient beliefs in order to strip off accretions and to analyse those parts which are mere tribalism and totemism, sources of emotional stimulus. Some traditional literary and other materials enable us to register, to stabilize in our minds, and to make use of, experiences which we might otherwise miss. The pioneer work in this area, still valid though necessarily to be expertly used, has been done in the East.

The establishment of authoritative spiritual schools in the East or the West is not the answer to the question of how one might find and employ such schools. One reason is that no such school can maintain the imagined authority sought: another is that the sincere and the adequately prepared will always find the source, and ample verbal materials now exist to guide them. They (the students) bear some responsibility for reaching and maintaining an adequate standard of honesty and eligibility. Too much is said about the dangers of people being taken in by fakes. The fact is that the majority of those who call themselves pupils are themselves fakes, or using false approaches. Vanity and impatience, assumptions about what a school should look like, and imaginings about how teachers should behave, these are the things which the would-be learner can investigate and study for himself. Indeed, he or she *must* do so before the question of discipleship or criticism, analysis or assessment, of a school arises at all. Tourists amuse themselves: students learn, after preparing themselves.

If you know what you need, that is something. If you

299

only know what you want, you should not pretend that it must therefore be what you need. For the two to coincide, you must have a certain degree and quality of knowledge. The only people who believe otherwise are fools; and the only people not being fools who hold the contrary opinion are trying, consciously or otherwise, to deceive you.

One thing must not be mistaken for another. A sour-faced religious devotee is not a saint; any more than an elated one is, benign face or not; something which is said to be metaphysics may not be that at all; people who value money or their own status more than they do learning are not students but valuers of status and possessions. These things are commonplaces of religious rhetoric; but in metaphysics, for the mystical quest, they are more: essential facts which have to find expression within the seeker if he is to start the search at all.

Sufis and others involved in this activity behave in a manner contrary to expectation largely because the expectation itself is conditioned by misconceptions. Learners generally either follow a too-restricted path (say, thinking that one idea or exercise will lead to all truth) or else they shift their ground like the man and the opera-house. Yet, on the contrary, only a flexible approach correctly guided to prevent the shifting of ground, though not of focus, will lead to self-realization.

The problem is to put religion and all other relative things where they belong; Knowledge and understanding, especially of the kind termed mysticism, cannot be *put* anywhere: it *stays* where it belongs — and you must go to *it*.

In the Middle East, the untrammelled investigation of higher knowledge has been continuing in parallel with the West's scientific and materialistic work for many centuries. One of the major public figures in this effort is Abdur Rahman Abu Zaid Ibn-Khaldun, the fourteenth-century genius who is accepted in both the East and West as the pioneer scientific historian of humanity. He is buried in the Sufi cemetery near Cairo, having died in

300

March, 1406 of the Christian reckoning.

As the Western grasp of human processes has developed, so appreciation of Khaldun, as a major overt exponent of the Sufi method of describing humanity, has grown. His work, *The Muqaddimah* — or Introduction to his Universal History — was characterized by Arnold Toynbee as 'undoubtedly the greatest work of its kind that has ever been created by any mind in any time or place'. Note what Khaldun says about the need to divide higher knowledge of mystical matters and objective reality from emotional and denominational concerns, while retaining the whole subject within the boundaries of religion:

'The attainment of sainthood is not restricted to the correct performance of divine worship, or anything else. When the soul is firmly established as existent, God may single it out for whatever gifts of His He wants to give it . . . God does not select His servants for gnosis only on the basis of the performance of some legal duty . . . This school is called that of the people of revelation, manifestations and presences. It is a theory that people cultivating (logical) speculation cannot properly grasp . . . There is also a great gap between the theories of people who have vision and intuitive experience and those of people who cultivate logical reasoning. (Sufi) systems are often disapproved of on the strength of the plain wording of the religious law, for no indication of them can be found in it anywhere. (As to Sufi experiences beyond sense perceptions) no language can express the things that Sufis want to say in this connection, because languages have been invented only for the expression of commonly accepted concepts . . .'*

The use, therefore, of Sufi words and movements are (1) instrumental, helping to conduct towards a higher understanding, not to describe it or inform about it; (2) to allude to experiences which others have also had, so

---

The Muqaddimah (An Introduction to History) Translated by N. J. Dawood, London: Routledge, 1967, pp.86, 363 and 366.

that those who share their knowledge may recognize the signals, as when I say 'Strawberry Jam', only those who have tasted it know what experience I am referring to.

7/.v.
An Important Aspect of Sufic Study

The instrumental function

The ordinary person thinks in two basic 'styles'. His first preoccupation is with himself. This means that, in general, he associates almost everything with his own interests or interprets all experiences in relation to what he takes to be himself. The accuracy of this, in operation, is only as great as his sense of himself. If he does not understand himself, he will not be able to further his own best interests. This sense is, ordinarily, automatistic.

The second 'style' which preoccupies the ordinary person is some sort of community to which he belongs, imagines he belongs, or would like to belong. This is his social milieu. He has a model of this in his mind, and he relates what happens to him to this model. His assessment of everything comes through this model. Hence, if someone says something to him, he will automatically check it with the possibility of its acceptability in the light of what he takes to be his social reference-frame. Again, his perception of that frame may or may not be accurate. Its automatism is not perceptible to him, though it may be so to others.

But there is a third field of action, development and understanding higher than the above two areas. This is the 'instrumental' modality. In Sufi teaching, the instructor provokes reactions in people, individually and/or collectively, in accordance with the potentialities of the people and their needs. He may, that is, say or do something in order to help the individual with his

302

problem: which is to understand himself and also his social milieu. The narrative or overt verbal level of this material or action is only a *minor* part of it.

But what if someone is already fully aware of himself, his needs and the social milieu into which he is, or is to be, integrated?

Under these circumstances, he has no need of Sufi study. He is either right in his contention that he knows himself and/or his social setting, in which case he understands the Sufi; or he is wrong, in which case he needs the Sufi's instrumental function to 'wake him up', though the degree to which he can really perceive this is extremely variable and may fluctuate.

If you know who you are, where you are, and where you belong, you have no need of Sufis: either because you are one of them, or because your perception is so fallacious that you are enclosed in an impenetrable system based on concepts which suffice your level of aspiration.

Then it is asked, why do people who have been described as self-satisfied and working on a lower level interest themselves in the Sufis at all? Simply because these people have a taste for dilettantism, for emotional or intellectual stimulus. They are not seeking what the Sufi offers. And it is the Sufi's role, expertise and duty to be able to diagnose this condition.

These are the people who have been described in the prayer: 'O Lord, let me repent — but not yet!'

7/vi.
Letter from a Sufi Teacher

On the present-day projection of Sufic studies

I think that it will be useful to mention, perhaps to

303

refresh your memory, a few characteristic human attitudes which we constantly meet, and which account for many of the individual and group pressures which people try to bring, and also to restate a few basic attitudes which are at work in the current projection of our teaching in this and in other cultural areas:

* The desire for attention, to receive someone's attention, or to call attention to oneself, is often marked. This, and not deeper motivations, sometimes obsesses people who use the 'work' areas not as teaching areas but as sounding-boards. When, as they imagine themselves to be, they are 'neglected', they may become hostile. It is obviously a mistake to imagine that psychologically-based agitation, in the absence of perceived sincerity, is honest spiritual desire.

* The human being lives in a world where he does not realize that many of his evaluation systems (in 'the work' as well) are frequently programmed ones; the result of indoctrination, deliberate and (more often) unwitting. He opposes what seems to him to be directed against 'the work', helps that which he imagines to be 'the work'. In reality, he usually has little real understanding of 'the work', 'though his fame ascend to heaven', as our proverb has it.

* The law, one might call it, is that series of ideas become crystallized in people's minds by selective adoption, into what can only be called cults. There is always the authority-figure, the canonical literature, the hierarchy, the myth, the locality, the sacred this and that. This formation inhibits rather than makes possible, real teaching and development. Most people who currently surround the 'work ideas' are to some extent in the grip of this infantile state. Almost all institutions seek to further these mechanical elements (even if they deny them), as the 'blood and bones of organization'. But they do not know that it is bricks and mortar only of a limited kind of construct, a non-organic one, one might call it, referring to the difference in vitality and sophistication as between a building and a plant.

304

* There are plenty of people who can only 'recognize' metaphysics if it is put in words which they have met before, or if it is claimed to be metaphysics. The real task is to balance this number of people with an appropriate number and quality of people who can truly recognize this pursuit wherever and however represented. Indeed, it is the latter people who save the former from useless groping.

* The instructional duty is as much to the second group as to the first, even though the first may be more vocal and demanding. The overriding principle is the activity and the operation, not social welfare and palliatives.

* Some, but not all of them without real effort, of the first type of people, may develop, through mutual striving and the right experiences, into the latter type, to the advantage of all. This is a very real part of the activity.

* It is unfortunate from a vulgar point of view that some of the crudely useful tendencies in man are harmful to their development and to the interests of the teaching. For instance, inculcated loyalty of the obsessional type, single-mindedness of the type which excludes versatility, material support from the wrong motivations, compromise with people because of their social, vocational or other usefulness, unless they have a potentiality and we can help them.

* We can never stay true to our mission and also pander to the lower desires of people (for fame, position, attention, sense of significance, something to do, to study, at all costs). We have chosen to stay true to our mission. 'Pious fraud' is not applied by us.

* There is all the difference in the world between tradition and traditionalism. As we use the terms, traditionalism is doing something because others have done it, whether we understand it or not, whether it applies in a given culture, time-scale, etc., or not. It may be simply dogmatism. Tradition itself enshrines the functional part of which traditionalism is the husk. Very many of the people with whom we have to deal in this

culture area appear not to have been informed of the distinction and kept up to it. The result is that they are often in social and psychological disarray.

* To learn, really learn, that the essence of something is crucial and not how it is presented, is a real form of effort and involves real discomfort. Hair-shirts and self-reproach are in comparison ridiculous imitations of this.

* Nobody's 'psychic life' is in suspension. People who are in groups and have no studies to do, people who have been in formal contact with us and do not receive regular letters, lectures, and so on, may be unaware of their continuing spiritual life — they are not disconnected from the work. It is sad if they imagine that their intellectual and emotional life is their spiritual life. It is not.

* The activities which are carried out in centres and at meetings, in various Sufi organizations may be participated in by those who are not formally present. The uses which are made of resources, and which will be made of them in the future, are as much concealed to ordinary people who imagine themselves to be students of higher learning as is anything else. What a sorry state such people are in when some sort of dramatic event spells activity and significance, and where the absence of a crude stimulus spells discontent or means that 'nothing is happening!'

* If the metaphysical activity had been dependent upon the hammer-and-chisel approach, had been manifested through the circus or the lecture alone, were to be found in the old ladies' tea-party, it would have been a wonder to end all wonders.

* Most of the people who pride themselves upon being 'seekers' and are hurt when they are not given anything to seek, while thinking that they are trying not to be proud, such people are passengers on those who are truly working with Reality. Like all delinquents they are a sorrow and a burden. Like delinquents, again, they do not in reality call the tune.

* What many such people need is: (1) Ordinary psychological help; (2) Suspension from the tensions of their

306

imaginativeness, a change of interest; (3) Information before they have knowledge. Without information they would spurn knowledge, because they would not recognize aright its manifestations. But they are often too proud to accept information, unless it titillates them. This titillation, however, they tend to call 'experience', which deprives it of a salutary effect.

* Certain materials, certain experiences, certain kinds of grouping, certain exercises, have been used in certain manners and with various kinds of people, in accordance with cultural peculiarities, for thousands of years. These things stem from an ancient and intact knowledge. What the so-called followers of esoteric ideas take for religion, teaching and so forth are almost always tattered and generally inoperative remnants of this great science.

* Attempts to summarize this information, and to lead people to understanding it in customary ways are not certain to succeed. People have turned the wrong face towards the ideas.

FOUR SUFI CLASSICS

Jami, Ghazzali and Sanai are the authors of these four classical expositions of Sufi thought and experience, giving a cross-section of traditional Sufic instruction materials studied in dervish schools — but which are also a part of the literature of the Middle East. Together they cover the major approaches of the Sufis: the allegorical, the interpretative, the psychological and the literary.

FOUR SUFI CLASSICS
'Salaman and Absal' translated by W. H. T. Gairdner;
'The Niche for Lights' translated by Edward Fitzgerald;
'The Way of the Seeker' and 'The Abode of Spring' translated and abridged by David L. Pendlebury.
Introduction by Idries Shah

The Octagon Press

A FOOL OF GOD: MYSTICAL VERSE OF BABA TAHIR

One of the earliest Persian Sufi poets, Baba Tahir is famous for his use of rustic dialect rather than polished style. In his mystical love-poetry are seen close analogies with Western mystical writings. He is one of the four great pioneers of the quatrain (the others were Abu Said, Ansari and Omar Khayyam) and his songs are still widely sung and revered in Central Asia. Known as 'The Naked' because of his disdain for outward show, Tahir was visited by Sultan Tughrul Beg and, it is believed, granted him victory over his enemies, providing that he always upheld justice. Perhaps for this reason, the recitation of his work is believed by some to grant the heart's desire of an honest man or woman.

A FOOL OF GOD: MYSTICAL VERSE OF BABA TAHIR
Persian text with a translation by Edward Heron-Allen

The Octagon Press

A PERFUMED SCORPION

The 'perfuming of a scorpion' referred to by the great Sufi teacher Bahaudin symbolises hypocrisy and self-deception: both in the individual and in institutions.

Idries Shah, in these lectures and meditations, directs attention to both the perfume and the scorpion — the overlay and the reality — in psychology, human behaviour and the learning process.

Crammed with illustrative anecdotes from contemporary life, the book is nevertheless rooted in the teaching patterns of Rumi, Hafiz, Jami and many other great sages. It deals with the need for, and ways to, knowledge as well as information, understanding which comes beyond belief, perception as distinct from emotion, self-development in addition to the desire for intellectuality.

'Suppose Einstein had "leaked" one aspect of his Relativity concept to an astronomer, another aspect to, say, a biologist and so on. It seems likely that revolutions would quickly have followed in different branches of science without anybody suspecting the existence of a master. Something like this may be happening today . . . Idries Shah, the 53-year-old Afghan appears to be the man-behind-the-scenes in all this . . .' — *Evening News*

A PERFUMED SCORPION
Idries Shah

The Octagon Press

THE RELIGION OF THE SUFIS

Constantly quoted and widely read for the three centuries since it was written, this book by a scholar of the East based in India gives an excellent insight into what the Sufis of the time gave out as their teaching, and what scholars and others thought of them. It well vindicates its prefatory phrase: 'containing what has been reported by those who know what is manifest, and see what is concealed; as well as by those who are attached to exterior forms, and by those who discern the inward meaning . . . without hatred, enmity and scorn, and without taking a part for the one, or against the other side of the question.'

'*The Dabistan* contains more recondite learning, more entertaining history, more beautiful specimens of poetry, more ingenuity and wit . . . than I ever saw collected in a single volume' — *Sir William Jones*

'A work by an Oriental and written for Orientals, but we of the West may equally profit by its contents'
— *Professor A. V. Williams Jackson,* Professor of Indo-Iranian Languages in Columbia University.

THE RELIGION OF THE SUFIS
Translated from 'The Dabistan' by David Shea and Anthony Troyer
Introduction by Idries Shah

The Octagon Press

TEACHINGS OF HAFIZ

Hafiz of Shiraz is unquestionably in the front rank of world classical poets. As a lyricist and Sufi master, his work is celebrated from India to Central Asia and the Near East as are Shakespeare, Dante or Milton: Goethe himself, among many other Westerners, was among the master's admirers.

As Professor Shafaq says:

'Hafiz attained perfect mystical consciousness: and his spiritual and mental power derived from this. The Path, projected by Sanai, Attar, Rumi and Sa'di each in his own way, is described by Hafiz with the very deepest feeling and highest expressive achievement.'

History of Persian Literature, Tehran

This collection is by the eminent linguist and explorer Gertrude Bell who (as Dr. A. J. Arberry says) 'early in her adventurous life conceived an enthusiasm for Hafiz which compelled her to write a volume of very fine translations'

TEACHINGS OF HAFIZ
Translated by Gertrude Bell: Introduction by Idries Shah.

The Octagon Press.

For further Information on
Sufi Studies please write:
The Society for Sufi Studies
Box 43, Los Altos, CA 94022